CONSCIENCE AND
CATHOLIC HEALTH CARE

CONSCIENCE AND CATHOLIC HEALTH CARE

From Clinical Contexts to Government Mandates

Edited by

DAVID E. DECOSSE AND
THOMAS A. NAIRN, OFM

ORBIS BOOKS

Maryknoll, New York 10545

Maryknoll, New York 10545

Founded in 1970, Orbis Books endeavors to publish works that enlighten the mind, nourish the spirit, and challenge the conscience. The publishing arm of the Maryknoll Fathers and Brothers, Orbis seeks to explore the global dimensions of the Christian faith and mission, to invite dialogue with diverse cultures and religious traditions, and to serve the cause of reconciliation and peace. The books published reflect the views of their authors and do not represent the official position of the Maryknoll Society. To learn more about Maryknoll and Orbis Books, please visit our website at www.maryknollsociety.org.

Library of Congress Cataloging-in-Publication Data

Names: DeCosse, David E., editor.
Title: Conscience and Catholic health care : from clinical contexts to government
    mandates / edited by David E. DeCosse and Thomas A. Nairn,
    O.F.M.
Description: Maryknoll, NY : Orbis Books, [2016] | Includes index.
Identifiers: LCCN 2016036119 | ISBN 9781626982123 (pbk.)
Subjects: LCSH: Medical ethics. | Conscience. | Medicine—Religious aspects.
    | Bioethics.
Classification: LCC R724 .C65 2017 | DDC 174.2—dc23
LC record available at https://lccn.loc.gov/2016036119

We dedicate this volume

to Sister Patricia Talone, RSM, PhD,

who recently retired as Vice President, Mission Services,

for the Catholic Health Association;

to Jerome J. DeCosse (1928–2001), the late Lewis Thomas

University Professor at Weill Cornell Medical College;

and to Sister Anne Patrick, SNJM,

our dear colleague and prophetic voice on conscience

whose essay graces this volume and

who entered eternal life on July 21, 2016.

CONTENTS

ACKNOWLEDGMENTS

Many people have been instrumental in helping bring this volume to completion. We especially thank Michael and Phyllis Shea for their very generous gift to the Markkula Center for Applied Ethics in support of the Project on Conscience and Roman Catholic Thought. Their generosity made this book possible. We are grateful to Jim Keane at Orbis for his enthusiasm for the project and his good-humored professionalism, and we are grateful to the whole Orbis team for their help with the book. We thank Sister Carol Keehan, DC, the president of the Catholic Health Association; Sister Mary Haddad, RSM, the vice president of mission services for the Catholic Health Association; and our Catholic Health Association colleagues Brian Smith, Charles Bouchard, OP, and Lynette Ballard. We also thank our colleagues at Santa Clara University who helped with many different stages of this project: Kirk Hanson, the executive director of the Ethics Center; Monica DeLong, the operations director at the Ethics Center whose support helped make possible our scholars seminar in February 2016 and other crucial aspects of this project; Lauren Ellis, a graduate assistant at the Ethics Center; Carol Bayley of Dignity Health and Karen Peterson-Iyer of Santa Clara University, both of whom attended our scholars seminar and whose wisdom contributed to this volume; Thomas Massaro, SJ, the former dean of the Jesuit School of Theology at Santa Clara University, and Paul Crowley, SJ, the Jesuit Community Professor at Santa Clara University and the editor of *Theological Studies*, for their unstinting enthusiasm for this project and for Catholic theology; and the many invaluable staff at Santa Clara who helped with logistics, travel, food, events, and much more. And we are deeply grateful to the contributors to this book for their collegial spirit, their enthusiasm, and their time and effort in working on such difficult topics and producing such excellent work.

INTRODUCTION

This book is an effort to clarify ethical and theological issues related to conflicts of conscience arising in Roman Catholic health care in the pluralist context of the United States. The book also draws on the Catholic tradition of moral theology to bring forward a compelling theology of conscience to assist Catholic health care in its mission. In all, the book aims to engage three distinct but overlapping audiences. One is the world of the Catholic theology of conscience, as reflected on by theologians, deployed by bishops, and shaped by the experience of countless patients and employees of Catholic health care institutions. Another is the practical world of Catholic health care institutions, where thousands of devoted men and women have constantly to make consequential decisions of conscience. And the third is the secular, pluralist culture in which Catholic health care, which provides one in six hospital beds in the United States, is practiced. We wish to be in dialogue with this secular, pluralist culture. Thus we are hopeful that the book's reflections can assist those grappling with issues of conscience on hospital and elder care staffs, in policy-making roles, in chancery offices, in secular organizations such as the ACLU, in academia, and in the Catholic and general public both in the United States and elsewhere.

A word is in order about the origin of this book. In 2015 Orbis Books published *Conscience and Catholicism: Rights, Responsibilities, and Institutional Responses*.[1] That volume was the first book in the Project on Conscience and Roman Catholic Thought at the Markkula Center for Applied Ethics at Santa Clara University, the Jesuit university in Silicon Valley. *Conscience and Catholicism* covered a broad range of contemporary topics in the Catholic theology of conscience (from the formation of conscience in a racist culture to the challenge of religious freedom in India in the face of a Hindu nationalist government). The book especially discussed conscience in light of context, relationship, history, and praxis; contributors to the volume came from the United States, Kenya, the Philippines, Japan, India, Ireland, and Argentina. Two of the essays in the first book focused on Catholicism and health care: "From Catholic Health Care West to Dignity Health: Conflicts of Conscience in American Catholic Health Care," by Carol Bayley, and "'To

---

[1] *Conscience and Catholicism: Rights, Responsibilities, and Institutional Responses*, ed. David E. DeCosse and Kristin E. Heyer (Maryknoll, NY: Orbis Books, 2015).

Pardon What Conscience Dreads': Navigating the Contours of Precepts and the Contexts of Life," by Agbonkhianmeghe E. Orobator, SJ. But as fine as the two essays are, the issues of conscience and Catholic health care ranged far and wide beyond what the first book could accomplish. And so we decided to write a second volume focused only on conscience and US Catholic health care. The donors who made possible the first book—Michael and Phyllis Shea—generously made a second gift that enabled us to forge ahead with this second major product of the Project on Conscience. *Conscience and Catholic Health Care: From Clinical Contexts to Government Mandates* is a joint effort of the Markkula Center for Applied Ethics and the Catholic Health Association of the United States, which represents more than one thousand Catholic health care institutions in the United States. As co-editors, we bring complementary skills to the project. David DeCosse is a moral theologian and was the co-editor of *Conscience and Catholicism*; he has also written widely on contemporary challenges of conscience and Catholicism. Thomas Nairn is a widely published moral theologian, a Franciscan priest, and the Senior Director, Theology and Ethics, for the Catholic Health Association. Father Nairn is exposed on an almost daily basis to myriad conscience issues arising in Catholic health care institutions around the country. The development of this book involved three stages. First, as co-editors, we invited a group of leading theologians and ethicists working in Catholic health care and in Catholic educational institutions to contribute essays to the project. Then, on February 11–12, 2016, this group—all the authors in this volume—met for a two-day scholars' seminar at Santa Clara University to discuss drafts of all of their essays. After the conference, the scholars then revised their essays in response to the discussions at the seminar. The outcome of this process is what you see in this book.

Certainly, the theme of the first book—a theology of conscience sensitive to context, relationship, history, and praxis—is evident again in this volume. Throughout *Conscience and Catholic Health Care*, essays take issue with a neo-Scholastic ("neo" because it sought to modernize the medieval Scholasticism of Thomas Aquinas) model of conscience popular in nineteenth- and twentieth-century Catholicism and still influential in many sectors of the Church today. In this model, conscience is rational and deductive; it is oriented toward judging individual acts and obeying unquestioned moral laws; and it is all but singularly formed by clear and unchanging Catholic moral doctrine. This model of conscience also exhibits a certain defensiveness: It is more concerned about what one should *not* do and how one should protect one's innocence or purity. By contrast, many of the essays in this book consider conscience in light of the theology and philosophy of personalism and thus as a complex moral phenomenon oriented to action and responsibility, immersed in relationships, and blending spirit, intellect, emotion, and embodiment. It has been common in the last years in American society, in issues of health care and more, to hear conscience invoked in rhetorical fashion as a trump card meant to end a discussion. Many of the essays in this book challenge such rhetoric and instead call for greater humility around decisions of conscience—a humility more aware of the provisional nature of many such decisions and of the effect of such decisions on many other people beyond one's self.

Those, then, are theoretical issues about the way conscience is conceived that have carried over from the first volume to *Conscience and Catholic Health Care*. What about concrete, real-time issues of context that hold special significance for this volume? Three such topics come to mind: The change in the theology of conscience brought about by the papacy of Francis; the significance of issues of sex, gender, and reproductive medicine in many of the conflicts of conscience and Catholic health care; and the changing economic landscape of Catholic health care. A brief word is in order about each.

From its beginning, Catholicism has affirmed the great value of conscience.[2] For instance, Paul's Letter to the Romans gives eloquent testimony to this value.[3] Nevertheless, the Catholic theological tradition has not had a univocal understanding of the concept, sometimes tightly linking a right conscience to obedience to church authority and sometimes loosening this linkage and recognizing the appropriateness of conscience as its own authority. Thus Augustine in the fifth century affirmed conscience but constrained its freedom to act, whereas Thomas Aquinas in the thirteenth century constrained church authority and affirmed the liberty of conscience. In the early modern period, great ecclesiastical battles between figures like Blaise Pascal and his rival Jesuit moralists over such terms as "laxism" and "probabilism" were in effect disputes over the degree of deference to be given to the authority of conscience (Lisa Fullam's essay in this volume discusses these battles of the early modern period). The Second Vatican Council from 1962 to 1965 represented a high-water mark in the theological tradition of conscience. The historian John O'Malley has identified "conscience" as one of the key thematic words of the council.[4] Certainly the treatment of conscience in conciliar documents such as *Gaudium et Spes* ("Conscience is the most secret core and sanctuary of a man. There he is alone with God, Whose voice echoes in his depths," no. 16) and *Dignitatis Humanae* ("In all his activity a man is bound to follow his conscience in order that he may

---

[2] The following discussion draws on Linda Hogan, *Confronting the Truth: Conscience in the Catholic Tradition* (Ottawa: Novalis, 2000), 1–126.

[3] In Romans, see 1:16–2:29 and 14.

[4] John W. O'Malley, *What Happened at Vatican II* (Cambridge, MA: Harvard University Press, 2010), 48–52.

come to God, the end and purpose of life," no. 3) constituted a powerful and positive theological affirmation of the value of the authority of the individual conscience. But the council was not univocal on the topic and also reaffirmed the more restricted, neo-Scholastic view of conscience that had been commonplace in church thought before the council.[5] Moreover, critical voices were quickly raised about the conciliar praise of conscience. Indeed, shortly after the council's conclusion, theologian Joseph Ratzinger (later to become Pope Benedict XVI) criticized the formulation of individual conscience in *Gaudium et Spes* for being susceptible to a problematic subjectivism in which the authority of conscience was almost recklessly unconstrained.[6] Ratzinger's sophisticated theological critique would become a decisive mode of interpretation of the theology of conscience for almost the next fifty years.[7] Both Pope John Paul II (for whom Ratzinger was the principal theological and doctrinal adviser) and Pope Benedict XVI certainly affirmed the importance of a person following one's conscience. But they carefully narrowed what might be acceptable reasons for doing so against the claims of church authority.[8] They also emphasized that a properly formed Catholic conscience would adhere strictly to Catholic moral doctrine, especially about sensitive matters that they called "intrinsic evil" like contraception, abortion, and sterilization.[9] Here was a defensive, heroic mode of conscience: Conscience as sentinel or witness announcing the Truth in a culture bent on relativism. And they insisted on a related, collective notion: The Catholic conscience adhering strictly to church teaching should be reflected uncompromisingly in the practices of Catholic institutions such as health care facilities and should be left unimpeded by government and civil society. (The case of the Little Sisters of the Poor opposing the contraception policy of federal health care reform represents this theological logic at work.)

Pope Francis has not adhered to a similar theology of conscience. Early in his papacy, he signaled this shift when he responded to an Italian atheist newspaper editor's question about the possibility of Christian forgiveness for a person who neither believes nor seeks God. "The question for one who doesn't believe in God," Francis said, "lies in obeying one's conscience. Sin, also for those who don't have faith, exists when one goes against one's conscience."[10]

---

[5] See, for instance, *Gaudium et Spes*, no. 50.

[6] Joseph Ratzinger, "The Dignity of the Human Person," in *Commentary on the Documents of Vatican II: Volume 5, Pastoral Constitution on the Church in the Modern World,* ed. Herbert Vorgrimler (New York: Herder & Herder, 1969), 134–36.

[7] See especially Ratzinger's essay, "Conscience and Truth," in *Crisis of Conscience,* ed. John M. Haas (New York: Crossroad, 1996), 1–19.

[8] *Catechism of the Catholic Church,* nos. 1790–94.

[9] *Veritatis Splendor*, no. 64.

[10] Lizzy Davies, "Pope Francis Tells Atheists to Abide by Their Own Consciences," *Guardian* (September 11, 2013).

Those familiar with the views of the previous papacies charged Pope Francis with subjectivism.[11] But in fact he was appealing to a Catholic theological tradition affirming the authority of conscience that had been attenuated in the papacies of the previous decades. Then, in *Amoris Laetitia,* his document on the family from the spring of 2016, he challenged his fellow church leaders to step back from overly controlling efforts to shape the consciences of the Catholic faithful. The church, he said, has "been called to form consciences, not to replace them" (no. 37). He has spoken strongly in defense of the "fundamental right" of religious freedom but has declined opportunities to insert the papacy into the culture war conflicts that animate many American battles over conscience.[12] And he has also underscored the importance of the ancient Christian doctrine known as the *sensus fidelium*, which holds that the truth of Catholic teaching should be the result of an ongoing interplay between insights derived from the consciences of the whole church (and especially the consciences of the poor) and authoritative judgments made by the hierarchical magisterium.[13] We are at an open moment in the Catholic theological tradition of conscience, the familiar thinking of the last decades giving way to the recovery of another vibrant stream in the tradition.

In considering this new moment in the theological tradition of conscience in light of Catholic health care, it is essential to note the significance of issues of sex, gender, and reproductive health care. Many of the essays in this book focus on these issues. Consider the major topics at the center of the most publicized conflicts of conscience involving Catholic health care in the United States. First, there is the dispute between the Little Sisters of the Poor and the Obama administration over contraception and the Affordable Care Act's mandate regarding preventive health services. Then there are repeated disputes and lawsuits over Catholic hospitals refusing to provide tubal ligations for women seeking sterilizations or over cases of a pregnant woman coming to a Catholic hospital with possibly life-threatening prenatal complications. Driving such clashes are, of course, profound differences between Catholic and broader cultural notions of sexuality, of valuing prenatal life, and of the gendered status of women. But it is also important to note the contested nature of such concerns within Catholicism itself.

A final key contextual issue is the changing organizational and economic landscape of Catholic health care in the pluralist culture of the United States. One set of problems comes with expansion when discrete secular or non-Catholic

---

[11] See, for instance, *New Oxford Review,* New Oxford Notes: "Pope Francis & the Primacy of Conscience," (December 2013).

[12] See "Address of the Holy Father," Philadelphia, September 20, 2015; http://w2.vatican.va/

[13] See *Sensus Fidei in the Life of the Church,* International Theological Commission, 2014; http://www.vatican.va.

health care institutions become part of Catholic health care systems. Such expansions have been a way to extend care in part by sharing costs across a wide number of facilities. But complexities of conscience have also followed these developments. Internal to Catholicism, important debates have emerged about the degree of autonomy in medical practice that should be accorded previously secular hospitals that have become part of Catholic hospital systems. Should a non-Catholic hospital that previously performed tubal ligations (which are formally against Catholic moral doctrine) be permitted to continue this practice when the non-Catholic hospital becomes part of a Catholic hospital system? Indeed, it was this dispute—and the directive given that any hospital in a Catholic network may *not* perform such sterilizations—that was a significant factor in causing the former Catholic Health Care West to give up its formal Catholic affiliation and become Dignity Health in order to allow secular hospitals in the Dignity network to perform such surgeries.[14] Another problem relates to the existence of a Catholic hospital as the only health care facility in a large geographical area where patients of all backgrounds have little option but to go to the Catholic hospital. What is the appropriate balance between a Catholic hospital's refusal to perform a procedure that is contrary to Catholic doctrine and the conscientious desire of a patient who does not agree with Catholic doctrine? This is especially problematic when the person is legally entitled to a standard of care and has no other health care option in the large area where she lives.

We hope the essays in this book will help clarify answers to these and other crucial questions of conscience. Let's now briefly consider the essays. Ron Hamel's essay that begins the book is the fruit of more than a decade of work as the Senior Director, Ethics, for the Catholic Health Association, a position from which he recently retired. In that role, Hamel was involved in myriad disputes of conscience ranging from the highest levels of federal health care policy to the daily decisions taking place in countless clinical contexts. Amid all of this, he argues in his essay, Catholic health care has turned to the language of conscience but often has done so with insufficient clarity or with a default turn to a model of conscience that is legalistic, individualistic, and top-down. By contrast, Hamel turns to the idea of the "reciprocity of consciences" taken from the work of the great twentieth-century German moral theologian Bernhard Häring, whose writing factored significantly in the powerful discussion of conscience in *Gaudium et Spes.* Hamel draws on the "reciprocity of consciences" as a way to think more clearly about the significance of the consciences of *all* of those involved in Catholic health care, from Catholic bishops with the responsibility of over-

---

[14] For an account of the change to Dignity Health, see Carol Bayley, "From Catholic Health Care West to Dignity Health," *Conscience and Catholicism,* 145–50.

sight to non-Catholic patients who land unwittingly in the emergency room of a Catholic hospital.

Whereas Hamel's essay seeks to restore a social dimension to conscience, Anne Patrick's essay aims at reimagining conscience less as a defensive posture protecting innocence and more as a creative stance ready to assume responsibility amid the ambiguities of history. Patrick turns to rhetorical analysis to show the way that metaphors of innocence and cleanliness and purity—all invoked in a defensive posture of conscience—can work as blinders to what in fact is morally at stake in many situations in Catholic health care and beyond. In particular, Patrick argues that thinking of the formation of conscience more in keeping with what she calls the development of "creatively responsible moral agents" is a needed change in order to begin to address challenges like the role of racism in enduring health care inequities.

With Hamel's and Patrick's essays, we see complementary analyses of crucial ways in which the theology of conscience in Catholic health care should recover a more social and egalitarian and dynamic dimension. With Roberto Dell'Oro's essay, we have the opportunity to engage directly the fundamental changes in the theology of conscience made at the Second Vatican Council and to consider the implications of these changes for Catholic health care. Dell'Oro's essay considers the discussions of conscience in *Gaudium et Spes* and *Dignitatis Humanae* and shows the profound shift that took place at the council in the movement from conscience being understood as a deductive judgment on a singular moral act to conscience being considered as a moral and spiritual entity representative of the deepest meaning of a person as such. He concludes his essay by reflecting on the need for the integration of this change in the theology of conscience into the *Ethical and Religious Directives for Catholic Health Care*.[15]

Among the theoretical issues that Dell'Oro engages is the relationship of conscience to moral truth. Conscience indeed does attain moral truth, he argues, but it does not do so with the certainty presumed to be possible by Catholic moral thought before the Second Vatican Council. Lisa Fullam's essay tackles the specific challenge of conscience seeking moral truth in medical matters. What, she asks, can the conscience of a medical practitioner do when he or she is confronted with enduring moral doubt? This may be doubt raised by the medical complexity of the case at hand or by rapid technological changes relevant to treatment or by confusion about the application of traditional moral norms to a new and unforeseen situation. To address such doubt, Fullam goes back to the Catholic moral tradition to recover the virtues of *epikeia* (a disposition for acting in justice when a traditional norm does not

---

[15] United States Conference of Catholic Bishops, *Ethical and Religious Directives for Catholic Health Care Services*, 5th ed. (Washington, DC: USCCB, 2010).

apply) and skepticism (understood *not* as all-encompassing doubt but instead as a fruitful and open-ended disposition to consider a wide range of arguments in the face of a new and unforeseen challenge).

Does an institution have a "conscience"? Or is saying that an institution has a conscience simply a rhetorical way of describing a quality of an institution that would be better called "identity" or "moral agency"? We are accustomed to thinking of conscience as a dimension of a person. But many of the conflicts in US society around Catholic health care pit a notion of personal conscience against a notion of institutional conscience. Should the conscience of a patient seeking a tubal ligation prevail over the institutional conscience of a Catholic health care facility that refuses to provide such a procedure because of Catholic moral doctrine forbidding sterilization? In his essay, Thomas Nairn explores the contested notion of institutional conscience as it applies to Catholic health care and identifies crucial questions that should be part of the evaluation when institutional conscience is invoked. What is the precise relationship between the traditional theological notion of individual conscience and the analogical notion of institutional conscience? How does the notion of the institutional conscience of a Catholic health care institution relate to being part of the larger church, the US legal system, and the medical profession? And are there ways of conceiving of institutional conscience that can either intensify or ameliorate the conflicts of conscience in which Catholic health care may find itself?

The United States Supreme Court case of the Little Sisters of the Poor—formally known as *Zubik v. Burwell*—factors significantly in the next three essays. Kristin Heyer's essay considers the case in terms of the individual and social dimensions of conscience. Her theological work has explored the concept of "social sin." Among other things, "social sin" is a way of speaking about the social nature of all morality. Sin is not simply a personal failing, but personal sin exists in dynamic interaction with sin present in social structures and prevalent cultures. Heyer has such matters in mind as she considers the contentious passage of the Affordable Care Act in 2010 and its rippling aftermath in the Catholic community. Much of the opposition by Catholic bishops to provisions of the law like the contraceptive mandate has been couched in the language of conscience (the Little Sisters case is opposed to the contraceptive mandate). But to what extent, Heyer asks, has such opposition on the grounds of conscience in fact occluded the full range of moral concerns at stake in structural and cultural matters related to the distribution of health care? Has conscientious opposition to the contraceptive mandate been at the expense of concern for the just distribution of health care? And what is it about the way that conscience is conceived that allows a more appropriately broad field of moral concern to be discounted?

In the next essay, medical ethicist John Paris along with M. Patrick Moore Jr. examines contemporary appeals to conscientious objection by health care providers. In particular, they consider two cases that recently reached the United States Supreme Court. One is the *Stormans v. Wiesman* case involving Washington State pharmacists who object to distributing the Plan B contraceptive (in June 2016 the US Supreme Court declined to hear the case, thus leaving in place a Federal Appeals Court ruling ordering the pharmacists to comply with Washington State law and distribute Plan B). And the second is the case of the Little Sisters, who object to signing a form declaring their opposition to contraception because they believe by doing so they are involved illicitly in facilitating use of contraceptives by their employees (in May 2016 the US Supreme Court declined to rule on the merits of the case and returned it to lower courts for additional argument). Paris and Moore affirm the time-honored significance of conscientious objection. But the essay provides a set of questions by which to assess the validity of such appeals, which can range from a rightful stance against arbitrary power to a blindered solipsism taking an easy way out. Paris and Moore ask as part of the assessment: What is the price an objector is willing to pay for his or her stand? What awareness does the objector have of the consequences of his or her actions on the lives of others?

In her essay, Cathleen Kaveny considers the case of the Little Sisters as a representative instance of the contemporary way in which moral and theological concerns about conscience are primarily contested in a sphere of law and litigation. Kaveny asks, What is the relationship between the litigation strategy of the lawyers arguing on behalf of the Little Sisters and the Catholic moral and theological tradition of conscience that is at issue in the case? Also, how might the arguments in the case affect the development of the moral and theological tradition around conscience? Kaveny has written extensively elsewhere about the moral principle of cooperation, which in the Catholic tradition is used to assess the degree of moral culpability in complex situations when the wrongdoing of one agent appears to be aided by the actions of a second agent (the lawyers argued that for the Little Sisters to sign a form saying they opposed contraception was in fact an unacceptable and immoral instance of "cooperation" with the evil of using contraception). Kaveny calls use of the principle of cooperation on behalf of the Little Sisters "nothing short of nonsensical," and goes on to review other aspects of the legal case that present significant challenges for the Catholic moral tradition.

In his essay, Lawrence Nelson addresses what is perhaps the most sensitive topic in the general theme of conscience and Catholic health care, cases related to the care in Catholic health facilities of women whose pregnancy complications raise the medical possibility of terminating a pregnancy that is threatening the life of the mother. Indeed, this was the general scenario that took place at St. Joseph's Hospital in Phoenix in 2009. In that case, the hospital ethics committee permitted the termination of the pregnancy. In reaction, Archbishop Thomas Olmsted of Phoenix barred St. Joseph's from continuing as a formal Catholic health care facility.[16] Whose conscience should prevail in such cases? The American Civil Liberties Union has been involved in litigation with Catholic health care institutions over such matters. In his essay, Nelson considers the specifics of these lawsuits and attempts "to point out some misunderstandings, misconceptions, or questionable assumptions on both sides and to offer some suggestions of what the ACLU might better learn and appreciate about [Catholic health care] and of what Catholic health care might take to heart about the problems the ACLU has with the way it serves the general public."

With Kevin T. FitzGerald's essay, the book takes up in succession concerns about conscience and biotechnology; conscience and end of life issues; conscience, race, and Catholic health care; and conscience and classroom teaching. FitzGerald is a scientist and an ethicist and an expert on the latest developments in biotechnology related to genetics and other groundbreaking life sciences. In his essay, he explores a difficult question: How can the consciences of the general public be formed morally in order to assess these biotechnologies? This is not an academic question. Rather, it is one of great public significance because of the implications of these technologies to help and to harm human life. Moreover, FitzGerald notes, there is a powerful drive within science itself to continue this work—in some respects whether the public understands and approves of the work or not. In response to this challenge, FitzGerald argues on behalf of a process of conscience formation that is capable of engaging complex technological matters, that is accessible to all, and that is able to foster broad agreement. He bases this approach on key elements of the Catholic moral tradition on conscience such as discernment; a confidence in a common set of moral aspirations across all consciences, Catholic and otherwise; and the preferential option to include the poor and marginalized in such a process.

Some of the most vexing conscience issues in health care pertain to patients at the end of life. Gerald Coleman's essay considers the increasing number of laws in the United States that sanction physician-assisted suicide (PAS) and in particular the law that came into effect in California in June 2016. The *Ethical and Religious Directives* prohibit PAS at any Catholic health care facilities. But Coleman's concern is with how this practice has been approved and legally sanctioned by the larger society. He argues that one of the key factors propelling support for PAS is an individualistic and radically autonomous understanding of conscience that is widespread in contemporary American culture. In this view, the capacity of a conscience simply to make a choice is paramount, without sufficient regard for what a choice is for or for

---

[16] For an account of the case, see Bayley, 141-45.

the context in which such a choice is made. In turn, this autonomous view of conscience interacts with powerful cultural and economic forces to lead people readily to think that life is not worth living and that PAS is an honorable and the only way out. By contrast, Coleman argues in his essay on behalf of a Pope Francis–inspired understanding of conscience in which mercy plays a central role. The perspective of mercy, Coleman says, opens up the possibilities and duties of care and relationship and hope at the end of life.

Margaret McLean's essay takes on a different vexing issue at the end of life: The case of the conscience of an unrepresented patient. What is Catholic health care to do when a patient at the end of life is not able to represent himself or herself (due, for example, to dementia), does not have a family member or friend to indicate his or her wishes, and does not have anything like an advanced health care directive to provide guidance to a treatment team? Studies indicate that more than 25 percent of adult general medical inpatients are incapacitated in this way. To those treating them, the conscience of such patients is inaccessible. McLean's essay surveys this tragic problem in health care and offers a practical program for caring for those appropriately understood as among the "poorest of the poor."

In the Catholic tradition, the formation of conscience has classically been thought to apply to individuals who either learn the teaching of the church or develop the virtues that constitute good character. But what if such methods of conscience formation leave untouched assumptions about justice and injustice that are the bitter fruit of the powerful cultural forces of racism? In her essay, Shawnee Daniels-Sykes considers the particular challenge of the consciences of African Americans as they interact with Catholic health care. Having a history of systematic and deliberate mistreatment by health care of all types, many African Americans can often doubt whether health care is intended to help much at all. To respond to this reality, Daniels-Sykes proposes that Catholic health care consider the practices of a black liberation bioethics as a way to form the consciences of African American patients and to foster better care on the part of medical teams working with such patients.

Carol Taylor's essay concludes the book. Taylor is a master teacher at Georgetown University School of Medicine. In her essay, she reflects on teaching about conscience in such a setting—at a Catholic institution, amid many changes within Catholicism itself, with medical students of many different religious and philosophical backgrounds, with awareness of the delicate clinical contexts in which many of her students will one day be working (Taylor herself practiced nursing for many years), and in a medical and scientific world of rapid change. In her essay, she explores how different models of conscience in Catholic moral theology have met with different levels of receptivity in the classroom. She also offers some helpful teaching tools for opening up classroom conversations around these topics.

We offer this book in a spirit of service to those on all sides of these challenging matters in the United States and around the world. We trust that this book will open up conversations of all those involved—a true "reciprocity of consciences"—and that the outcome of those conversations will be a deeper respect and care for the men, women, and children touched by the sacred and priceless ministry of Catholic health care.

David E. DeCosse
Markkula Center for Applied Ethics, Santa Clara University

Thomas A. Nairn, OFM
Catholic Health Association of the United States

"Reciprocity of Consciences" and Catholic Health Care

Opportunities and Challenges

Ron Hamel

The exercise of conscience is an omnipresent reality in Catholic health care. Day in and day out, decisions are made of an ethical nature that bring conscience into play. Yet despite its omnipresence, considering conscience in Catholic health care is a significant challenge largely because of the diversity of contexts, persons, and understandings of conscience that are in play.

Regarding contexts, Catholic health care has a foot in two very different worlds—the religious world of Catholicism and the secular world of US health care.[1] It has a fundamentally religious identity and purpose (carrying on the healing mission of Jesus), while also carrying out a secular purpose (delivering health care) within an enterprise (US health care) that is thoroughly secular, in a society in which there is enormous moral and religious pluralism with a very strong dose of secularism. In addition, as part of the US health care system, Catholic health care has relationships with federal, state, and local government agencies. It interacts with and is dependent on numerous payers and vendors. To more adequately meet the health care needs of the innumerable communities it serves and to more effectively carry out its mission, Catholic health care has been and is, by necessity, increasingly partnering with a broad array of secular health care organizations. All of these various relationships create challenges in the exercise of conscience.

So do the various "persons" who are part of Catholic health care. Leadership, once the purview of "the Sisters," is now in the hands of laypeople, many of whom are not Catholic, some of whom are not Christian. The medical and nonmedical staffs of Catholic hospitals represent a broad spectrum of ethnic, religious, and moral diversity, and, increasingly, physicians

---

[1] See Thomas A. Nairn, "Catholic Health Care Must Stand in the Middle," *Health Progress* 94, no. 4 (July–August 2013): 87–89; Joseph Bernardin, "Catholic Identity: Resolving Conflicting Expectations," in *Selected Works of Joseph Cardinal Bernardin*, ed. Alphonse Spilly, vol. 2: *Church and Society* (Collegeville, MN: Liturgical Press, 2000), 167–75.

are becoming employees of these organizations. Probably most patients who come to Catholic hospitals are not Catholic. They too, along with their families, represent considerable diversity. Catholic health care facilities exist in communities in which there is religious and moral pluralism. In these myriad interactions, conscience is at play.

But what understanding of conscience? Conscience as subjective opinion? As simple obedience to policies, rules, laws, and authorities? Conscience as discernment in concrete situations? Conscience seeking to do what is self-serving or expedient, or conscience seeking to do what is right? And to what extent have these myriad consciences been formed? And by whom or by what?

The reality is that when one speaks about conscience in Catholic health care, one is not speaking about one thing. There are multiple understandings of conscience, and there are even more actual consciences representing a broad spectrum of how conscience operates and how and by what consciences have been formed. The challenges posed by this diversity are intensified by the fact that the exercise of conscience is most often implicit, and there is rarely if ever an explicit awareness that conscience is in play, or there are rarely discussions about conscience (what it is, what it entails, etc.), even though there are appeals made to it by administrators, staff, patients, and others.

Given the omnipresence of decisions of conscience in Catholic health care, the likely great diversity in consciences, and the fact that conscience is not something that is generally explicitly considered, there may be some value for Catholic health care to raise questions about and examine the understanding of conscience and explore some of its implications for the Catholic health ministry.

In what follows, I examine the understanding of conscience articulated by the German moral theologian Bernhard Häring, one of the most prominent and influential Catholic moral theologians of modern times, and then explore what that understanding might entail for Catholic health care. What is most appealing about Häring's description of conscience, particularly as found in *Free and Faithful in Christ*,[2] is not only his biblical and personalist emphasis but also his view of conscience as fundamentally relational. Although conscience is deeply personal and individual, it is not individualistic or relativistic. Häring's approach avoids the extremes of an individualistic subjectivism and relativism, as well as legalism. As such, it is an important corrective to much of what occurs in descriptions of, appeals to, and the

---

[2] Although Bernhard Häring discusses conscience extensively in volume 1 of *The Law of Christ* (Westminster, MD: Newman Press, 1965), 135–213, and in passing in other of his works, his treatment of conscience in *Free and Faithful in Christ*, volume 1 (New York: Seabury Press, 1978), 223–301, represents his most developed thought and will serve as the prime source for this discussion.

exercise of conscience. This relational aspect of conscience Häring terms the "reciprocity of consciences."

Conscience and the "Reciprocity of Consciences" in Bernhard Häring's Thought

The Nature of Conscience

For Häring,[3] drawing on biblical insights, conscience is the "heart" of the person, the core of one's being,[4] "an inner disposition and call to do good, to search honestly for God's will, in readiness to do it,"[5] and to seek the good of others. It is "the person's moral faculty, the inner core and sanctuary where one knows oneself in confrontation with God and with fellowmen."[6] Upon the heart is written the law of love that enables the heart to "grasp what is good and right."

Häring also speaks of conscience as the source of our very deepest yearning for wholeness and integrity.[7] According to Häring, we are created for wholeness, and conscience, the deepest part of ourselves, "is keenly sensitive to what can promote and what can threaten our wholeness and integrity," guiding us toward the Other and others.[8] In concrete situations, conscience's "longing for wholeness" helps guide the individual in discerning what God is calling him or her to do. Maintaining wholeness in the core of one's being results in a healthy conscience. If, however, intellect and will are in conflict, if they oppose each other, then the unity of the self is split.[9] This conscience, this yearning for wholeness and integrity, is a gift of God and is related to the idea that human beings are made in the image and likeness of God.

For the Christian, conscience takes on an added dimension. A Christian conscience is grounded in faith, in "an all-embracing Christ-consciousness."[10]

---

[3] Häring's understanding of the nature and function of conscience ideally should be considered in the context of the basic structure of his ethics which is one of word and response. God reveals God's self, inviting human beings into a salvific response. In his person and life, Christ is the fullness of God's self-revelation and call to fellowship, and the human response. See *Law of Christ*, 1:35–51, 51–53; *Law of Christ*, 2:47–50, 55–84 (Westminster, MD: Newman Press, 1963); *Free and Faithful in Christ*, 1:8–15, 66, 74–82.

[4] Häring, *Law of Christ*, 1:137–38, and *Free and Faithful in Christ*, 1:225–29.

[5] Häring, *Free and Faithful in Christ*, 1:225.

[6] Ibid., 224.

[7] Ibid., 34–38.

[8] Ibid., 234–36. Häring says something similar in *Law of Christ*, 143.

[9] Häring takes a holistic approach to conscience seeing it as neither just in the intellect (Aquinas) nor just in the will (Bonaventure), but rather in both and more. It involves all dimensions of the self, compenetrating in the core of one's being. It is the entire self as moral agent. See *Free and Faithful in Christ*, 1:230–32, 234–39; also, *Law of Christ*, 1:142–44.

[10] Ibid., 249.

It entails "being-in-Christ" and "putting on the mind of Christ." Such a grounding results in the "freedom of the children of God" (Rom 8:21), not a freedom to do what one wants, but rather a freedom to love as exemplified in the person and life of Christ. It is a freedom that requires ongoing response and responsibility toward all of God's creatures and all of God's creation.[11] This freedom means that the disciple is now under the law of Christ (Rom 8:2, 6:14) and no longer primarily subject to external, impersonal, minimal laws. Rather, the disciple is subject to the requirements of a faithful, loving, personal relationship.[12] The new law is interior, not imposed from without as was the "old (Mosaic) law" or any other laws. Furthermore, it is not one of requirements, restrictions, and prohibitions, but of the ever-increasing realization of the "works of the Spirit" (Gal 5:22–23), the ideals of the Sermon on the Mount (Mt 5), and the goal of perfect love. These "goal-commandments" are, for Häring, *normative* ideals.

Häring sees conscience as closely associated with a person's basic life direction. In the depths of the self, a person makes the fundamental choice to respond lovingly or unlovingly to the call to fellowship with God and with fellow human beings. This fundamental direction of a person's life is more important for Häring than determining the rightness or wrongness of particular actions, though this basic orientation does find expression in a person's attitudes, dispositions, motives, and actions.[13] Ongoing conversion is required to the extent that these latter are not consistent with an individual's basic life direction or fundamental orientation.[14] Discipleship and a choice for a positive life orientation or "fundamental option" facilitates knowing by connaturality, that is, a type of intuitive knowledge resulting from being deeply committed to or being attuned to the good and to love. It is the knowledge born of love.

The Primacy of Conscience

Consistent with the Catholic theological tradition and the teaching of Vatican II,[15] Häring affirms the primacy of conscience. "A sincere conscience is, for everyone," he states, "the supreme authority under God."[16] He also recognizes, of course, that conscience is not infallible. He notes the statement

---

[11] Häring, *Law of Christ*, 1:35–37, 45–51; 2:347, 381–89; 406; *Free and Faithful in Christ*, 1:66, 74–82.

[12] Bernhard Häring, *Christian Maturity*, trans. Arlene Swidler (New York: Herder and Herder, 1967), 9–23; also *Free and Faithful in Christ*, 1:67–75.

[13] Häring, *Free and Faithful in Christ*, 1:164–218.

[14] Häring, *Law of Christ*, 1:387–419; *Free and Faithful in Christ*, 1:215–18, 417–26.

[15] Thomas Aquinas, *Disputed Questions on the Truth*, 16 and 17; Alphonsus Liguori, *Theologia moralis*, I, tr. 1, ch. 2, art. 1 and 2; John Henry Newman, *Letter to the Duke of Norfolk*, sec. 5, 246. *Gaudium et Spes*, 16, 17; *Dignitatis Humanae*, 3, 14.

[16] Häring, *Free and Faithful in Christ*, 1:282.

in *Gaudium et Spes* (no. 16) that conscience errs rather frequently. However, Häring is quick to observe that the council acknowledges that conscience can err without personal guilt, without conscience losing its dignity. "This is so," Häring explains, "whenever the intentions are right and the conscience is sincerely seeking the best solution. By 'best solution,' I do not mean the abstract best, but what is for the person here and now, in this particular situation, the most fitting step in the right direction."[17] It is worth quoting Häring at some length here to better appreciate his reverence for a sincere conscience:

> When a person is truly looking for what is good and right, there is a kind of indefectibility in the conscience. With unwavering certainty, it orders the will to conform with the intellect. . . . This imperative, written in the heart, has moral majesty even though it may have a background of defective moral knowledge, indeed even if it makes a fully erroneous judgment. If the error in evaluation is in no way due to negligence and ill will, there is nothing in the faculty of conscience itself which would murmur against acting on the ground of that erroneous judgment. . . .
>
> An inculpably erroneous dictate of conscience obliges in the same way as a correct conscience. . . . Hence, Cardinal Newman is correct in his famous statement, "I have always contended that obedience even to an erring conscience was the way to gain light."[18]

Given the dignity and primacy of conscience, Häring maintains that no one has the right to interfere intentionally with the exercise of another person's conscientious decision (unless to prevent harm to another), and no one ought to refrain from acting on the same. This assumes, of course, that the conscience is sincere and that it has not become dulled by sin or unconcerned with the search for truth and goodness.

Häring explains further. Drawing on the thought of Saint Alphonsus de Liguori, the founder of Häring's religious congregation (the Redemptorists) and the patron saint of moral theologians, he observes that there are times when a sincere conscience cannot internalize a law of the church or of secular society, or some teaching based on natural law. This may be due not to an erroneous assessment, but rather to an impossibility in accepting the teaching or law. It may be the best the person can do "in the direction toward more light." Furthermore, "it would be a most serious fault against the dignity of the conscience if a pastor, a confessor, or anyone else were to press the person to act against his sincere conscience, or indiscreetly try to inculcate the

---

[17] Ibid., 239–40.
[18] Ibid., 240.

objective norm if this would disturb the person who simply cannot accept a particular precept or norm."[19]

The "Reciprocity of Consciences"

Although Häring's understanding of conscience is profoundly personal, it is not, as previously noted, either private or individualistic. At its core, conscience is fundamentally relational—in relationship with the Other, with Christ (for Christians), with the self (seeking integrity and wholeness), and with human others whose good one must constantly seek. Häring's notion of the "reciprocity of consciences," quite possibly his most important contribution to an understanding of conscience, further develops the interpersonal and communitarian aspects of conscience and is critical to conscience formation and to avoiding subjectivism and relativism.

Häring begins his discussion of the reciprocity of consciences by noting that the root words of conscience (*con* and *scientia*, "to know together") indicate a "mutuality of consciences."[20] He goes on to explain:

> We have to see the reciprocal action. The healthy conscience allows wholesome relationships with neighbor and the community. Equally and perhaps more fundamentally, wholesome relationships in mutual love and respect, and a healthy community and society, greatly promote the development and health of the individual conscience.[21]

Hence, the mutuality of consciences involves, in part, the individual conscience promoting the good of the other and of the community; in turn, the other and the community, when good, contribute to the development of the individual's conscience.

More specifically, Häring maintains that it is only through the experience of relationship with the other that one is able to come to one's own self-awareness, identity, and integrity. But this also involves accepting the other in his or her selfhood and uniqueness. "Without this synthesis between the reverence that allows the other to be who he is and the solidarity by which the persons are a source of identity, integrity and authenticity for each other, there can be neither true freedom nor creative fidelity."[22] Consciences are fully alive and creative, according to Häring, when they are free not only to give and receive knowledge and experience, but also to give themselves to one another.

---

[19] Ibid., 241.
[20] Ibid., 265.
[21] Ibid.
[22] Ibid., 266.

This leads to a profound respect for the conscience of the other. Here Häring appeals to Romans 14 where Paul addresses a particular instance of reciprocity of consciences. The issue is the eating of ritually clean and unclean foods. Paul urges Christians who, like him, see no difference between the two to respect the consciences of those who refrain from eating ritually unclean foods and these latter to respect the consciences of those who see no difference. "The person who eats must not hold in contempt the other who does not, and he who does not eat must not pass judgment on the one who does; for God has accepted him" (Rom 14:2–3).[23] Häring comments on this passage: "This mutuality of conscience is rooted in our faith relationship with Christ. If we live for the Lord, we also live for each other in concern and respect for one another's conscience."[24]

Not only does the reciprocity of consciences involve a mutual respect of consciences when there may be disagreement on a particular matter, it also involves a sensitivity to the conscience of the other and at times requires refraining from acting in a particular way so as not to disturb the conscience of the other or of others. Here Häring appeals to 1 Corinthians 10 where some in the community brag about the freedom of their consciences when it comes to eating meat sacrificed to idols. Paul asks them, "But does everything help the building of the community? Each of you must regard not his own interests but the other person's. . . . Whatever you are doing, do all for the honor of God: give no offense to Jews or Greeks or to the Church of God" (1 Cor 10:23–24; 28–32).[25] Hence, the reciprocity of consciences for Häring means also that one must always consider the impact of one's decision of conscience and one's actions on the conscience of others and on the good of the community.

Reciprocity of consciences also means building up the community. Paul urges the community to be as concerned about each other as they are about themselves (Rom 12:16). And this concern extends even to those who are hostile. Häring here quotes Romans 12:20: "If your enemy is hungry, feed him; if he is thirsty, give him a drink. . . . Do not let evil conquer you, but use good to defeat evil."[26] By building up the community for good, we are also creating an environment for the development of healthy consciences in the direction of the good. This community emphasis in Häring's understanding of conscience helps to protect against individualism in the conception, development, and exercise of conscience as well as relativism in moral judgments. Seeking truth together, taking account of others in judgments of conscience can provide an important guide and corrective.

---

[23] Ibid., 268.

[24] Ibid.

[25] Ibid.

[26] Ibid., 267.

Seeking truth together is a further dimension of a reciprocity of consciences. Häring makes it quite clear that no one, not even the hierarchical magisterium of the church, has a monopoly on truth. The entire pilgrim People of God must be engaged in an ongoing search for truth, deciphering the signs of the times and not being bound by "ossified formulations."[27] The never-ending search for truth with others is an essential element of conscience for Häring.

> We understand conscience, then, as man's innermost yearning toward "wholeness" which manifests itself in openness to neighbor and community in a common searching for goodness and truth. Man's conscience is unthinkable without an active sharing of experience and insights with others searching for truth in mutual responsibility.[28]

This search for truth is not limited to members of the Christian community, but rather involves all persons who seek the good.

There are two other relevant elements that Häring discusses in conjunction with the reciprocity of consciences. The first has to do with the formation of conscience. Häring strongly rejects the notion that the formation of conscience for the community of believers consists in simply aligning one's conscience with or submission to the teaching of the church or formulations of natural law. This is contrary to his entire understanding of conscience, as we have seen. Such an approach would contribute to a superego-type conscience. Church teaching, formulations of natural law, moral principles, and the like are essential in the search for truth and in the process of making concrete decisions, but they do not replace this process. And, for Häring, what is more important and a part of the reciprocity of consciences is the "exemplary person who lives truthfully under the authority of his conscience and respects wholly the conscience of others."[29] He praises as gifts to the entire church the "'authority' of the prophets and the many humble saints who live fully the reciprocity of consciences under God and in full co-responsibility with and for all of God's people."[30]

The remaining significant aspect of the reciprocity of consciences is what Häring outlines as the "rules of prudence for taking moral risks."[31] These

---

[27] Ibid., 283.

[28] Bernhard Häring, *A Theology of Protest* (New York: Farrar, Straus and Giroux, 1970), 65. See also *Free and Faithful in Christ*, 2:24–25; *Morality Is for Persons* (New York: Farrar, Straus and Giroux, 1971), 158; *Law of Christ*, 1:48.

[29] Häring, *Free and Faithful in Christ*, 1:282.

[30] Ibid. Häring here also discusses the roles of the magisterium and theologians. See 282–84.

[31] Ibid., 290–94. This discussion follows and occurs in the context of Häring's "new

rules provide further insight into Häring's understanding of conscience and its workings. Häring observes that the risk of making mistakes is unavoidable if one operates out of one's conscientious convictions and courageously searches for truth and goodness beyond what might be demanded by a superego-type conscience which would likely not permit such risk. The first "rule" or "requirement" is that church authorities assist people in creatively seeing "the enormous realm of the good" beyond legal boundaries. Focusing only on legal boundaries may blind one to the real needs of people. Second, when it comes to convincing a conscience of the goodness of an opinion, appeal should be made not to authority, but rather to substantial, well-grounded reasons. Third, while the teaching of the church must be taken seriously, it is also important to realize that some formulations are no longer adequate to new historical contexts and persons may feel "obliged to give precedence to higher and more urgent values."

Next, all need to be involved in an ongoing learning process in a reciprocity of consciences that might lead to a revision of earlier positions. Persons' consciences must always strive to come to the best possible solution in the current situation with current knowledge. Fifth, arbitrary decisions of conscience are not acceptable. They violate the dignity of conscience. Rather, there should be "a careful evaluation of the present opportunities, of the needs of fellowmen and community in view of God's gifts, and always in light of our vocation to holiness."[32] Finally, Häring maintains that if members of the church do not meet in dialogue and a mutual respect that manifests creative fidelity toward tradition and creative responsibility for the here and now and for the future of humankind and the church, then divisions can emerge around any number of issues. Here he quotes *Gaudium et Spes* (43) where the faithful are urged to "always try to enlighten one another through honest discussion, preserving mutual charity and caring above all for the common good."

A word needs to be said here about prudence, which is central to Häring's understanding of conscience. He refers to it as "vigilant prudence." The "vigilance" is essentially attentiveness to God's call in the here and now, being attentive to the voice of conscience, symbolized by the virgins in the Gospel who are always ready for God's coming. "Vigilant prudence," says Häring, "gives the conscience the delicate tact for the situation and deciphers even in the most confused and confusing events the present opportunities and needs. . . . Thus, the conscience is sensitive for the Lord's calling and trustful of his grace."[33] Vigilant prudence has a twofold task: first, it must correctly and thoroughly perceive the reality of the situation in all its complexity, and,

---

look at probabilism," 284–90.

   [32] Ibid., 292.

   [33] Ibid., 254.

second, it must ensure that conscience's response both respects God's gifts and adequately and appropriately addresses human needs. While prudence is a divine gift, it can be developed through personal effort. It is best developed, for Häring, by intensifying one's relationship with God.[34]

Conscience, the Reciprocity of Consciences, and Catholic Health Care

Can Bernhard Häring's description of conscience be of any help to Catholic health care? I would like to consider three possible contributions (though there may certainly be others): respect for the dignity and inviolability of conscience, the formation of conscience, and creating communities of moral deliberation.

Respect for the Primacy of Conscience

As we have seen, Häring, echoing the Catholic tradition, maintains the supremacy and inviolability of conscience. The question for Catholic health care is how to exercise the utmost respect for conscience in all the interactions and relationships that occur within Catholic health care. These relationships are too many and too broad in scope to address here. But it is important to raise the question: How does Catholic health care respect the consciences of the individuals and groups with whom it interacts, and is it adequate? It is quite safe to say that there is respect for conscience when the "other" decides or acts in a manner consistent with the beliefs and value commitments of the organization.

But what happens, for example, when a staff member of a hospital or long-term care facility refuses to participate in some procedure or some behavior or practice? The majority of facilities most likely have policies that attempt to accommodate the individual's beliefs. Such accommodation is a part of respect, allowing the individual to act on the basis of his or her conscience. But then how is this individual viewed and treated by staff and administrators? What does "respect for conscience" entail in these circumstances? Is there a price to pay for standing on conscience?

More challenging yet is the situation of the physician who comes to the conscientious decision that a tubal ligation is necessary to prevent serious and possibly lethal harm from occurring to a particular patient for whom there are few if any other plausible options. The physician truly believes that this procedure is the right thing to do in this set of circumstances, and that the good of this patient, her health and life and the good of her family, are more important than preserving the integrity of a biological process. The physi-

---

[34] Häring discusses prudence at considerable length in *The Law of Christ*, 1:498–513.

cian believes herself or himself morally bound to do this and not to do it to be morally wrong. What would respect for the inviolability of conscience mean here when church teaching and the *Ethical and Religious Directives*[35] (in which church teaching is specified for different areas of medical practice) forbid all direct sterilizations? And what of the conscience of the patient who has come to a conscientious decision that a tubal ligation is the right thing to do for her own well-being and that of her family?

Does the prohibition of sterilization force these individuals to act contrary to their consciences? Does it impose on them an obligation they are not "ready" to accept, as Häring (and Alphonsus Liguori) would put it? Is there any room in these types of situations for Häring's creative freedom and responsibility? Several authors on the issue of conflicts of conscience suggest the importance of "tolerance" in certain situations.[36] Is there space for tolerance in difficult circumstances? And are there boundaries to such tolerance?[37] To use Häring's language, what is God's call in these circumstances? And might there be a need to give precedence to a more urgent value? As the theologian Anne Patrick observes in *Liberating Conscience: Feminist Explorations in Catholic Moral Theology*, "Surely there is need to study anew the Gospel stories of Jesus breaking rules for the sake of his neighbor's welfare and proclaiming that a person's need can preempt even important obligations of religious law."[38] And how does the Catholic health care organization maintain its moral integrity in these types of situations when it is at once a ministry of the church, carrying on Jesus' ministry of healing, and a provider of health care seeking the good of those in need? Häring speaks of the need to sometimes rethink certain moral teachings that may no longer adequately apply to new realities. Is it time for an honest and open dialogue on the possibility of tubal ligations for serious medical indications and perhaps an acknowledgment that the teaching needs to be adapted to new realities?

---

[35] United States Conference of Catholic Bishops, *Ethical and Religious Directives for Catholic Health Care Services* (Washington, DC: USCCB, 2009).

[36] See, for example, Daniel Sulmasy, "Institutional Conscience and Moral Pluralism in Health Care," *New Theology Review* 10, no. 4 (1997): 13. He defines "tolerance" as "mutual respect for conscience." See also Thomas May, "Rights of Conscience in Health Care," *Social Theory and Practice* 27 (January 2001): 111–28.

[37] Sulmasy also proposes "boundaries of tolerance." See 15–19. Sulmasy maintains that "the grounds for contravening someone's conscientious disagreement must be very strong," stronger to compel someone to perform an action than to require them to refrain from acting (16). While this may be generally true, it may not always be the case. Being compelled to refrain from acting could be as serious a violation of conscience with as serious or more serious consequences as being compelled to act.

[38] Anne E. Patrick, *Liberating Conscience: Feminist Explorations in Catholic Moral Theology* (New York: Continuum, 1996), 194.

These are just two examples where respect for conscience can be a challenge. There are numerous others. But if conscience is to be taken seriously, Catholic health care will need to grapple with how to achieve respect for the dignity of conscience in concrete circumstances, paying attention to all the relational dimensions suggested by Häring. These relational dimensions call for a balancing of the claims of conscience. There is much work to be done to further address these issues.

Formation of Conscience

Formation of conscience is critical to Häring's understanding of conscience as it is to any conception of conscience. As we saw with Häring, one's natural orientation toward the good, toward wholeness and integrity, toward the Other and others must be nourished and strengthened. If this does not occur, conscience can become dulled or even blinded. For Häring, one must make the tree good at its roots in order for the fruit to be good. In addition, formation of conscience must occur prior to and in the process of judgments of conscience. Formation prior to judgments is intimately tied to an aspect of the reciprocity of consciences, learning the right and the good from the communities to which one belongs. And formation in the process of judgments refers to the fact that in and through our moral choices we shape ourselves to become certain kinds of persons and that in turn disposes us to decide and act in certain ways in the future.

Formation is so important for Häring because, as we have seen, he does not perceive conscience in a superego sense, that is, as rigidly obedient to the commands of various sources of authority. Rather, conscience seeks the good, the appropriate response to its multiple relationships in concrete situations, and with creative freedom, fidelity, and responsibility. Häring's conception of conscience requires even more formation than a view of conscience that is subservient to the commands of authorities. It is essential in order to prevent subjectivism and relativism.

Furthermore, formation is an essential aspect of a relational understanding of conscience, of the reciprocity of consciences. One's conscience is shaped by the others and the communities with which one is in relation. It is also shaped in the search for truth, which is largely a community endeavor.

As noted at the beginning of this essay, there are hundreds of conscience decisions made in Catholic health care organizations every day by an innumerable diversity of consciences. This pluralism of individual consciences is a reality in Catholic health care and cannot be changed. However, Catholic health care organizations have their own religious and moral identity. They too are called to wholeness and integrity. In view of this, it seems reasonable, indeed fitting, for these organizations to expect that decisions that are made in the name of the organization or by individuals as individuals within the organization at minimum not contravene the identity of the organization and, most preferably, are consistent with, advance, and deepen that identity.

For this to occur, individuals need to embody in their decisions the fundamental value commitments of the organization. Ideally, they will be espoused, incorporated into their own consciences, but at minimum they need to be known and operative in decisions and behaviors. This requires some degree of formation—formation in appropriate aspects of the religious and moral identity of Catholic health care. Many will appropriate these dimensions into their own consciences; some will not internalize them, but nonetheless apply them; others may ignore or resist them, a sign that they probably should not be working in the organization.

This formation is a formation into the ethos or culture of the organization, into its religious and moral identity. It should be an ongoing and deliberate process, employing various methods. It will likely not be recognized as or called "formation of conscience," but it in fact is. And consistent with Häring's approach to formation of conscience, the emphasis is not on rules or policies, though these are certainly important and even necessary, but rather on helping individuals come to appreciate and appropriate the mission and value commitments of the organization. In this process, it would be well not to forget the witness, the exemplary example, of those who best embody and reflect the identity of the organization and not neglect the "prophets"—those who call the organization to conversion. As Häring notes, both of these types of people are critical to the formation of conscience.

If Catholic health care is to take conscience seriously, it must be engaged in conscience formation so that the myriad decisions made on a daily basis by individuals and the organization reflect and strengthen the identity of the organization.[39]

Communities of Moral Discourse

As previously discussed, Häring's notion of the reciprocity of consciences involves "knowing together," which for him entails a searching for truth together. While such a search may occur for believers within a community of believers, it is not limited to believers. "Conscience unites us with all men in the search for truth," says Häring. "Since the Christian community did not receive all the answers from the very beginning and does not yet have all the

---

[39] Formation of conscience frequently occurs with regard to patients and their families as they face difficult treatment choices. See USCCB, *Ethical and Religious Directives for Catholic Health Care Services*, no. 28.

answers or the whole truth, natural law has both the possibility and the need for growth through shared human experience and co-reflection."[40]

What Häring says about the reciprocity of consciences in the search for truth would seem to have applicability to Catholic health care organizations. If conscience were taken seriously in these organizations, conscience that has some resemblance to what Häring describes, then the search for truth by Catholic health care organizations and within such organizations would seem to be a necessity as well as an opportunity. A Catholic health care organization can be, to use ethicist James Gustafson's term, a "community of moral discourse" within which there are smaller communities of moral discourse. What this means is that those who speak for the organization as well as other discrete groups within the organization gather as appropriate to explicitly discern the right thing to do from an ethical perspective. This would be an exercise of the "reciprocity of consciences."

Such an exercise does not reside solely in an organization's ethics committee. As theologian/ethicist John Glaser has reminded us, health care ethics committees "are only one—and not alone the most important one—of many centers of ethical deliberation and action in a health care institution," one of many centers of moral responsibility.[41] Other such critical moral agents include, according to Glaser, all major individuals and groups within the health care organization, from the CEO and board of trustees to key positions (e.g., business development) and committees (e.g., finance).[42]

Häring would probably add that anyone who has some competence to address an issue should also be part of a community of moral discourse and not just "major individuals and groups." He would probably also agree with James Gustafson's observation that communities of moral discourse "also need to bring into participation persons who represent various interests, conflicting loyalties and values, so that whatever consensus emerges is informed by the feelings and judgments of various groups."[43] Gustafson affirms that discourse among morally serious individuals is more likely to result in fitting and responsible judgments than decisions that are made individually. This echoes Häring's reciprocity of consciences.

Glaser goes on to identify four elements for such ethical deliberation to occur: (1) a community of reflection as the primary agent of ethical decision-making, that is, "the group of persons needed to surround the problem at

---

[40] Häring, *Morality Is for Persons*, 158.

[41] John Glaser, "Hospital Ethics Committees: One of Many Centers of Responsibility," *Theoretical Medicine* 10 (1989): 278.

[42] Ibid., 278–79, 281.

[43] James M. Gustafson, "The Church: A Community of Moral Discourse," in *The Church as Moral Decision-Maker* (Philadelphia: Pilgrim Press, 1970), 92.

hand—with their minds, imaginations, and hearts";[44] (2) a consensus on some fundamental value priorities, primarily the values of Catholic health care as well as the organization's value commitments; (3) engaging the complexity of ethical issues in a manner that is logical, systematic, critical, consistent, and adequate to the issue at hand; (4) a process, a "fullness of reflection," that is adequate to the complexity of the community of concern and the complexity of the issue being addressed.[45]

Other of Häring's themes would also be critical to communities of moral discourse. These might include a creative fidelity to the Gospel and the church, creative freedom and responsibility, attention to the goal-commandments, vigilant prudence, building up the community, and respect for and sensitivity to the conscience of others.

Vatican II retrieved and affirmed the best of the Catholic tradition regarding conscience and proposed an incipient personalist understanding. Many moral theologians, Häring chief among them, contributed to and further developed that understanding. Unfortunately, in the years following the council, that understanding was eclipsed by an emphasis on conscience as obedience to the magisterium.[46] The role of personal conscience as a creative activity was diminished. That is changing, however.

Perhaps the best example of this change, within the church itself, is the teaching of Pope Francis as reflected in his two apostolic exhortations, his many other writings, his speeches and homilies, as well as his interviews. The clearest articulation is perhaps found in *Amoris Laetitia* where Francis states that the church and its pastors "have been called to form consciences, not to replace them" and that they "also find it hard to make room for the consciences of the faithful, who very often respond as best they can to the Gospel amid their limitations" (37).[47] He affirms that the faithful "are capable of carrying out their own discernment in complex situations" (37) and that conscience "can also recognize with sincerity and honesty what for now is the most generous response which can be given to God, and come to see with a certain moral security that it is what God himself is asking amid the concrete complexity of one's limits, while yet not fully the objective ideal" (303).

---

[44] Ibid., 282.

[45] Ibid., 283, 285, 285–86.

[46] For further discussion of this point, see Linda Hogan, *Confronting the Truth: Conscience in the Catholic Tradition* (Mahwah, NJ: Paulist, 2000); Robert Smith, *Conscience and Catholicism: The Nature and Function of Conscience in Contemporary Moral Theology* (Lanham, MD: University Press of America, 1998).

[47] Pope Francis, *Amoris Laetitia* (Rome: Libreria Editrice Vaticana, 2016). There is much in *Evangelii Gaudium* (2013) that echoes themes in Häring's moral theology and discussion of conscience. See, for example, 35–37, 39, 43, 44.

Similar to Häring, Francis states that "a subject may know full well the rule, yet have great difficulty in understanding its 'inherent values', or be in a concrete situation which does not allow him or her to act differently and decide otherwise without further sin. As the Synod Fathers put it, 'factors may exist which limit the ability to make a decision'" (301). Also, like Häring, Francis appeals to the "law of gradualness" which he borrows from Saint Pope John Paul II (295).

Francis goes further, recognizing the difficulty of applying general norms to concrete situations. Appealing to Aquinas (*Summa Theologiae*, I-II, q. 94, art. 4), Francis states that

> it is reductive simply to consider whether or not an individual's actions correspond to a general law or rule, because that is not enough to discern and ensure full fidelity to God in the concrete life of a human being. . . . It is true that general rules set forth a good, which can never be disregarded or neglected, but in their formulation they cannot provide absolutely for all particular situations. (304)

Much more could be said about Francis and conscience, but the point should be clear. Pope Francis is rehabilitating conscience and doing so in a manner that echoes many of the themes found in Häring's understanding.

Rehabilitating the understanding and role of conscience, affirming its primacy and inviolability, and conceiving it in personalist and relational terms, as does Bernhard Häring, has actual implications and consequences. At least in Catholic health care, it is not at all clear that these implications and consequences have been fully perceived and addressed. Nor does it seem to be the case that Catholic health care espouses and employs a robust understanding of conscience. Appealing to conscience only in very limited situations is insufficient. Conscience as a whole must be engaged, and here there is considerable work yet to be done before respect for the inviolability of conscience, the reciprocity of consciences, and formation of conscience are adequately addressed, along with the practices, processes, policies, and guidelines needed to support them. This will require intentional efforts and difficult work, surely a significant challenge, but also a significant opportunity for more deeply and fully carrying on the healing ministry of Jesus.

THE RHETORIC OF CONSCIENCE

Pope Francis, Conversion, and Catholic Health Care

Anne E. Patrick, SNJM

> Why complicate something so simple? Conceptual tools
> exist to heighten contact with realities they seek to explain,
> not to distance us from them. This is especially the case
> with those biblical exhortations which summon us so force-
> fully to brotherly love, to humble and generous service, to
> justice and mercy toward the poor. Jesus taught us this way
> of looking at others by his words and actions. So why cloud
> something so clear?
>
> —Pope Francis, *Evangelii Gaudium*

"Will not someone in authority in the Church tell the Little Sisters that they can fill out the form with a clear conscience?" This cri de coeur was voiced by Michael Sean Winters online after the July 2015 decision of the US Tenth Circuit Court of Appeals against the Little Sisters of the Poor.[1] They had objected to cooperating with the Affordable Care Act even to the extent of completing paperwork to indicate unwillingness to be a party to an insurance policy that they believed facilitated access to contraceptive services for their employees. The sisters have since appealed to the United States Supreme Court, which in April 2016 remanded the case to lower courts for further argument.

"It's this clean white conscience that is the biggest impediment to racial justice," declared Maureen H. O'Connell in another cri de coeur, expressed online after Trayvon Martin, an African American teenager, was killed by a white neighborhood "watchman," George Zimmerman. The February 2012

---

[1] Michael Sean Winters, "The Becket Fund, Not the Little Sisters, Lose," July 16, 2015, http://ncronline.org.

shooting of a boy carrying snacks home from a store drew national attention to the vulnerability of African American males in a racist society, but
as O'Connell noted, the incident failed to elicit "much by way of statements
by Catholic leaders or empathetic rituals by Catholic parishes." This led her
to conclude, "It is time we examine our culture, as well as our individual
consciences."[2] Bryan N. Massingale has also argued that racism "cannot be
attacked through strategies aimed at individual conscience formation alone,
whether this is conceived of as a process of information gathering or moral
maturation." As he explains, "One's sense of right and wrong, one's grasp
of morality, and one's very conscience become blunted and twisted by one's
socialization in a culture of racism."[3]

Both of these concerns—the case of the Little Sisters and the evil of
intransigent, unconscious, systemic white racism—are important. To address
them effectively, we will do well to examine how the term "conscience" is
used in Catholic culture, and perhaps make a firm purpose to amend some
of the ways we understand and use the term, or at least to employ it more
thoughtfully. Massingale calls for a "new direction in conscience formation"
that involves "cross-racial solidarity" and requires not simply information, but
rather "conversion."[4] Such a conversion also has the potential to lessen the
drift toward sectarian opposition to legislation that is necessarily imperfect
under the conditions of democratic pluralism, not to mention human finitude,
which we see in the case of the Little Sisters.

Massingale's call for repentance and cross-racial solidarity has gained
urgency as we learn of more incidents of violence against African Americans, ranging from the brutal shooting of Laquan McDonald by Chicago
police officer Jason Van Dyke in October 2014 to the massacre of nine black
Christians at Mother Emanuel Church in Charleston in June 2015 by twen-
ty-one-year-old white supremacist Dylann Storm Roof. Moreover, with
anti-Muslim sentiment gaining ground in the wake of terrorism inspired by
the group calling itself the Islamic State, especially massacres in Paris and
San Bernardino and Orlando in 2015 and 2016, it seems clear that conversion to cross-cultural solidarity is also needed. Pope Francis has only upped
the moral ante by pleading for the conversion required to heal the earth in
Laudato Si': "A healthy relationship with creation is one dimension of overall
personal conversion, which entails the recognition of our errors, sins, faults

---

[2] Maureen H. O'Connell, "Catholics and Racism: From Examination of Conscience
to Examination of Culture," March 30, 2012, http://ncronline.org.

[3] Bryan Massingale, "Conscience Formation and the Challenge of Unconscious
Racial Bias," in *Conscience and Catholicism: Rights, Responsibilities, and Institutional
Policies*, ed. David E. DeCosse and Kristin E. Heyer (Maryknoll, NY: Orbis Books, 2015),
63–64.

[4] Ibid., 64–65.

and failures, and leads to heartfelt repentance and desire to change." Individual conversion and efforts are not enough: "The ecological conversion needed to bring about lasting change is also a community conversion."[5]

Many factors are required for progress toward the conversion that is needed. Here I isolate just one, the rhetoric of conscience, and suggest that some improvement in Catholics' use of the language of conscience may yield promising results. I recommend that we give more attention to the metaphoric nature of language about conscience and inquire, paradoxically, whether lessening attention to something called "formation of conscience" may prove helpful, at least temporarily. Something might be gained if we spoke instead of forming creatively responsible moral agents.[6] I highlight the issue of white racism in this country, because this evil continues to be linked with great disparities in health insurance, health care, and medical outcomes, and this problem deserves more attention from white academics. Racism is an evil that most white Catholics acknowledge intellectually, but it is not usually central to our personal sense of moral obligation. Acknowledging that the Catholic Health Association has shown leadership in promoting efforts to address both health disparities and climate change, I will indicate that Pope Francis's teaching, both in style and substance, invites believers to make such concerns more of a priority, and thus to "bring forth fruit in charity for the life of the world," as the Second Vatican Council hoped would be the result of a renewed moral theology. The council's criterion of practical benefit to the world suggested that past emphasis in moral theology had been too preoccupied with the state of believers' souls to take sufficient notice of its effects on the well-being of persons within and beyond the Catholic community.[7] Fifty years after the council, Pope Francis voiced a similar desire for practical benefit to the world when he proclaimed a special "Jubilee of Mercy," so that "the witness of believers might grow stronger and more effective." His rhetoric bypasses discussions of how to form consciences and simply says, "Let us open our eyes and see the misery of the world, the wounds of our brothers and sisters who are denied their dignity, and let us recognize that we are compelled to heed their cry for help!"[8]

In what follows I first discuss how metaphor influences our understanding of conscience and moral growth, and then suggest that Pope Francis

---

[5] *Laudato Si'*, 218, 219.

[6] I develop this point more fully in Anne E. Patrick, *Women, Conscience, and the Creative Process* (New York: Paulist Press, 2011), 52–54.

[7] Second Vatican Council, *Decree on Priestly Formation (Optatem Totius*, no. 6), quoted here from *The Documents of Vatican II*, ed. Walter M. Abbott (New York: America Press, 1966), 452. I draw here on Anne E. Patrick, *Liberating Conscience: Feminist Explorations in Catholic Moral Theology* (New York: Continuum, 1996), 11–12.

[8] *Misericordia Vultus*, 3, 15.

is opening up new lines of thought regarding conscience, responsibility, and creativity in the church. I next describe two types of responsibility and indicate certain problems in the US bishops' 2007–15 documents on political responsibility, especially the emphasis on conscience formation and opposing intrinsic evils. I conclude by suggesting some implications of the conversion that Pope Francis is inspiring for those involved in Catholic health care.

Examination of Metaphor
and the Rhetoric of Conscience

Our rhetoric of conscience is heavily dependent on metaphor. By "rhetoric" I mean the use of language to communicate effectively and persuasively. The authors cited above exemplify this tendency, as when Winters uses a metaphor of clarity, O'Connell one of cleanliness, and Massingale one of an instrument "blunted and twisted by one's socialization in a culture of racism." Although such metaphors can be useful, they can also be misleading and problematic. The metaphors of clarity and cleanliness, for example, can lend themselves to preoccupation with personal innocence, especially when practices of "examination of conscience" are focused on commandments instead of on the impact of one's deeds and omissions on the lives of other people, including those beyond our immediate relational circles. Moreover, metaphors of clarity, cleanliness, and instrumentality can contribute to the reification of conscience, that is, the tendency to regard it as a thing that is either different from the self (for example, "the voice of God") or compartmentalized within the self (for example, a "faculty" of the soul). Taken to the extreme, the reification of conscience may lead to the supposition that conscience is like a piece of moral radar equipment that allows one to home in on the right deed like a plane landing in a fog. From there it is a short step to understanding the phrase "formation of conscience" in a way implying that moral education is simply a matter of shaping the radar dish and plugging in the right wires.[9] When conscience is thus isolated from the moral agent, it is ripe for co-optation by external authorities and unscrupulous politicians. Instead of regarding conscience as a thing that can be abstracted from the moral agent, we do better to understand it as an aspect of the self, perhaps on a par with "intelligence." We all have some of it, but degrees vary greatly, and even a lot of it is no guarantee we'll always be right. Conscience is a dimension of the self, one central to our experience of moral agency. I define it as personal moral awareness, experienced in the course of anticipating future situations and making moral decisions, and in the process of reflecting on one's past decisions and the quality of one's

---

[9] Patrick, *Women, Conscience, and the Creative Process*, 63.

character. Although conscience is experienced by individuals, it is a very social phenomenon because every individual is always a self-in-relation to others, and our awareness of moral obligation is intimately bound up with our experiences of others who are significant in our lives.[10]

If white Catholics are to repent effectively of racism, we must be proactive in attending to the complex reality of persons of color. When these "others" have thus gained emotional significance for us, we will begin to experience, though never completely, some of the pain that racism causes them, and sharing in their suffering can move us to act to alleviate it. Cultivating deep friendships and seeking other ways to put ourselves "into the racist world of the oppressed," as Joe R. Feagin has expressed it, are required.[11] Bryan Massingale, citing research by Feagin and Eileen O'Brien, observes that "loving and committed relationships give one the visceral outrage, strength, and motivation to break free from the 'rewards of conformity' that keep most whites complacent with white privilege."[12] To overcome the unconscious bias involved in racism, Massingale insists, it is necessary to get beyond "current reflection on conscience formation," which is "overly rational and abstract" and "lacks the appreciation of the nonrational depths needed to move people to see social reality differently and then act against their own social interests and malformed racial identities."[13] Without emphasizing the categories of "conscience" or "conscience formation," the theologian M. Shawn Copeland has wisely commended a spirituality that recognizes in the bodies of those suffering from racial, economic, and sexual injustice the crucified body of Jesus, thereby drawing on powerful Eucharistic symbolism to inspire a sense of moral obligation that cannot be reduced to a checklist of sins avoided and evils opposed, but rather requires creative and collaborative efforts, with the expectation of a need for continual conversion and forgiveness.[14]

In *Conscience: Development and Self-Transcendence*, the theologian Walter E. Conn stresses the metaphorical nature of the rhetoric of conscience, observing that "the term 'conscience' does not refer to any power or faculty, but is rather a metaphor pointing to the specifically moral dimension of the human person, to the personal subject as sensitive and responsive to value." Understood broadly, he argues, "conscience" amounts to "personal moral

---

[10] Patrick, *Liberating Conscience*, 35–36.

[11] Joe R. Feagin, *Racist America: Roots, Current Realities, and Future Reparations* (New York: Routledge, 2001), quoted in Massingale, "Conscience Formation," 65–66.

[12] Massingale, "Conscience Formation," 66.

[13] Ibid., 67.

[14] See, for example, M. Shawn Copeland, "Toward a Critical Christian Feminist Theology of Solidarity," in *Women and Theology*, ed. Mary Ann Hinsdale and Phyllis H. Kaminski (Maryknoll, NY: Orbis Books, 1995), 3–38; and M. Shawn Copeland, *Enfleshing Freedom: Body, Race, and Being* (Minneapolis: Fortress, 2010).

consciousness."[15] The philosopher Douglas C. Langston has also argued against regarding conscience as a "faculty" or "substantial entity," preferring to see it as a "relational entity" that develops as an agent grows in maturity and virtue. For Langston, conscience "provides the checks on morally good agents so that their behavior is not at odds with the demands of their societies and prevents the morally good person from slipping into self-delusion."[16] Langston's metaphors of "checking" and prevention of "slipping" highlight negative features of the experience of conscience and miss the aspect that needs attention if we are to be awakened to possibilities for action to benefit our neighbors.

The theologian H. Richard Niebuhr, also highly aware of the importance of metaphor for morals, captures an important aspect of the experience we name "conscience" in "The Ego-Alter Dialectic and the Conscience." He notes that the experience involves a sort of conversation "in which a reasoning and feeling self takes toward itself the attitude of an other which it represents to itself or which is presented to it."[17] Niebuhr concludes that a purely secular approach leaves no room for forgiveness of sins or consolation, but when the "other" in conversation with the self is "the Holy Spirit," the recognition of transgression is not the end of the story:

> Instead of excluding the self from companionship with the divine other the latter remains within the self, a source of consolation, and of inspiration toward the keeping of the principles which have been transgressed. The choice does not lie between the good conscience of a self which has kept all its laws and the bad conscience of the trans-gressor, but between the dull conscience which does not discern the greatness of the other and the loftiness of his demands, the agonized conscience of the awakened, and the consoled conscience of one who in the company of the spirit seeks to fulfill the infinite demands of the infinite other.[18]

Pope Francis, Conscience, and Creativity

Niebuhr's analysis is interestingly close to the way Pope Francis mentions conscience in "The Face of Mercy," his announcement of the year celebrating God's mercy, which began December 8, 2015. For Pope Francis, the jubilee

---

[15] Walter E. Conn, *Conscience: Development and Self-Transcendence* (Birmingham, AL: Religious Education Press, 1981), 1–2.

[16] Douglas C. Langston, *Conscience and Other Virtues* (University Park: Pennsyl-vania State University Press, 2001), 177.

[17] H. Richard Niebuhr, "The Ego-Alter Dialectic and the Conscience," *Journal of Philosophy* 42 (1945): 355.

[18] Ibid., 359.

invites intense reflection on the "*corporal and spiritual works of mercy*," and "will be a way to reawaken our conscience, too often grown dull in the face of poverty."[19] Both thinkers employ metaphors of dullness and awakening for conscience, and both emphasize the fact that God's disposition toward us is one of friendliness and mercy, which should have the effect of freeing us for significant action, indeed for carrying forward Jesus' own mission. Our focus should be on the physical and spiritual needs of our neighbors, and not on a misguided quest for innocence. God's mercy provides the context in which we can accept our sinfulness, and while striving to observe the commandments, we can be aware that "the rule of life for [Jesus'] disciples must place mercy at the center, as Jesus himself demonstrated by sharing meals with sinners."[20] With consciences thus consoled by the assurance of God's mercy, revealed as love like "that of a father or a mother, moved to the very depths out of love for their child,"[21] we can act confidently and creatively to promote the well-being of others, and accept the fact that "life means 'getting our feet dirty' from the dust-filled roads of life and history."[22]

Pope Francis spoke these last words to prisoners whom he met in Philadelphia on September 27, 2015. In the same breath, he voiced his own need of having his feet washed by Jesus, conveying a spirituality that seeks not innocence, but rather forgiveness. His words to the prisoners echoed an ideal he had expressed earlier in a homily at the canonization mass of Junípero Serra:

> The Church, the holy People of God, treads the dust-laden paths of history, so often traversed by conflict, injustice and violence, in order to encounter her children, our brothers and sisters. The holy and faithful People of God are not afraid of losing their way; they are afraid of becoming self-enclosed, frozen into elites, clinging to their own security.[23]

The idea that creativity is required of disciples is something the pope also emphasized in Philadelphia. Reflecting on St. Katherine Drexel, a white heiress who devoted her life to serving Native and African Americans, he declared to bishops, priests, and religious gathered in the cathedral that for the faithful to fulfill their responsibility "as a leaven of the Gospel in our

---

[19] *Misericordia Vultus*, 15.

[20] Ibid., 20.

[21] Ibid., 6.

[22] Pope Francis, "Jesus Saves Us from the Lie That Says No One Can Change," in *Pope Francis Speaks to the United States and Cuba: Speeches, Homilies, and Interviews* (Huntington, IN: Our Sunday Visitor Press, 2015), 154.

[23] Pope Francis, "Keep Moving Forward!" in *Pope Francis Speaks to the United States and Cuba*, 77.

world" there is need for "creativity in adapting to changed situations . . . [and] above all by being open to the possibilities which the Spirit opens up to us and communicating the joy of the Gospel, daily and in every season of life."[24] He also called for creativity in his encyclical on the environment, *Laudato Si'*, when speaking of the conversion required by the ecological crisis: "By developing our individual, God-given capacities, an ecological conversion can inspire us to greater creativity and enthusiasm in resolving the world's problems and in offering ourselves to God 'as a living sacrifice, holy and acceptable'" (Rom 1:1).[25] Likewise in his 2013 apostolic exhortation, *Evangelii Gaudium,* the pope asked all Christians to respond to the call to be concerned for the poor and for social justice in "creative ways," which go beyond "discussion with no practical effect," and declared: "Any Church community, if it thinks it can comfortably go its own way without creative concern and effective cooperation in helping the poor to live with dignity and reaching out to everyone . . . will easily drift into a spiritual worldliness camouflaged by religious practices, unproductive meetings and empty talk."[26] Without criticizing the hierarchy or his predecessors in papal office—on the contrary, his writings quote many statements of popes and episcopal conferences appreciatively—Pope Francis is opening up new lines of thought regarding conscience, responsibility, and creativity in the church.

Official Teaching and
Two Kinds of Responsibility

As Albert R. Jonsen has demonstrated, the term "responsibility" gained new prominence in Christian ethics following the Second World War, as may be seen in the works of H. Richard Niebuhr, Dietrich Bonhoeffer, and Bernhard Häring.[27] In reflecting on this development, I have distinguished two types of responsibility, one that is more passive and the other more creative. The former involves obeying the commandments and fulfilling the duties of one's state in life, whereas the latter looks beyond the obligations of rules and social roles and seeks to accomplish good on a wider scale. To the extent that recent teaching by the hierarchy has emphasized opposition to intrinsic evils, it has encouraged the more passive type of responsibility, especially when taking an authoritarian approach. Responsibility's passive dimension has been greatly stressed in Catholic literature, whereas there has been less emphasis

---

[24] Pope Francis, "What About You?" in *Pope Francis Speaks to the United States and Cuba,* 126.

[25] *Laudato Si',* 211.

[26] *Evangelii Gaudium,* 207.

[27] Albert R. Jonsen, *Responsibility in Modern Religious Ethics* (Washington, DC: Corpus Books, 1968).

on creative responsibility, which involves the ability to think imaginatively and independently, and take risks for the sake of helping to improve things. Both types of responsibility are needed, like the black and white keys on the piano, but socialization has equipped many of us too well for the one and very poorly for the other.[28] If complex problems such as poverty, racism, and environmental degradation are to be addressed effectively, moral agents must be willing to take risks and collaborate across religious and political boundaries. Pope Francis's emphasis on the reality of God's mercy is crucial for encouraging believers to take such risks, for it reminds us that success, indeed salvation, is God's work, while our task is to invest our talents to the full for the sake of helping neighbors near and far, of this and future generations.

Creatively Faithful Citizenship

At their November 2015 meeting the US bishops voted to approve a revised version of their 2007 document on political responsibility, "Forming Consciences for Faithful Citizenship," despite some eloquent arguments that the project should be completely rethought in light of new emphases in papal teaching.[29] The 2007 document demonstrated that the hierarchy was not advocating a single-issue approach to elections, and it offered much wisdom on social ethics. At the same time it embodied an unresolved conflict within the bishops' conference, between those who took an "abortion trumps all" approach to political responsibility, and those recognizing abortion as one of a number of evils with which public policy must contend. Moreover, its emphasis on "forming consciences" led to the need to explain the meaning of conscience, and these explanations tended to be abstract and confusing, with readers given information implying that the safest course is to agree with the clearest prohibitions and priorities voiced by the bishops.[30]

---

[28] I develop these points more fully in *Liberating Conscience*, 183–88, and *Women, Conscience, and the Creative Process*, 55–60.

[29] Tom Roberts, "US Bishops Pass Revised 'Faithful Citizenship' as Some Call for New Document," November 17, 2015, http://ncronline.org.

[30] *Forming Consciences for Faithful Citizenship: A Call to Political Responsibility from the Catholic Bishops of the United States* (Washington, DC: USCCB, 2007). To accompany this forty-page document they also published a two-page summary, "The Challenge of Forming Consciences for Faithful Citizenship" (USCCB Publication No. 7-027). In 2008 USCCB staff members published articles about the document, both of which were ambiguous in explaining "conscience" and decisions about voting. See Mary Ann Walsh, "Conscience and the Catholic Voter," *America*, October 6, 2008, 13–16, and J. Brian Bransfield, "Conscientious Election," *America*, October 13, 2008, 17–19. None of these works dealt with the metaphorical aspect of language about conscience, with the result that readers might well wonder how something they were responsible for "properly forming" could also be the voice of God. In 2011 the bishops reissued their 2007 document with a new introduction emphasizing religious liberty and warning against "misguided appeals

The 2015 revision is more substantial than press accounts suggested, with changes in many paragraphs and much new material added, including mention of newer issues and lengthy quotations from Pope Benedict XVI and Pope Francis.[31] As before, the bishops rely on "intrinsic evil" as a category carrying special weight in reaching political judgments, and their language of conscience formation implies that good Catholics will agree with their judgments. Moreover, the greater length and complexity of the new document make it unlikely that its nuances will be well understood by most readers. Compare, for example, the changes to a key sentence in paragraph 34, with changes indicated in italics:

> A Catholic cannot vote for a candidate who takes a position in favor of an intrinsic evil, such as abortion or racism, if the voter's intent is to support that position. In such cases a Catholic would be guilty of formal cooperation in grave evil. (2007)

> A Catholic cannot vote for a candidate who *favors a policy promoting an intrinsically evil act,* such as abortion, *euthanasia, assisted suicide, deliberately subjecting workers or the poor to subhuman living conditions, redefining marriage in ways that violate its essential meaning, or racist behavior,* if the voter's intent is to support that position. In such cases a Catholic would be guilty of formal cooperation in grave evil. (2015)

Neither version explains the difference between "intrinsically evil acts" and other evil acts or structural realities, or between formal and material cooperation, but because the category of intrinsic evil is given great weight, readers are encouraged to play it safe by agreeing with their priorities. The new version of paragraph 37 adds policy language, but is otherwise unchanged: "In making these [voting] decisions, it is essential for Catholics to be guided by a well-formed conscience that recognizes that all issues do not carry the same moral weight and that the moral obligation to

---

to 'conscience' to ignore fundamental moral claims, to reduce Catholic moral concerns to one or two matters, or to justify choices simply to advance partisan, ideological, or personal interests" (p. v). In 2012 they followed up with a two-page publication drawing on the *Catechism of the Catholic Church* and other official sources to answer the questions, "What Is Conscience?" and "How Do I Form My Conscience?" Authoritative definitions and suggestions for useful activities are provided, with no attention to metaphor or to the mystery involved in one's relationship with God.

[31] *Forming Consciences for Faithful Citizenship: A Call to Political Responsibility from the Catholic Bishops of the United States with Introductory Note* (Washington, DC: USCCB, 2015). www.usccb.org.

oppose *policies promoting* intrinsically evil acts has a special claim on our consciences and our actions."

In 2008 M. Cathleen Kaveny offered an excellent critique of the first version's emphasis on intrinsic evil, arguing that this language is prophetic but it does not offer help to voters looking for strategies to address such evil, and, indeed, "preventing intrinsically evil acts is not always our top moral priority" because "sometimes preventing harm caused by other kinds of wrongdoing, or even harm caused by natural disasters can take priority."[32] Her criticism is equally applicable to the 2015 version. To it I would add the judgment that the abstract label "intrinsic evil" may carry less weight among voters considering whether to approve physician-assisted suicide in their state than would empirical evidence that legalizing this practice has led to overall increases in suicide rates in states that have done so, especially among the elderly.[33]

In 2013 Bishop Robert W. McElroy also pointed out the limitations of the category of intrinsic evil, observing that this category "is vital in identifying the exceptionless evil inherent in certain types of actions," but structural sin, especially poverty, "is not a one-time action." Rather, poverty is "the result of countless specific human actions with varying degrees of responsibility that give rise to social structures and practices imbued with selfishness and evil." With regard to racism McElroy observes that this evil lies "partly within the scope of government and partly outside." Laws are needed to prevent discrimination in housing and employment, but they cannot deal with "contemptible racism expressed in private conversation." Pointing out similar issues with other instances of structural sin, including war and exploitation of immigrants, he concludes: "There is no single category of sin or evil, social good or virtue, that is the filter for discerning the priorities of the church in the public order."[34]

McElroy argues that poverty should have equal status with abortion in the US church's public stance, and that our political conversation should be transformed by "prioritizing the issue of poverty, focusing not only on intrinsic evils but also on structural sin, and acting with prudence when applying Catholic moral principles to specific legal enactments."[35] He recognizes that disagreement on legislative ways to implement even the clearest moral principle is inevitable, and he strongly rejects the idea "that issues pertaining to intrinsic evils do not necessitate prudential judgments." Declaring that Pope

[32] M. Cathleen Kaveny, "Intrinsic Evil and Political Responsibility," *America*, October 27, 2008, 17–18.

[33] Aaron Kheriaty, "Assisted-suicide Laws' Contagious Effect," *Washington Post*, November 22, 2015, A-27.

[34] Robert W. McElroy, "A Church for the Poor," *America* (October 21, 2013): 13–16, 15.

[35] Ibid., 14.

Francis challenges us to recognize that "Catholic teaching on economic justice is clear and binding," McElroy indicates that the immediate task will require both vision and creativity: "We are called to create a Catholic political conversation that proclaims the greatest problems of our day can only be solved with a vision rooted in the transcendent dignity of the human person."[36] Significantly, he mentions neither conscience nor conscience formation, instead appealing directly to the minds and hearts of his readers. The imagery of vision and hearing, however, is embedded in the essay. He criticizes the tendency of US citizens to "turn our eyes away from the growing domestic inequality that ruins lives and breaks spirits"[37] and quotes Pope Francis responding to the deaths of hundreds of would-be immigrants to Italy who died in a shipwreck at Lampedusa:

> "Who is responsible for the blood of these brothers and sisters of ours?" Francis asked. "Nobody! That is our answer. It isn't me; I don't have anything to do with it; it must be someone else, but certainly not me. Yet God is asking each of us: 'Where is the blood of your brother that cries out to me?'"[38]

McElroy's approach, so strongly influenced by Pope Francis, speaks directly to conscience without theorizing about its "formation." In this respect his rhetoric is similar to that of the pope, whose moral instruction summons readers to a spirituality of attentiveness and employs imagery of hearing ("attentive to the cry of the poor")[39] and seeing ("go beyond the surface of conflict, see others in their deepest dignity")[40] without mention of "forming consciences."

If the US bishops hope to have greater influence in the future, they would do well to leave off the rhetoric of "conscience formation," which has the effect of reifying the mysterious reality involved and implying that external authority has full access to moral and political truth. It is not simply a matter of making the issues of poverty (and the attendant racism that so plagues this country) and environmental degradation more central to the church's political agenda, but of recognizing that Catholics need encouragement to develop a spirituality of attentiveness to the poor and instruction in ways of increasing both prudence and creativity in their exercise of responsibility. If more of our bishops can model creativity like that of Pope Francis, who surprised homeless persons in Rome with a gift of sleeping bags and who has in so many

---

[36] Ibid., 16.
[37] Ibid., 14.
[38] Ibid., 15.
[39] *Evangelii Gaudium,* 187.
[40] Ibid., 228.

ways colored outside the lines of papal protocol, so much the better. Certainly the conference of bishops would do well to emulate the pope in using rhetoric that appeals more directly to the minds and hearts of believers instead of focusing on the complicated language of conscience formation. Indeed, they would also do well to encourage faithful citizens to deal with political opponents with the hearts of peacemakers, who go "beyond the surface of the conflict"[41] to recognize the human dignity of their adversaries, and seek to find common ground for the sake of the common good.

Pope Francis has not written systematically about conscience or its formation, but his moral teaching presumes a much richer notion of conscience than is conveyed in the US bishops' documents on political responsibility. In his discussion of spiritual accompaniment in *Evangelii Gaudium* he declares, "As for the moral component of catechesis, which promotes growth in fidelity to the Gospel way of life, it is helpful to stress again and again the attractiveness and the ideal of a life of wisdom, self-fulfillment and enrichment."[42] Those who accompany others in the process of spiritual growth must realize that "reaching a level of maturity where individuals can make truly free and responsible decisions calls for much time and patience," and "each person's situation before God and their life in grace are mysteries which no one can fully know from without."[43] In his 2016 apostolic exhortation *Amoris Laetitia* he discusses ethical education in terms of the need to go beyond a disembodied rationality: "We have to arrive at the point where the good that the intellect grasps can take root in us as a profound affective inclination, as a thirst for the good that outweighs other attractions and helps us to realize that what we consider objectively good is also good 'for us' here and now."[44] "Education," he observes, "includes encouraging the responsible use of freedom to face issues with good sense and intelligence. It involves forming persons who readily understand that their own lives, and the life of the community, are in their hands, and that freedom is itself a great gift."[45] Such persons would not have been shocked to hear the pope declare in February 2016 that Catholics might use contraception rather than risk severe fetal abnormalities due to the Zika virus, for "avoiding pregnancy is not an absolute evil."[46]

In suggesting earlier that Catholics might profitably abstain, for a time, from language of "conscience formation" in favor of language of "forming creatively responsible moral agents," I have been wanting to restore more

---

41 Ibid.

42 Ibid., 168.

43 Ibid., 171, 172.

44 *Amoris Laetitia,* 265.

45 Ibid., 262.

46 Pope Francis, quoted in Joshua J. McElwee, "Francis Allows for Discernment on Contraception in Emergency Cases, Spokesman Says," February 22, 2016, http://ncronline.org.

mystery and complexity to our understanding of moral agency, something I believe is quite congenial with Pope Francis's approach to these matters. I recognize, of course, that "forming the conscience" can be a useful phrase and that many of my colleagues, including those represented in this volume, employ it to our profit. My suggestion of a temporary rhetorical shift is made in the hope that it might contribute to a shift of emphasis from seeking innocence in relation to ideals and laws to seeking effective action in our ambiguous circumstances.

Implications for Catholic Health Care

Could such a shift of emphasis contribute to improved motivation on the part of agents within the Catholic health care system to reprioritize the moral claims they experience? Could it inspire them to devote new energy to addressing the issues of poverty and the environment? The Catholic Health Association has provided excellent resources on these matters, especially by its attention to health care disparities and to the effects of climate change on health.[47] Both concerns are linked to racism, for in general patients with darker skins suffer more from unequal access, lower quality of care, and poorer health outcomes than do white patients, and they are disproportionately affected by heat waves, smog, and water pollution because of economic disadvantages resulting from a history of slavery and racial discrimination. If the approach of Pope Francis takes hold, and more Catholics examined their lives not only in light of traditional commandments and definitions of evil, but with attention to the extensive suffering of humanity and the precarious condition of the planet, what developments might we see?

At the level of *policy*, efforts to prevent evils long stressed by the hierarchy could continue, but with a new willingness to appreciate the limits of law in preventing evil and a new honesty about ambiguities in such positions as Saint John Paul II's view of contraception as "intrinsically evil."[48] One might hope too for greater emphasis on issues that disproportionately affect the poor and racial minorities, especially disparities in access to education, nutrition, and health care, and exposure to environmental

---

[47] The website of the Catholic Health Association of the United States (https://www.chausa.org) contains a statement of its commitment to the "importance of diversity—both in the workforce and in meeting the needs of diverse patients" and provides links to resources on these issues. Likewise, the CHA website documents its commitment to environmental responsibility and offers links to resources. The organization has also published *Faithfully Healing the Earth: Climate Change and Catholic Health Care* (Washington, DC: CHA, 2009), and Laura Anderko, Stephanie Chalupka, and Brenda M. Afzal, *Climate Change and Health: Is There a Role for the Health Care Sector?* (Washington, DC: CHA, 2012).

[48] *Veritatis Splendor*, 80.

hazards including tainted water and easily available guns. *Providers*, especially those who benefit from white privilege, might be inspired to give more time to listening to and learning from patients and colleagues of color. They might also attend more fully to the situations of medical technicians, clerical staff, and service employees, who often come from less advantaged backgrounds. *Patients* might be inspired to treat such workers with the same respect they offer their doctors, and to see the lives of others waiting outside the office as deserving the same care and compassion as their own. Those with lighter skins and greater fluency in English might bring to all our clinical encounters a recognition that inbred bias against and fear of those with darker skins and foreign accents undermine our best intentions to be just and loving, and involve an aspect of our sinfulness requiring ongoing repentance and conversion.

One white thinker whose research could benefit Catholics at all levels of our health care system is Aana Marie Vigen, whose *Women, Ethics, and Inequality in US Healthcare* interprets the experiences of several black and Latina breast cancer patients and draws attention to how problems that affect all patients with serious illness—including imbalances of power in relation to providers, difficulties with bureaucratic procedures, and financial worries—are compounded by racial assumptions and stereotypes. As she writes,

> Stereotypes do not have to be spoken to exist or to have unsettling effects on human behavior. The simple act of putting on gloves when you do not need them sends a strong message. . . . Indeed, negative postures and dismissive practices can be communicated in many ways: By body language and eye contact, by the presence or absence of touch, by how hurried or distracted one seems while another is speaking or by a cool, professional demeanor that communicates distance, self-protection, and disinterest.[49]

Vigen listened carefully to the women she interviewed, and in referring to a woman who endured both physical suffering from treatment and mental anguish from losing health insurance, she writes, "Sophia's story rings in my ears and pierces my conscience."[50] The category of conscience is not an explicit interest of hers, but Vigen's imagery here is significant. She might well have written instead "heart." Her afflicted white conscience is not reified or separate from herself, but is central to her being. It is the opposite of the "clean white conscience" that Maureen O'Connell found an "impediment to

---

[49] Aana Marie Vigen, *Women, Ethics, and Inequality in US Healthcare: "To Count among the Living"* (New York: Palgrave Macmillan, 2011), 150–51.

[50] Ibid., 151.

racial justice." Vigen has served the health care community well by subjecting medical culture to such a critical examination.

If the consciences of all white Catholics were to be similarly pierced, what might our conversion involve? Might racial disparities become the lens through which we look at policy issues and health concerns? Might we regard diversity training and disparities workshops not as administrative tasks required for accreditation or government funding, but as invitations to shake off the moral blinders of white privilege? Might our improved vision give us a greater sense of the complex effects of various policies and lead us to adopt more collaborative, less confrontational ways of influencing public policy? Might we understand that our gifts and talents have not been given to be buried out of fear, but to be invested in creative activity for the benefit of the world? Confident in the availability of God's mercy, might all of us, including the Little Sisters of the Poor, be less timid about "'getting our feet dirty' from the dust-filled roads of life and history"?[51] Might we, in short, begin to realize the hope that Pope Francis voiced in proclaiming the Jubilee of Mercy, namely that our witness as believers "might grow stronger and more effective"?[52]

---

[51] Pope Francis, "Jesus Saves Us from the Lie That Says No One Can Change," 154.

[52] *Misericordia Vultus,* 3.

CONSCIENCE AFTER VATICAN II

Theological Premises for a Discussion of Catholic Health Care

Roberto Dell'Oro

In this chapter, I reflect on the Catholic understanding of the notion of conscience, looking specifically at post-Vatican II theological developments.[1] Thus, the essay will be a kind of background framework for the articulation of contemporary issues in faith-based health care. The latter articulation will remain somewhat latent in my observations. Rather, the focus will be on unpacking different facets of a "pre-comprehension," so to speak, that is, a set of theological premises about moral conscience that nourish, explicitly or implicitly, normative criteria, attitudes, and value judgments. A hermeneutic reconstruction remains inevitably embedded in specific systematic preoccupations: We revisit the past in order to find better solutions for the present. We do so impelled by the present's historical location and questions, all the time mindful of the fact that new developments, especially when called for by dramatic changes, are never possible without a retrospective outlook on the tradition within which we stand: The consistency of such tradition and its dynamic integrity are at stake.

Recent public debates in health care seem characterized by an almost inflationary reference to the notion of conscience. Indeed, appeal to conscience has become the argument privileged by faith-based organizations, as they defend the right to stand by their own normative principles. For an

---

[1] The literature on conscience is quite vast. For a recent assessment, see James F. Keenan, "Redeeming Conscience," in *Theological Studies* 76, no. 1 (2015): 129–47. An interesting take on the historical journey of the topic is provided by Richard Sorabji, *Moral Conscience through the Ages: Fifth Century BCE to the Present* (Chicago: University of Chicago Press, 2014). From the international literature, in addition to the works indicated in the individual notes, I have benefited from Eberhard Schockenhoff, *Das umstrittene Gewissen: Eine theologische Grundlegung* (Mainz: Grünewald, 1990), and Aristide Fumagalli, *L'eco dello Spirito: Teologia della coscienza morale* (Brescia: Queriniana, 2012). Most recently, and with reference to Catholic health care, David DeCosse and Kristin Heyer, eds., *Conscience and Catholicism: Rights, Responsibilities, and Institutional Responses* (Maryknoll, NY: Orbis Books, 2015).

example, religious conservatives invoke constitutional protection for their conscientious moral judgments. Grounding their claim on the Free Exercise Clause of the First Amendment and the Religious Freedom Restoration Act, they have refused to comply with the contraception mandate enacted by the Department of Health and Human Services in the regulations implementing the Affordable Care Act. The objection of the Little Sisters of the Poor, who are involved in a lawsuit against the Obama administration, is a case in point: For the Sisters, even the most remote connection to the governmental mandate to provide insurance coverage for contraception constitutes a burden on their consciences.[2]

The Catholic tradition can certainly claim for itself a rich heritage of reflection on the doctrine of conscience. The rhetoric of conscience, however, gives pause, for here a discrepancy seems to emerge between the strong appeal to *institutional* conscience and the relatively lukewarm deference paid to conscience as a dimension of *personal* decision-making. A category that, especially in the magisterial teaching, tends to be looked at with suspicion when predicated of the individual's power to self-determination[3] receives now an all too facile endorsement when invoked as a condition for institutions to operate freely according to their own cherished moral principles. Thus, in what appears like an ambiguous lack of consistency, Catholic rhetoric promptly calls for respect of institutional conscience while undermining the space of freedom that protects *conscientious* decision-making by individuals, whether health care professionals or patients, within its very institutional space. I am tempted to call this state of affairs an "inconsistent ethic of life."

To be sure, the judgment in question warrants careful scrutiny. It points to the need, on the one hand, to distinguish between the personal and the institutional spheres of conscience, and to respect the relative autonomy of each; on the other, it calls for avoidance of conceptual ambiguity and dangerous double standards. The celebration of conscience constitutes a welcome retrieval of an important, if too often neglected, aspect of the Catholic tradition. The plausibility of such retrieval, however, rests on a coherent rehabilitation of conscience that speaks to the moral agency of mature individuals, and,

---

[2] The case is discussed by Cathleen Kaveny in her contribution to this collection. In more general terms, Kaveny points out that the debate about religion, law, and morality in the American public square has shifted from one on the *enactment* of generally applicable laws to one on *exemptions* from such laws.

[3] See *Veritatis Splendor*'s considerations about "creative" conscience. "There seems to be an emphasis within *Veritatis Splendor* on the suppression of conscience and a move of power toward the Magisterium," writes Jayne Hoose in "Conscience in *Veritatis Splendor* and the *Catechism*," in *Conscience: Readings in Moral Theology No. 14*, ed. Charles E. Curran (New York: Paulist Press, 2004), 89. For a critical reading of moral theological developments under the pontificate of John Paul II, including *Veritatis Splendor*, see Paul Valadier, *Eloge de la conscience* (Paris: Seuil, 1994).

by *analogical* extension, of institutions alike. Thus, the retrieval will be convincing, provided the rights of the latter are defended as central to an ethos that equally cherishes and cultivates those of the former.

This chapter proceeds in three stages. First, it lays out some central aspects of the doctrine of conscience developed by the Second Vatican Council, especially in the statements of *Gaudium et Spes* and *Dignitatis Humanae*, and shows how the council's "turning point" integrates and corrects important aspects of the traditional understanding of conscience. Second, it looks at the theological conceptual framework that supports a renewed understanding of conscience, with reference, in particular, to the meaning and function of moral normativity, the particular character of moral truth, and the centrality of freedom. Third, I allude, in the conclusions, to some implications of the above reconstruction for Catholic health care today.

The Doctrine of Conscience at a Turning Point: The Second Vatican Council

The council's statements on conscience, specifically in *Gaudium et Spes* and *Dignitatis Humanae*, speak to "the dignity of conscience" (*GS*, 16), the "excellence of freedom" (*GS*, 17), and the right of the individual "not to be forced to act against conscience, nor be prevented from acting according to conscience" (*DH*, 3). The positive recognition of the centrality of conscience goes hand in hand, perhaps not without contradiction, as Linda Hogan has observed,[4] with a more sober recognition that "as it often happens . . . conscience goes astray through ignorance, which it is unable to avoid, without thereby losing its dignity" (*GS*, 16). To prevent conscience from embarking along erroneous paths in the perilous journey of life, there stands, unequivocal and clear, the "holy and certain teaching of the church," to which "the faithful must pay careful attention in forming their conscience" (*DH*, 14).

Despite possible conflicts of interpretations, I stand with those authoritative readers of the council's statements who see in them a clear development, perhaps even a shift in paradigms both in tone and content, with respect to the previous tradition of neo-Scholastic theology.[5] Indeed, one finds in the council's texts an understanding of conscience that interprets its function

---

[4] Linda Hogan, "Conscience in the Documents of Vatican II," in *Conscience: Readings in Moral Theology No. 14*, ed. Charles E. Curran (New York: Paulist Press, 2004), 82–88: "Two strands of conscience that had been successfully integrated by Aquinas are present in the documents, not together but as competing accounts."

[5] See especially two classic studies by Domenico Capone on the history of redaction of *Gaudium et Spes* 16: "Antropologia, coscienza e personalita," *Studia Moralia* 4 (1966): 73–113, and "La teologia della coscienza morale nel Concilio e dopo il Concilio," *Studia Moralia* 24 (1986): 221–49.

beyond the limitations of normative concerns, that is, in terms of the relation of conscience and law. In this latter perspective, conscience concerns the
practical judgment on the objectivity of the norm; as the "ultimate practical
judgment on an act to be made, or an act that has been made" (*judicium ulti-
mo-practicum de actu ponendo vel de actu posito*),[6] conscience tends to be
reduced to a post-factum mechanism of praise, when the action is done in
conformity to the law, or regret, when contradicting it.

Three aspects are central to this traditional understanding of conscience:
first, the restriction to an act-centered morality; second, the dualism of
subjectivity and objectivity; third, the overall syllogistic character of moral
reasoning, understood as a deductive conclusion from clearly defined premises. The focus, to begin with, is on the ontic facticity of the act, which will
be more clearly defined in its ethical meaning the more it is isolated from
the idiosyncratic features of the acting person. Thus, while the norm prede-
termines the rightness of the act (*finis operis*), conscience speaks only to
the goodness, that is, the motivational and intentional structure, of the agent
(*finis operantis*). Because the relation between the two is extrinsic rather than
intrinsic, conscience functions only as a subjective, rather than objective,
determinant of the action's morality. Furthermore, the classic neo-Scholastic tradition distinguishes between "original conscience" (*synderesis*) and
"conscience in situation," each one with their different degree of certainty:
the former absolute, the latter fallible. For Thomas Aquinas, *synderesis* is the
habit of practical reason, by which one knows the first principles of natural
law, that is, do good and avoid evil.[7] Conscience in situation, however, is
the act of applying the first principles known in *synderesis* to the conduct at
stake. The application in question is virtually equivalent to the conclusion of a
syllogism: The major premise expresses the moral law; the minor refers to the
act to be done in the particular situation, and for which the law is supposed
to obtain; the conclusion states whether the action comes under the moral
law. One can see that, for the neo-Scholastic manuals of moral theology, the
reasoning of conscience is a form of deductive syllogism.[8]

---

[6] As quoted in Bruno Schüller, *Die Begründung sittlicher Urteile*, 2nd ed. (Düssel-
dorf: Patmos Verlag, 1980), 45.

[7] When confronted with the Augustinian tradition, the contribution of Thomas
Aquinas is certainly precious in terms of its systematic power. However, it also contributes to what has been labeled an "intellectualization" of the notion of conscience: For
Thomas, the measure of action is not so much conscience, but practical reason. To act
according to conscience means to act according to *recta ratio*. Furthermore, with respect
to the Franciscan school, Thomas stands by the pure *cognitive* character of the judgment
of conscience, as he claims that "iudicium conscientiae consistit in pura cognition" (*De
Veritate* 17, 1, ad 4).

[8] See Charles E. Curran, "Conscience in the Light of the Catholic Moral Tradition,"
in idem, *Conscience*, 3–24. The difference between Thomas and the neo-Scholastic tradition should not go unnoticed. See, for an example, the classic manuals of Merkelbach,

When confronted with the previous tradition, the council's statements on conscience cannot fail to impress, not only for their deeper theological quality, but also for the, at least initial, overcoming of the methodological flaws of traditional doctrine. In its various statements, the council looks at conscience not only as a function of practical judgment on individual actions, but as the very definition of personal selfhood. The retrieval of the biblical notion of "heart" constitutes an attempt to root the notion of conscience in a more clearly biblical understanding, which sees in the heart the ultimate space of one's communication with God.[9] Furthermore, the theological grounding supports a more holistic anthropology. By using the heart metaphor, the council reconciles in a higher synthesis the more intellectualistic strain of the Thomistic tradition with the emphasis on the will by the Franciscan school. According to Karl Golser, the council's text even echoes an understanding of conscience developed in the German mystical tradition of Meister Eckhart with the notion of *Seelengrund*.[10] The heart alludes to a complex set of dimensions that synergistically bring together knowledge, decision, and power of ratification by a moral agent.[11] Also, there is a reference to a more inductive, rather than deductive, way of proceeding, alluded to in *Gaudium et Spes* 16, by a call for collaboration with others within society, in the search of common values and criteria for action.

Insofar as it expresses the whole moral history of the person, with its successes and failures, conscience is more than a purely syllogistic deduction from established premises, one that could function without reference to the moral character of the agent. Rather, conscience is always "in act," already actualized, so to speak, by a concrete history of freedom, in which moral disposition and knowledge condition each other.[12] This is why conscience

---

Aertnys/Damen, and Zalba. Although the latter develop in the "effectual history" of the former, the two differ in important points, especially with regard to the character of the judgment of conscience in question. Unlike the neo-Scholastic tradition, which emerges from the confrontation with a modern conception of ethics *more geometrico demonstrata*, Thomas distinguishes *determinatio* from *conclusio* in *S.Th.*, I-IIae, q. 95, a.2. See Schockenhoff, *Das umstrittene Gewissen*, 77–82. Thomas underscores the autonomy of *practical* reason, and the singularity of practical judgment vis-à-vis theoretical reason. On this, among others, Martin Rhonheimer, *Natural Law and Practical Reason: A Thomist View of Moral Autonomy* (New York: Fordham University Press, 2000).

[9] On the biblical notion of conscience in light of biblical anthropology see Schockenhoff, *Das umstrittene Gewissen*, 48–55.

[10] Karl Golser, "Das Gewissen als verborgenste Mitte im Menschen," in *Grundlagen und Probleme der heutigen Moraltheologie*, ed. Wilhelm Ernst (Würzburg: Echter Verlag, 1989), 116.

[11] For a philosophical anthropology inspired by the "heart tradition" see Andrew Tallon, *Head and Heart: Affection, Cognition, Volition as Triune Consciousness* (New York: Fordham University Press, 1997).

[12] This is, of course, not a new idea, for Thomas Aquinas already underscores the relation between knowledge and freedom: one knows only when one *wants* to know. Thus: "Vis cognitiva non movet, nisi mediante appetitive" (*S.Th.*, I, q. 20, a. 1, ad 1), or "Intelligo

cannot be fully accounted for in terms of a function of ratification or application: It stands for the moral identity of the subject, for the agency that commits itself to a particular principle of action with a free insight supported by an existential openness to the good, or, conversely, by a progressive blindness to it.[13] Indeed, conscience exceeds mechanical compliance with the norm; it exceeds the concern for correspondence between subjective and objective dimensions of morality: For conscience underlines, and, in so doing, *grounds*, both the objective and subjective presuppositions, and the conditions of possibility, of such correspondence.[14] Conscience speaks of the incommunicable "idiocy" of the self, a knowing-of-oneself irreducible to abstract universality.[15] To say that "in her [or his] conscience" a person is given-over-to-herself [or himself] most radically is to identify a reality in which insight and decision toward the good exist in unity. Thus, conscience is the voice of *transcendence* because it is also the reality to which all dimensions of moral agency, that is, commanding, prohibiting, inviting, and so on are *transcendentally* reduced in the identity of a moral subject who is fully himself or herself when before God (*coram Deo*).[16] In conscience, the person sees his or her ultimate destination, in a *visio* irreducible to a purely intellectualistic anticipation

---

enim quia volo" (*De Malo* 6). On this, Klaus Demmer, *Sein und Gebot: Die Bedeutsamkeit des transzendentalphilosophischen Denkansatzes in der Scholastik der Gegenwart für den formalen Aufriss der Fundamentalmoral* (Munich: Schöningh, 1971).

[13] Phenomenologists speak, in this context, of *value blindness* (*Wertblindheit*). See especially Dietrich von Hildebrand, *Sittlichkeit und ethische Werterkenntnis: Eine Untersuchung über ethische Strukturprobleme*, 3rd ed. (Vallendar-Schönstatt: Patris Verlag, 1982), 47–86. Bernard Lonergan has developed a similar perspective in *Insight: A Study of Human Understanding* (New York: Harper and Row, 1957), 595–618.

[14] The recent magisterium seems to look skeptically at the attempt to expand the notion of conscience beyond practical judgment. In *Veritatis Splendor* one finds a kind of alternating between the language of moral personalism and the traditional essentialism of neo-Scholastic theology: "The judgment of conscience is a *practical judgment*. . . . It is a judgment which applies to a concrete situation the rational conviction that one must love, do good and avoid evil. The first principle of practical reason is part of the natural law . . . but whereas the natural law discloses the objective and universal demands of the moral good, conscience is the application of the law to a particular case. . . . Conscience thus formulates *moral obligation* in the light of the natural law (59).

[15] "Idiocy" refers, in its etymological meaning, to the *idios*, i.e., the intimate. For an articulation of the "idiotic" as a potency of the ethical, I am indebted to William Desmond, *Ethics and the Between* (Albany: State University of New York Press, 2001). John F. Crosby's notion of "incommunicability" speaks to the same phenomenological reality. See his *The Selfhood of the Human Person* (Washington, DC: Catholic University of America Press, 1996), 41–81.

[16] For a transcendental reinterpretation of the notion of conscience and the interplay of "reduction" and "deduction" see Klaus Demmer, especially *Fundamentale Theologie des Ethischen* (Freiburg: Herder, 1999), 183–233, and Demmer, *Sein und Gebot*, 15–119. In an analogous vein, Lonergan speaks of the transcendental notion of value. See Walter E. Conn, "Conscience and Self-Transcendence in the Thought of Bernard Lonergan," in *Conscience*, ed. Charles E. Curran, 151–62.

of one's ultimate fulfillment. The apprehension of a particular value system entails, at the same time, a fundamental option, a *decision* to the absoluteness of the good that binds knowledge to action, insight to freedom. In the sacred space of conscience, the person sees himself or herself in light of the value system to which he or she has committed. Conscience occupies a position of (transcendental) ultimacy with respect to moral action and to the norms that regulate it: It is the original source from which ethical principles and norms depend; as *derivative* functions of conscience, moral norms are grounded by the horizon of understanding and interpretation that generates them.

Theological Premises of a
Renewed Doctrine of Conscience

In the second part of this chapter, I reflect on the meaning of the shift initiated by the Second Vatican Council. I said that the theological premises of such a shift do not always come to the fore unequivocally. Thus, the importance of a more systematic articulation that unpacks what is implicit or latent, and this in the context of the larger turning point of post-Vatican II theology, known in the language of Peter Eicher as the "anthropological turning point."[17] The attempt to reduce the meaning and function of moral conscience, pushing theological reflection back, behind the theoretical threshold set by the council, can be understood as a critique of the broader anthropological turning point in question. Thus, the ambiguity inherent in the *letter* of the council's documents very quickly leads conservative readers to a dismissal of the aggiornamento that unequivocally grounds their *spirit*.[18] In this systematic reconstruction, unpretentious as it may be, I start from the premise that the "anthropological turning point" in theology constitutes, at least methodologically, a point of nonreturn, even when remaining open to the possibility of more nuanced developments.[19] Karl Rahner, one of the main exponents of such a turn, explains its meaning thus:

---

[17] See Peter Eicher, *Die anthropologische Wende: Karl Rahners philosophischer Weg von Wesen des Menschen zur personalen Existenz* (Freiburg: Universitätsverlag, 1970).

[18] Consult, as an example, the articles of Germain Grisez, Russell Shaw, and William E. May, in the collection previously quoted: Curran, ed., *Conscience*. The work of Janet E. Smith follows in the same direction. The contribution of Joseph Ratzinger on the topic cannot be homologized to that of the authors above, for it stands out for historical precision and systematic depth. Ratzinger's commitment to a more Augustinian anthropology has made him ambivalent about too optimistic a celebration of conscience. This can be seen already in his commentary on *Gaudium et Spes* for the 1986 edition of the *Lexikon für Theologie und Kirche* (Ergänzungsband III, 313–54), and more recently, in his rendition of *synderesis* in terms of the Platonic notion of *anamnesis*. See Joseph Ratzinger, *On Conscience* (San Francisco: Ignatius Press, 2006), 30–37.

[19] The critique of Hans Urs von Balthasar of Rahner might be taken here as symptomatic of the reaction. See his very polemical *The Moment of Christian Witness* (San Francisco: Ignatius Press, 1984).

Theology wants to tell man what he is, and what he still remains even
if he rejects the message of Christianity in disbelief. Hence theology
itself implies a philosophical anthropology, which enables this message
of grace to be accepted in a really philosophical and reasonable way,
and which gives an account of it in a humanly responsible way.[20]

For Rahner, anthropology is the hermeneutical locus and the point of entry to
the theological question.[21] For an anthropologically oriented moral theology,
conscience designates the sacred space in which, in faith, the moral subject
confronts the ultimate telos of his or her moral experience. In conscience, the
moral subject encounters, in all its clarity and urgency, the central question of
Christian morality: How can the disclosure of moral truth in the Christological event represent a meaningful alternative to the reality of moral conflict
experienced by every human being?

Conscience and Norms:
The Meaning and Function of Moral Normativity

In his 2013 Apostolic Exhortation, *Evangelii Gaudium*, Pope Francis states:

The centrality of the kerygma calls for stressing those elements
which are most needed today: it has to express God's saving love
which precedes any moral and religious obligation on our part; *it
should not impose the truth but appeal to freedom*; it should be
marked by joy, encouragement, liveliness. . . . All this demands on
the part of the evangelizer certain attitudes which foster openness
to the message: approachability, readiness for dialogue, patience, a
warmth and welcome which is non-judgmental. (165)

Truths about the human being are implications of truths about God's free
and forgiving self-communication, reaching its eschatological measure in
the Christ-event. Consequently, Christian morality represents the practical
articulation of a renewed anthropological understanding, flowing from the
encounter with the Christ-event and its "effectual history" in the life of the
Christian tradition. To posit a structural correlation between theological
anthropology and ethics entails a shift in moral discourse: First and foremost,
one is "invited" to share in an anthropological ideal. Of course, the latter finds
expression in models of moral conduct and norms; yet, the "good news" of

---

[20] Karl Rahner, *Foundations of Christian Faith: An Introduction to the Idea of Christianity* (New York: Seabury Press, 1978), 25.

[21] Such an anthropological turning point must be understood in Christological terms.

Christian moral discourse consists in the fullness of meaning disclosed by a renewed human teleology, on which any prescriptive or normative functions depend. Norms are always relative to an anthropological self-understanding articulated in ideologies of human fulfillment:

> Before we ask what we must do, there is a more fundamental question: "What can I be?" This question is prompted by a self-understanding that perceives ethical truth as a promise of existential possibilities. Morality is no oppressive burden but an empowerment to act, which leads to ever-greater freedom.[22]

In conscience, the person encounters the question of his or her own ultimate identity. Thus, the intentional correlate of conscience is already beyond the normative level. For sure, the communication of moral claims—be they values, ideals, or virtues—takes place through the mediation of normative language. Yet the moral language of rules and norms is secondary to the reality of human conscience. It is *in* conscience and *through* conscience that the communication of ethical insights and notions of human flourishing takes place. Here the meaning of moral experience discloses itself to a subject willing to recognize its power of fascination and attraction. I am speaking of "experience" not just in its empirical meaning but also as the interpreted sedimentation of lived intuitions of the good, which have matured historically within a moral tradition through progressive confrontations with and solutions to situations of conflict. It is such experience that saturates the moral identity of a community and defines its *institutional* conscience. Moral norms are *grounded* in the community's experience: They express the concrete existential potential of a moral community, articulated through trial and error over time. One could say that moral norms convey a standard of "moral performance," a consensually defined moral threshold behind which the community stands as a definition of its moral identity. Because they are an interpretation of experience, norms are also being kept in constant movement by the very experience that grounds them: Institutional conscience refers to a dynamic, rather than static, reality.

The discussion of moral norms, however, needs preliminary clarifications. This is so because moral normativity is *analogical*, rather than univocal: It entails different levels of meaning, which, in turn, must be analyzed in their own specific nature. Moral principles, such as the first principle of practical reason, the categorical imperative, or the Golden Rule, cannot, by themselves, provide standards for action. They can do so when the substance of

---

[22] Klaus Demmer, *Living the Truth: A Theory of Action* (Washington, DC: Georgetown University Press, 2010), 11.

their moral normativity is unpacked, or "broken down," in concrete moral norms.[23] The path to concreteness in the language of morality signals a move from the *formal* orientation of moral principles, aimed at the goodness of the moral agent, to a progressively *content-filled* determination of moral norms, directed at the rightness of the action. Whereas the former refers directly to conscience, the latter is driven by the work of practical reason.

Consider the relevance of the last observation when applied to the distinction between "transcendental" and "categorial" norms.[24] Transcendental norms appeal to moral values and, consequently, directly speak to the moral intentionality, that is, the conscience, of the agent. In categorial norms, however, the language of values is enriched with reference to particular goods, which now become the intended object of a specific action. In the passage from intention to action, from goodness to rightness, values intermediate with goods in a creative synthesis that ultimately aims not only at the pursuit of partial goals, but at the complete flourishing of the moral agent. Moral norms, now clearly understood as action norms, will be the result of a kind of "probing" of experience, in which both standards of practicability and consequences of action converge into the definition of the morally right. Far from being understood as fixed determinations, moral norms will be seen as "signposts" (Heidegger) in the historical between. Their epistemic status remains that of prima facie rules, namely, rules that have a presumption of validity, as long as their claim can be supported by experience. This might happen in two ways: first, in relation to a change of the circumstances envisioned by a norm as the concrete conditions of its own practicability, and, second, in relation to a possible shift in the standards of freedom presupposed by the norm. The practicability of a moral norm traditionally considered true might be falsified by the evidence of changed historical circumstances or by the existential condition of the community to whom the norm is directed.[25] When this happens, a shift in paradigms sets in:

---

[23] We need images to articulate the meaning of this process. See Thomas R. Kopfensteiner, "The Metaphorical Structure of Normativity," *Theological Studies* 58 (1997): 331–46. Demmer privileges the notion of "sedimentation," especially with reference to a community of moral discourse: "It is not a misunderstanding to say that action norms represent the consensus *sedimented* [*geronnene*] within a community of moral discourse." Klaus Demmer, "Sittlicher Anspruch und Geschichtlichkeit des Verstehens," in *Heilsgeschichte und ethische Normen*, ed. Hans Rotter (Freiburg: Herder, 1984), 75.

[24] For an analysis of the distinction see Klaus Demmer, *Shaping the Moral Life: An Approach to Moral Theology* (Washington, DC: Georgetown University Press, 2000), 46–47.

[25] John T. Noonan has shown the logic of moral development in relation to the cases of usury, marriage, slavery, and religious freedom. See "Development in Moral Doctrine," in *The Context of Casuistry*, ed. James F. Keenan and Thomas A. Shannon (Washington, DC: Georgetown University Press, 1995), 188–204. More broadly Albert R. Jonsen and Stephen Toulmin, *The Abuse of Casuistry: A History of Moral Reasoning* (Berkeley: University of California Press, 1988).

Each science attempts to remember its own past. The guiding question is whether or not fundamental paradigms have been exhausted in their ability to provide adequate explanations. Only when this has been determined is it possible to responsibly speak of a shift of paradigm. One can discover new paradigms; indeed this happens when the chasm between empirical verification and theoretical explanation becomes disjointed.[26]

Thomas Kopfensteiner has shown the importance of such development in the meaning of moral norms by reference to the change in the interpretation of the principle of totality.[27] Issues pertaining to the ethics of transplantation provide a context for the application of the principle.

In a different context, defined by the discovery of new medical possibilities, an expanded understanding of the notion of therapy, and the development of the field of transplantation, also the principle of totality and the norms supported by it undergo a "shift of paradigm." In the end, moral norms safeguard the integrity of freedom by protecting *historically* defined standards of moral performance from possible erosion. Moreover, they articulate goals for action, making progressively more transparent their relation to the ideologies of human fulfillment on which they depend.[28]

Conscience and Moral Truth

In light of the previous reflections on the meaning and function of moral normativity, it becomes clear that the moral truth conveyed by concrete norms

---

[26] "Klaus Demmer, "Theological Argument and Hermeneutics in Bioethics," in *Catholic Perspectives in Medical Morals: Foundational Issues*, ed. Edmund D. Pellegrino, John P. Langan, and John Collins Harvey (Dordrecht: Kluwer Academic, 1989), 103. Demmer's moral epistemological analysis of "paradigms" is inspired by Thomas S. Kuhn, *The Structure of Scientific Revolutions* (Chicago: University of Chicago Press, 1962). For an intensive confrontation with Kuhn's thesis see Klaus Demmer, *Moraltheologische Methodenlehre* (Freiburg: Herder, 1989), especially 34–52.

[27] See Thomas R. Kopfensteiner, *Paradigms and Hermeneutics*, diss., Pontifical Gregorian University (Rome, 1988). Also "Historical Epistemology and Moral Progress," *Heythrop Journal* 33 (1992): 45–60. Traditionally, the principle rests on a physicalistic and individualistic understanding, seeing the removal of an organ in the body as a "mutilation" justified by the axiom *pars propter totum*. A body part can be surgically mutilated only for the good of the whole. However, in 1944 Bert Cunningham made possible a further expansion of the principle. See Bert Cunningham, "The Morality of Organic Transplantation," *Studies in Sacred Theology*, no. 86 (1944). For an analysis of Cunningham's thesis, see David F. Kelly, *The Emergence of Roman Catholic Medical Ethics in North America: An Historical, Methodological, Bibliographical Study* (New York: Edwin Mellen Press, 1979), 332–41.

[28] Thomas R. Kopfensteiner, "Science, Metaphor, and Moral Casuistry," in *Context of Casuistry*, ed. Keenan and Shannon, 207–20.

is always the mediation of two dimensions: one orienting the conscience of
the moral agent to a value-attunement, and the other measuring such orientation with the concrete reality of moral goods to be protected for the sake of
the agent's integrity and dignity:

> Human beings learn by reflecting on their own reactions in the face
> of challenging demands. In this way, the concept of moral value can
> be concretized within one's own *experienced* context. This concret-
> ization does not invalidate the universality of values. The morally
> true [*das sittliche Wahre*] is always also the possible [*das Mögliche*].
> But what is possible is grasped through the experience of one's own
> freedom.[29]

A reflection on conscience needs to highlight the distinctive phenomenological character of moral truth as truth pertaining to meaning. As Klaus
Demmer has repeatedly observed, moral theology hardly seems to have any
interest in the theoretical discussion on truth; as a result, it rarely engages in
serious confrontation with contemporary theories of truth, feeling rather at
home in the Scholastic definition it inherits from the tradition.[30] Unfortunately,
in so doing, it precludes itself from becoming aware of several difficulties
affecting a naïve use of the notion of truth, especially one that fails to distinguish between the truth of empirical states of affairs, which presupposes an
objective distance between subject and object, and historical, anthropological,
and ethical truths, which entail a reference to a meaning recognized and interpreted by a subjectivity.

It is customary for moral theology to rely on Thomas's definition of
truth as the *adequatio intellectus et rem*, the conformity of the knowing
intellect to its object (*De Veritate* q. I, a. 1). This definition conveys an understanding of truth in terms of a formal notion expressing a relation; as such,
it presupposes as its condition of possibility the ontological truth of things,
manifesting itself to a *receptive* mind, open to the manifestation of the object.
Although certainly not wrong, the above definition must be further nuanced
when applied to moral truth. This can be done by looking at the analogical
relation of knowledge and truth. The knowledge of an object entails an act
of receptivity on the part of the mind toward the object, a receptivity which,

---

[29] Klaus Demmer, "Sittlich Handeln aus Erfahrug," *Gregorianum* 59 (1978): 677.
More broadly on experience and truth see Roberto Dell'Oro, "Esperienza e verita' morale,"
Rivista di teologia morale 109 (1996): 63–82.

[30] Klaus Demmer, "Wahrheit und Bedeutung: Objektive Geltung im moralthe-
ologischen Diskurs," *Gregorianum* 81 (2000): 59–99. The relation of freedom to truth
constitutes a central theological topos of John Paul II's magisterial teaching. The emphasis
is on the correspondence of freedom to truth.

however, is grounded in the active anticipation (*Ausgriff*) of the totality of being. Following Karl Rahner's reinterpretation of Thomas Aquinas's meta-physics of knowledge, one could say that the relation between *intellectus possibilis* and *intellectus agens* is one in which the former always presup-poses the activity of the latter.[31] In an analogous way, the truth of the object is already grounded in the active anticipation of its meaning by the mind, against whose horizon the truth of this object can be recognized as such, that is, as true. What is meant with this analogy? As truth pertaining to meaning, moral truth is, by its very nature, the truth *intended* by an agent, not by a detached spectator. Moral truth is the truth that measures one's life-project, the happiness and moral fulfillment pursued by a moral subject in a delicate balance of personal expectations and disposition to sacrifice. Moral reason is *practical* because its knowledge of the truth is always energized and sustained by freedom's desire of the good.[32] In Thomistic terms, the anticipation of the mind (*excessus mentis*) toward being as true always corresponds to an antic-ipation of the will (*excessus voluntatis*) toward being as good.[33] Finally, the singular character of moral truth can be recognized when seen as the result of an *intersubjective* or communal engagement. Although truth cannot be reduced to consensual agreement or social constructionism (*consensus non facit veritatem*), it is nevertheless important to recognize that moral experi-ence intermediates the historical meaning of values and ideals relative to a specific lifeworld and its interpretive framework. Standards of moral perfor-mance can be gained only through a "process of communication" within a community of moral discourse, in which all the participants bring to the table their own contribution, in a spirit of freedom and fairness. In such an *ideal* community, echoing the Kantian "kingdom of ends," theoretical presupposi-tions must be disclosed in order to exclude positions that ground their claim on the basis of privilege or other uncontrollable sources, and to ensure the best results in terms of intellectual honesty and transparency.[34]

---

[31] Karl Rahner, *Spirit in the World* (New York: Continuum, 1994).

[32] The practical nature of truth, as well as its beauty, is already presupposed by the unity of the transcendentals. On this aspect insists especially von Balthasar: "Because . . . it is a formal relation of correspondence, [the true] displays a certain correctness, but this is not yet the same as saying why anyone should care about this adequation. Thus, even the light of truth could seem cold and joyless if it did not also have the warmth of the good." Hans Urs von Balthasar, *Theo-Logic/Volume I: Truth of the World*, trans. Adrian J. Walker (San Francisco: Ignatius Press, 2000), 221.

[33] "Dicendum quod verum et bonum in se invicem coincident, quia et verum est quoddam bonum, et bonum est quoddam verum; unde et bonum potest considerari cogni-tione speculative, prout consideratur veritas eius tantum" (*De Veritate* III, q. 3, ad 9). Also: "Vis cognitiva non movet, nisi mediante appetitive" (*Summa Theologiae* I, q.20, a.1, ad 1).

[34] This is the basis of "communicative" or "discourse ethics," especially in the version of Jürgen Habermas. See Maureen Junker-Kenny, *Habermas and Theology* (London: T&T Clark, 2011), 81–94; more recently, Maureen Junker-Kenny, *Religion and*

Moral Truth and Freedom

How to understand, in the end, the relativity of moral truth to freedom?[35] More specifically, how can the "transcendental reduction"[36] of moral truth to freedom avoid the pitfall of a possible *reductionism* of moral truth to a pragmatic function of self-preservation and self-interest? The problem is clearly at the heart of the magisterial preoccupation, as the following quotation from *Veritatis Splendor* shows:

> The way in which one conceives the relationship between freedom and law is thus intimately bound up with one's understanding of the moral conscience. Here the cultural tendencies—in which freedom and law are set in opposition to each other and kept apart, and freedom is exalted almost to the point of idolatry—lead to a *"creative" understanding of moral conscience*, which diverges from the teaching of the Church's tradition and her Magisterium.[37]

One must keep in mind that the term "freedom" does not denote freedom of choice in its empirical facticity, but rather a fundamental disposition toward the good, which, in turn, constitutes the ontological condition for the possibility of each concrete and free choice. We could speak here of *transcendental* freedom, understood as the original source that grounds and sustains empirical freedom. In its dynamic actualization (*Vollzug*), however, freedom is not pitted against its own metaphysical and, ultimately, theological ground, as in the Kantian version of autonomy; rather, it is released to its own identity as love. Each moral decision can be considered good when it mediates the transcendental ground of love upon which it rests; only thus can each human decision articulate, in a historical way, the radical openness (*Vorgriff*) of human freedom to its own *true* fulfillment (*finis ultimus*).[38] Freedom

---

Public Reason: A Comparison of the Positions of John Rawls, Jürgen Habermas, and Paul Ricoeur (Berlin: De Gruyter, 2014), 103–83.

[35] For the reflections on the relation of freedom and moral truth, I am indebted to Schockenhoff, *Das umstrittene Gewissen*, 115–33.

[36] The term "reduction" is, of course, technical, in that it refers to the transcendental movement of grounding.

[37] *Veritatis Splendor* 54. Later on in the encyclical one reads: "In their desire to emphasize the 'creative' character of conscience, certain authors no longer call its actions 'judgments' but 'decisions': Only by making these decisions 'autonomously' would man be able to attain moral maturity" (55).

[38] James F. Keenan, *Goodness and Rightness in Thomas Aquinas's Summa Theologiae* (Washington, DC: Georgetown University Press, 1992). For a reinterpretation of the notion of *finis ultimus* in contemporary moral theology, see Joseph Fuchs, *Moral Demands and Personal Obligations* (Washington, DC: Georgetown University Press, 1993).

expresses the ultimate nature of conscience, and this is why I can say, I *am* my conscience; that is, I am the act of a radical openness to the source that gives to be, a source giving out of love, and whose call is, in the end, the call to love. Perhaps the Christian *form* of conscience might be properly reformulated in terms of a de-mystification of autonomy: conscience released to its own true self in love, as a freedom beyond autonomy. A conscience grounded in the Christological event turns autonomy into a free service for the good of the other, beyond the calculative self-interest of utilitarian prudence, beyond the determination of self-legislating will. It is an *agapeic* service, which serves the good of the other out of a release of freedom toward the other, a release that is an overflow of generosity.[39]

The systematic reconstruction of the notion of conscience offered above entails implications for Catholic health care. The very meaning of a Catholic normative system for health care, the interplay of norms and experience, and the risky nature of individual decision-making within the framework of a faith-based institution—all these questions will be affected, one way or the other, by the way we understand conscience.

Those who work in Catholic health care, whether professionals or patients, look at the *Ethical and Religious Directives for Catholic Health Care Services* as a basic normative statement. They guide both institutional and personal decision-making not against, but *through* the mediation of conscience. And this is so because their prescriptive character remains intimately tied to the recognition of an agency that commits to them. Unlike traffic signs, or the orders of a military commander, both of which obtain independently of the agent's appropriation of their claim, principles and norms do so because they bind as *moral*, rather than legal, norms.[40] Thus, the *Directives* ought to serve, first and foremost, as a guide in the formation of responsible decision-makers and their conscience. This holds true despite the fact that the *Directives'* reference to conscience is, to say the least, sparse.[41]

---

[39] For a demystification of autonomy, and the articulation of an ethics of generosity and service in a philosophical perspective, see the work of the Leuven philosopher William Desmond, in particular, *Ethics and the Between*.

[40] The statement in question does not contradict the recognition that the *Directives* are not only morally, but also *legally*, binding within Catholic institutions.

[41] At the end of the "General Introduction," one finds allusion to "a correct conscience based on the moral norms for proper health care." Later, at the end of the introduction to Part 1 ("The Social Responsibility of Catholic Health Care Services"), the *Directives* speak to the fact that . . . "within a pluralistic society, Catholic health care services will encounter requests for medical procedures contrary to the moral teachings of the Church. Catholic health care does not offend the rights of individual conscience by refusing to provide or permit medical procedures that are judged morally wrong by the teaching authority of the Church."

A richer understanding of conscience is needed to articulate both the importance of *institutional* conscience and the respect accorded to its *individual* exercise. Trust in the maturity of responsible decision-makers need not be pitted against the clarity of normative provisions. It is precisely the positive interplay of both that nourishes, as Pope Francis reminds us, the paradoxical conviction of Christian ethics: "The centrality of the kerygma . . . *should not impose the truth but appeal to freedom.*" Only in freedom can moral norms adequately convey the truth that sustains them. The grammar of love neither stifles the vitality of freedom nor hinders the intelligence needed for a faithful discernment of the good; through the latter, our hearts are open to a generosity mindful of human measure, yet ultimately guided by divine mercy.

DEALING WITH DOUBT

Epikeia, Probabilism, and the Formation of Medical Conscience

Lisa Fullam, DVM, ThD

Conscience seeks truth, and its function is to translate knowledge into a decision about prudent action. This has at least two immediate implications. The first is that we are called to form character (our own and others') both to pursue truth assiduously and to enact truth boldly. The second is epistemological: given the central importance of pursuing and enacting truth, one must not present as true something that is not known to be true. In other words, a well-formed and well-forming conscience seeks truth and avoids misrepresenting *dubia* as certain.

These two implications together serve to counter a common misunderstanding—that an appeal to conscience acts as a moral trump card that halts further conversation. In fact, if one takes truth seriously, then an appeal to conscience does not mean the end of an exchange, but is an opening to a deeper dialogue about the matter at hand, so that, even if ultimate agreement is not achieved, all parties can affirm that they have not rushed to premature certainty in matters that still admit to reasonable doubt.

And doubt is everywhere, especially, perhaps, in this time of rapid technological and scientific advancement. In medicine, practitioners and patients alike are faced with complexities both of fact (as the science changes) and meaning ("how does this affect me?") of a scope previously unknown, or at least vastly underappreciated. How are we to deal with doubt? In Catholic moral tradition, two main strategies arose for dealing with doubt in moral matters: epikeia and probabilism. I will begin with the history of these two traditions, then explore their implications for formation of conscience in medical contexts, and conclude with some examples of how these serve to refocus some questions of medical ethics.

Epikeia

The sabbath was made for humankind, not humankind for
the sabbath.

—Mark 2:27 (NRSV)

Epikeia (Greek ἐπιείκεια) means "reasonableness," "fairness," or "equity,"
and was described by Aristotle as "a sort of justice."[1] In an Aristotelian worldview,
laws are induced from the complexities of human reality, and are of necessity
imperfect.[2] Thomas Aquinas agreed, noting that in a particular case, if
following a generally just law would yield injustice, the just person acts
against the requirements of the law and in favor of justice. Epikeia, then,
does not challenge the rightness of a law itself (in most cases), but asks
whether its application in a particular instance achieves a just lawgiver's
intention of justice. Epikeia corrects imperfect law.[3] Thomas's example is
this: Ordinarily, one must return what is borrowed. But if a man demands the
return of his sword while in a state of madness or to commit treason, then "it
is good to set aside the letter of the law and to follow the dictates of justice
and the common good."[4]

---

[1] Aristotle, *Nicomachean Ethics*, trans. and intro. Terence Irwin, 2nd ed. (Indianapolis: Hackett, 1999), 84 (book 5, chap. 10).

[2] Epikeia can be framed in a Platonic worldview also. For Plato, the quotidian world is an imperfect reflection of the ideal realm of forms. Societies are best ruled by a philosopher king or queen who grasps those ultimate truths better than hoi polloi. Barring such a person, an absolutely authoritative body of written laws would have to do. (The later Plato understood that such laws could also protect against an evil ruler.) Where law required adaptation to human reality, this was seen as a diminution or even corruption of the law, not its perfection. When people invoke "pastoral solutions" to various kinds of problems, they are invoking epikeia, but in most cases using a Platonic understanding of the term. The doctrine is not called into question, but mitigated as a concession to human imperfection. In this view, the problem isn't the doctrine, but the people who cannot live up to it.

[3] The operative understanding of law generically here is that of Thomas Aquinas: "an ordinance of reason for the common good, made by him who has care of the community, and promulgated" (*Summa Theologiae*, I IIae, q.90.4c). In this view, ordinances that are unreasonable or do not serve the common good are not laws at all.

[4] *ST* II IIae, q. 120.1 c. Thomas's understanding of justice, and how epikeia fits in, is complex. He starts with Justinian's definition of justice as "a habit whereby a man [*sic*] renders to each one his due by a constant and perpetual will" (*ST* II IIae, q. 58.1c.). Thomas describes epikeia as a subjective part of the virtue of legal justice, which directs the exterior actions of any virtue to the service of the common good. Particular justice (e.g.,

Both Aristotle and Thomas are considering human or civil law in their discussions of epikeia: Where do natural law and moral norms fit in?[5] According to Thomas, natural law is the indwelling (i.e., natural or "imprinted" in the human being by God) first principles of practical reason, including the most basic definition "good is to be done and pursued, and evil is to be avoided," and those precepts that follow closely on this first principle. This *habitus* of first principles is abstract, universal, and not subject to epikeia. An exhortation to virtue like "Be just!" can be seen to belong to the realm of deductions so close to that basic definition "Do good!" that epikeia has no place.

But the devil is in the details: What, exactly, does justice require? Once we begin to formulate moral norms beyond those abstract first principles ("Do good!" "Be just!"), then we enter a realm of secondary principles; these norms are human formulations analogous to civil law, thus subject to correction when they don't apply.

> The natural law, as to general principles, is the same for all, both as to rectitude and as to knowledge. But as to certain matters of detail, which are conclusions, as it were of those general principles, it is the same for all in the majority of cases, both as to rectitude and as to knowledge; and yet in some few cases it may fail.[6]

This follows from the contingent nature of moral knowledge generally: both Aristotle and Thomas recognize that while principles are universal, when we apply those principles we enter a pluralistic realm:

> In speculative matters truth is the same in all men [*sic*], both as to principles and as to conclusions. . . . But in matters of action, truth or practical rectitude is not the same for all as to matters of detail, but only as to the general principles.[7]

Epikeia is not the whole of justice; it is the virtue by which one evaluates the justice of laws, both human civil laws and moral norms derived from the first principles of the natural moral law. Without epikeia, justice devolves to legalism, to rote enforcing of laws regardless of their human cost, a stance

---

commutative justice) applies immediately to rectifying relationships among individuals, and mediately (via legal justice) to the common good. *ST* II IIae, q. 58.7, ad 1.

[5] My argument here follows that of Josef Fuchs, SJ, "Epikeia Applied to Natural Law?" *Personal Responsibility and Christian Morality* (Washington, DC: Georgetown University Press, 1983), 185–99.

[6] *ST* I IIae, q. 94.4 c.

[7] *ST* I I IIae, q.94.4 c.

that is unworthy of responsible and intelligent moral agents. According to Joseph Fuchs, a robust virtue of epikeia is necessary for reforming moral norms, especially in changing times:

> If some norms were formulated for realities fundamentally different from the realities that exist today, or with a fundamentally different understanding of these realities, the question arises whether a norm formulated in this way can be helpful or "valid." Should it not be replaced by another norm? . . . This reformulation would require as some propose (e.g., Virt and Demmer), reinstating the virtue of epikeia in moral theology.[8]

So the virtue of epikeia applies in situations in which a law or norm generally (or historically) serves justice, but in a particular instance (or time) may not. In such cases, the just person recognizes that the letter of the law or the particulars of the norm must yield to the purpose of the law, that is, to an outcome that fosters flourishing and serves the common good.

Epikeia is a virtue for all who apply laws or norms—not only those in authority, but anyone wrestling with a moral question in which it is not certain that the relevant moral norm should be applied. Such cases were presumed to be unusual—good laws and norms do apply in most cases, and prudent exercise of epikeia refines, corrects, or revises a norm that was too simple for the complexity of human moral life. But what happens when we're faced with a situation in which the arguments we construct or the authorities we consult yield a plurality of reasonable stances on a given question? What if the norm itself is a matter of doubt?

Probabilism: *"Lex dubia non obligat"*

Probabilism arose in the sixteenth century at a time when moral theology was widely understood to be expressible in lawlike dicta. When must conscience obey a rule and when is it free to do what is contrary to it? In other words, how do we move from practical doubt about the right course of action to the moral certitude required to act?[9]

---

[8] Josef Fuchs, SJ, "Historicity and Moral Norm," *Moral Demands and Personal Obligations*, trans. Brian McNeil (Washington, DC: Georgetown University Press, 1993), 105–6.

[9] Moral certitude (also called "practical certainty of conscience," or, in Thomas's somewhat confusing terminology, "probable certitude" is the degree of certitude required to act, and is distinguished from speculative certitude, about which there can be no doubt. Again, the contingent nature of prudential decisions marks the difference. In a right triangle, $a^2 + b^2 = c^2$, always, everywhere, and for everyone. But the practical decision

The Dominican scholar Bartolomé de Medina (1527–81) is credited with the first explicit statement of probabilism in his 1577 commentary on Thomas Aquinas's *Summa Theologiae,* I IIae, q. 19, art. 6, "Whether the will is good when it abides by erring reason?" Thomas's answer is that if the error is of invincible (nonnegligent) ignorance of a circumstance of the act, then the will is "excused."[10] Medina wrote, "It seems to me that, if an opinion is probable, it is licit to follow it, even though the opposite opinion is more probable."[11]

"Probable" in this sense is not the common English usage meaning "more likely," but rather "capable of surviving a test." Probabilism helps the moral agent navigate in cases where more than one reasonable stance on a given question exists. "The thesis of probabilism simply asserts that a person who is deliberating about whether or not he is obliged by some moral, civil, or ecclesiastical norm or law may take advantage of any reasonable doubt about whether the law obliges him."[12] Probability requires "good and solid reasons for thinking that a certain line of action is morally correct."[13]

According to Medina, a probable opinion is so "because wise men propose it and confirm it by excellent arguments."[14] The Jesuit Gabriel Vasquez (1551–1604) named these intrinsic probability—supported by solid arguments—and extrinsic probability—held by reliable authority.

Two extreme positions were later condemned by ecclesiastical authority: tutiorism, which held that in situations of practical doubt one should choose the "safer" (tutior) position, granting obeisance to the law or norm, or when those were in conflict, the option less liable to lead one to sin. The other

---

about how to rightly punish a kid caught shoplifting a candy bar doesn't admit to that kind of certainty. Nevertheless, in order to act, one must have decided, in conscience, that THIS act is "a good and appropriate," or, ideally, "the best" way to address this question, here and now.

[10] "If then reason or conscience err with an error that is voluntary, either directly, or through negligence, so that one errs about what one ought to know; then such an error of reason or conscience does not excuse the will, that abides by that erring reason or conscience, from being evil. But if the error arise from ignorance of some circumstance, and without any negligence, so that it cause the act to be involuntary, then that error of reason or conscience excuses the will, that abides by that erring reason, from being evil" (*ST* I IIae, Q. 19.6). His example is that of a man who has sex with a woman he innocently mistakes for his wife. Surely, the celibate reasons, such an act is an understandable and nonnegligent error.

[11] Bartolomé de Medina, *Expositio in Summae Theologiae Partem I II, q. 19, a. 6,* cited in Albert R. Jonsen and Stephen Toulmin, *The Abuse of Casuistry: A History of Moral Reasoning* (Berkeley: University of California Press, 1988), 164.

[12] Jonsen and Toulmin, *Abuse of Casuistry,* 166.

[13] Henry Davis, *Moral and Pastoral Theology,* vol. 2 (New York: Sheed and Ward, 1943), 78.

[14] Medina, *Expositio in Summae Theologiae Partem I II, q. 19, a. 6,* cited in Jonsen and Toulmin, *Abuse of Casuistry,* 166.

extreme was laxism, which held that one could adopt even a very weak argument or authoritative opinion.

Ruling out these extremes left two middle positions, probabilism and probabiliorism. Probabiliorism is the position that one must follow the stronger argument and/or more influential expert opinions. The risk of probabiliorism is a drift into tutiorism, that an extant law or opinion of the current experts could be given an epistemological certainty it does not, in fact, possess.

The other middle position is probabilism, which exploded in the moral literature in the decades following Medina's proposal. In what might be called "the problem of moralists with too much time on their hands," probabilism took off in flights of justificatory fancy.[15] Moralists forgot that extrinsic probabilism wasn't merely a matter of counting the experts but is connected to intrinsic probabilism, the strength of their arguments. For example, in our time any number of advocates and practitioners of homeopathy may be counted up, but that doesn't mean that their practice is justified either in theory or by experimental data. Nonsense remains nonsense, regardless of the number of those credulous enough to fall for it.

If the risk of probabiliorism is a drift into tutiorism, the risk of probabilism is a drift into laxism; Jansenism, expressed par excellence in the savage anticasuist[16] rhetoric of Blaise Pascal (1623–62), tarred all probabilism with the laxist brush. For all his linguistic brilliance, however, it seems Pascal the mathematician missed the distinction between moral and speculative certitude. Jonsen and Toulmin note:

> He rightly recognized the inherent tendency of probabilism to slide toward moral skepticism, where every opinion is as good as any other, and into moral laxism, where all law falls before liberty. . . . Yet he missed the main point. His own words reveal this: "I am not satisfied with probability. I want certainty."[17]

---

[15] Two samples of laxist propositions condemned by the Holy Office: "An innocent man is permitted to kill a false accuser, false witness, and even the judge about to pass an unjust sentence, it is the only way to avoid harm," and "It is not breaking a fast day to eat little but often." John Mahoney, *The Making of Moral Theology: A Study of the Roman Catholic Tradition* (Oxford: Clarendon Press, 1989), 140.

[16] According to Jonsen, "Casuistry is the exercise of prudential or practical reasoning in recognition of the relationship between maxims, circumstances and topics, as well as the relationship of paradigm cases to analogous cases." See Albert R. Jonsen, "Casuistry as Methodology in Clinical Ethics," *Theoretical Medicine* 12, no. 4 (December 1991): 295–307. Probabilism is the paradigmatic tool of casuists: "marshaling, comparing and contrasting 'probable opinions' became a central feature of casuistry" (Jonsen and Toulmin, *Abuse of Casuistry,* 155).

[17] Jonsen and Toulmin, *Abuse of Casuistry,* 171, citing Pascal, *The Provincial Letters,* Letter 5, trans A. J. Krailsheimer (Baltimore: Penguin Books, 1967), 81.

Pace Pascal, there is much to recommend in probabilism. Medina's stance of probabilism, that one may follow the less probable opinion, respects the work of the conscience in seeking truth. It expands the realm of relevant moral knowledge beyond that possessed by dominant experts and expressed in the extant moral norms of a given time and place. For this reason, probabilism shines in the confessional. When one is clear about the relative merits of two positions, then prudence surely favors the more probable. But the confessor's role is different, as Bernhard Häring insisted:

In the tribunal of penance the confessor is never permitted to refuse absolution to any penitent who holds and follows an opinion proposed by prudent and learned moralists, even if the confessor himself looks upon it as false.[18]

And while they tend toward opposite stances when pushed to extremes, probabilism and probabiliorism need not necessarily be seen as an either/or choice:

Unfortunately, the casuists saw the probabilist and probabiliorist views as exclusive options, whereas they can be plausibly understood as alternatives for different situations. When faced with complex issues that you have no chance to reflect on yourself, accepting an opinion that appears reasonable from any sound doctor ("probabilism") may be prudent practical policy; but if you have time to undertake a fresh analysis of the issues, the other ("probabiliorist") course, which demands that you look for the sounder doctor and the more reasonable opinion, is surely preferable.[19]

Alphonsus Liguori (1696–1787) resurrected probabilism by renaming it. Liguori began his career as a probabiliorist, moved to probabilism, then to his own stance of equiprobabilism, in which a law is doubtful if the arguments and authorities on each side roughly balance out. Equiprobabilism can perhaps be seen less as a stance of mathematical equality and more like the equipoise that defines morally licit arms of a medical research trial—there has to be more than a whim to justify one's position. In the end it is prudence that distinguishes between reasonable and unreasonable stances. Bernhard Häring, CSsR, said of equiprobabilism:

When an upright conscience has equally or almost equally good reasons for creative use of freedom in view of present needs, it is

---

[18] Bernhard Häring, CSsR, *The Law of Christ*, trans. Edwin G. Kaiser, CPPS (Westminster, MD: Newman Press, 1961), 187.

[19] Jonsen and Toulmin, *Abuse of Casuistry*, 261.

not bound by law which is, in itself, or in its concrete application, doubtful. Law should have no right to stifle creative freedom unless it has clearly stronger reasons for doing so.[20]

Epikeia is, per Aristotle and Thomas, a virtue, "a sort of justice." Probabilism is not itself a virtue—it is a practice of engaging opinions and weighing expertise in contexts of plural contending voices, and of being capable of taking seriously the "less probable" argument, certainly when one is in a position of judgment of others (as in confession) and, more generally, when one is confronted with moral pluralism involving multiple arguable stances. What's the virtue that builds one's capacity to be a responsible probabilist?

I would call it skepticism.[21] As a virtue, skepticism practices the winnowing of opinions, between the poles manifested in practices of laxism and rigorism. It is a part of the cardinal virtue of prudence, perfecting the aspect of practical reason that deals with doubts of the kind we've addressed here. Like all virtues, it is connected to other traits of character necessary to enact it: general courage, for example. Like prudence in all its forms, it is also related to the aim of the virtue(s) at work in the situation at hand: fidelity in doctor-patient relationships, justice in matters of medical practice or policy, and so on.

Skepticism is an essential aspect of prudence—without skepticism prudence would lack the bold creativity that is the hallmark of the truly virtuous moral agent. Without skepticism, one's ability for responsible decisions of conscience is hamstrung—one is stuck in practical doubt. And in a Christian context, without skepticism, there is no real discipleship—not every word is from the Lord, and not all who speak in Jesus' name are to be believed.

---

[20] Bernhard Häring, CSsR, *Free and Faithful in Christ: Moral Theology for Priests and Laity,* vol. 1: *General Moral Theology* (Middlegreen: St. Paul Publications, 1978), 50. Of course, what counts as "equally or almost equally good reasons" is itself a prudential discernment—I read Häring's stance here as implying a practice of probablism more than equiprobabilism.

[21] I am not using the term in its formal philosophical sense that holds that certain moral knowledge is impossible to attain. Rather, the *virtue* of moral skepticism in the sense I mean here is closer to its colloquial sense either of resisting instant credulity or of threshing the harvest to separate the wheat from the chaff. The vices that exceed the virtuous mean of reasonable skepticism are, on one side, radical skepticism, rejecting the idea that truth is available to human reason, and on the other side, radical, filterless credulity. Skepticism here may be understood as Thomas's two virtues of docility (ability to learn from others, as in extrinsic probabilism) and shrewdness (ability to figure things out for oneself, as in intrinsic probabilism). These are reckoned as quasi-integral parts of the virtue of prudence (*ST* II IIae, q. 49.2–3). I have written about the virtues of curiosity and skepticism before: see Lisa Fullam, "Virtue for Genomics: Curiosity and Skepticism in Genetic Research," *Irish Theological Quarterly* 68 (2003): 307–23.

Epikeia and Probabilism in Medical Contexts

Formation of conscience in an ethics of virtue means formation of character, including, but not limited to, the intellect. Timothy O'Connell parses conscience into three aspects: an ineliminable capacity (which Thomas called *synderesis*), a process, and a judgment of conscience (*conscientia*).[22] The process aspect of conscience can be seen as moral reasoning in a given moral methodology. In virtue ethics, the process aspect of conscience is understood in a more holistic way than cogitation alone: a person's character (including and beyond intellect) is shaped and reflected in one's actions; it is one's whole character that structures one's decisions of conscience. My purpose in the remaining section of this essay is not to lay out an entire virtue ethics of medical practice, of course, but to begin to point to some ways in which the traditions of epikeia and probabilism may be helpful in medical contexts.

But before I separate them, I want to point to an important way in which the two are connected. Although epikeia differs from probabilism as different questions about laws or norms, there is also flow from one to the other. Uncontroverted law is inevitably liable to instances in which epikeia is appropriate, due to the nature of law itself. However, if a law is continually being "epikaically" sidestepped in case after case, perhaps reexamination of the norm itself is indicated, and the process of probabilism begins. This is usually on a small scale at first, and then if the arguments supporting revision are sound, other experts may also adopt the new stance and develop it further. In a healthy moral system, the virtue of epikeia first suggests and then spurs the practice of probabilism; this is the way doctrine develops. The converse can also happen: a new question (or a reframing of an old question by the process I just described) can produce a flurry of probable stances, which may then narrow as they are weighed and found adequate or wanting, yielding in time a more stable stance that is subject to the judgment of epikeia in its use. Either wide practice of epikeia or the proliferation of probabilism may be a snapshot in time of a norm in flux.[23]

---

[22] See Timothy E. O'Connell, *Principles for a Catholic Morality*, rev. ed. (San Francisco: Harper Collins, 1990), 111. He speaks of these three as conscience/1, conscience/2, and conscience/3.

[23] This may be the situation in Catholic practices concerning divorce and remarriage, for example. Ecclesiastical annulment of marriage requires evaluation of the relationship in light of canonical norms for declaring a marriage null from the start. In our time, however, we see rapid changes in ecclesial practices in the United States: first, beginning in the 1970s, the number of applications for annulments skyrocketed. Despite a very high (90 percent or higher) rate of granting annulments, the percent of divorced Catholics seeking annulment began to decline in favor of "internal forum" solutions, in which no formal annulment is sought, the decision resting with the consciences of the parties to the marriage in consultation with trusted advisers (usually parish priests or lay ministers.) The recent

Epikeia

Epikeia has an echo in medicine: in an analogous scientific sense, epikeia is a virtue for much of day-to-day medical practice. Acting on medical norms which work *ut in pluribus*, the practitioner may be confronted with situations in which prudence suggests that the rule be set aside in this case, since the aim of the treatment would not be achieved otherwise. Doses are adjusted, different drugs are used, surgery is elected or not, and so on. There are clear scientific norms, and their application requires a virtue that sometimes adjusts, corrects, or tosses out a norm. A deft practitioner possesses a "feel for the organism" that guides particular decisions in a given case. Rote application of treatment norms is a sure sign of the neophyte, whereas the virtue of epikeia (like other virtues) requires practice for its perfection. Epikeia raises medical practice from science to art.

Epikeia regarding moral norms is also practiced in medicine. Consider pain control in terminal illness, for example. When prescribing medications for pain control, physicians rightly take into account the effects of those medications on the patient's life as a whole, including both the positive and negative.[24] One concern is the possibility of abuse or addiction, a fear sometimes shared by patients and physicians alike. In terminal illness, however, especially in a time when physician-assisted dying is increasingly accepted as part of end-of-life care, the ordinary norm shifts even more strongly—perhaps absolutely—toward aggressive pain control, while concerns about addiction seem absurd. Since pain significantly impairs enjoyment of life, and since pain and fear of pain are a significant (though not the primary) reason citied by patients for electing assistance in dying,[25] failure to control pain adequately in terminal illness can be both abusive and deadly—in terminal patients, adhering to the norm that requires worry about abuse or addiction and moderating opiate use for that reason violates justice and the common good.

Synod on the Family opened the door to greater use of the internal forum. So a previously unchallenged norm (the indissolubility of marriage, with few annulment petitions until the 1970s) yielded to a widespread practice of epikeia, first in the Platonic sense (diocesan marriage tribunals), then in the Aristotelian sense (internal forum). Debates concerning how we understand indissolubility as a norm for Catholic marriage have proliferated since the 1980s—probabilism is being practiced and is likely influencing the practice of the internal forum.

[24] Despite the awareness of the negative effects of poor pain management for patient outcomes in all kinds of medical circumstances, the problem remains. See Frank Brennan, Daniel B. Carr, and Michael Cousins, "Pain Management: A Fundamental Human Right," *Anesthesia and Analgesia* 105, no. 1 (July 2007): 205–21.

[25] Pain or fear of pain was cited by 25 percent of patients in their decisions to elect for assistance in dying since the inception of the Death with Dignity Act of 2013 in Oregon which allowed physician-assisted dying. See "Oregon Death with Dignity Act: 2015 Data Summary," https://public.health.oregon.gov.

Probabilism

Probabilism is also a facet of the science of medicine, most clearly in the concept of the standard of care, the range of medical options that are supported by good science and competent authorities. The push toward evidence-based medicine (EBM) defined by Sackett et al. as "the integration of best research evidence with clinical expertise and patient values,"[26] can also be seen as an exercise in probabilism. EBM draws on the best empirical evidence (which is the scientific analog of intrinsic probabilism) including meta-analyses of available data, to substantiate—or not—practices based in clinical experience of physicians (extrinsic probabilism) in dialogue with the patient's expressing of his or her values (a new voice of extrinsic probabilism, recognizing patients as authorities in their own lives) to optimize medical outcomes.

Examples of probabilism also are found in ethical debates around some of the besetting moral dilemmas of the day; for example, Carol A. Tauer explores the stringency of Catholic magisterial protection of human embryos, arguing that the Congregation for the Doctrine of the Faith invokes, then misuses, probabilism in formulating its absolutist stance.[27]

A second example: in many or most cases, institutional review boards (IRB) practice probabilism with regard to medical trials. An innovative procedure, device, or medication is posited by a researcher who presents the process to the IRB, who serve as a prudential body to assess the (at least apparent) likelihood of gaining meaningful knowledge in light of the (at least apparent) risks undertaken by subjects. They are not assessing the likelihood that the trial will succeed in treating the condition for which it is proposed— that question is both outside the scope of the IRB's collective expertise and unknown to the experts who propose the trial.

Rather, they mediate between the medical profession's need for innovative treatments, the patient's safety and privacy, the adequacy of the information about the study offered to the patient, and the community standards of the locality. Jonsen and Toulmin began their study of casuistry by noting that the National Commission for the Protection of Human Subjects of Biomedical and Behavioral Research (on which Jonsen had been a commission member, Toulmin a staffer and consultant) worked by a method they described as "a 'casuistry' of human experimentation."[28]

---

[26] David L. Sackett et al., *Evidence-Based Medicine: How to Practice and Teach EBM*, 2nd ed. (Edinburgh: Churchill Livingstone, 2000), 1.

[27] Carol A. Tauer, "The Tradition of Probabilism and the Moral Status of the Early Embryo," *Theological Studies* 45 (1984): 3–33.

[28] Jonsen and Toulmin, *Abuse of Casuistry*, 338.

Why Epikeia and Probabilism?

I began this chapter with the observation that conscience seeks truth, and a well-formed conscience is epistemically rigorous in evaluating truth claims. We ought not claim as true something that is a matter of reasonable doubt. To settle for illusory certainties is as deadly to the conscience as the failure to pursue truth at all: the first is a short-circuit of conscience, and the latter is its total nonfunction. These important aspects of the good working of conscience are recognized, but, I contend, undervalued in the contemporary medical ethical landscape.

Medical ethics is dominated by the principlism of Beauchamp and Childress's monumental *Principles of Biomedical Ethics*, currently in its seventh edition. Medical ethics begins with four principles drawn from common morality: (1) respect for autonomy, (2) nonmaleficence, (3) beneficence, and (4) justice. These principles yield different kinds of norms: principles, rules, rights, and virtues, the latter proposed as corresponding to different principles, rules, and ideals of action. The practice of medical ethics in this framework consists in applying these norms, which involves processes of weighing and balancing:

> Balancing is concerned with the relative weights and strengths of different moral norms, whereas specification is concerned primarily with their scope. . . . Balancing seems particularly well suited for reaching judgments in particular cases, whereas specification seems especially useful for developing more specific policies from already accepted general norms.[29]

In chapter 2 of their text, they offer "five focal virtues for health professionals: compassion, discernment, trustworthiness, integrity, and conscientiousness,"[30] which are important in creating practitioners who possess the virtue of caring, which they call "the fundamental orienting virtue in health care."[31] In their presentation of virtues overall, they present them as a distinct domain of ethics, coherent with but neither inferior nor superior to that of principles. They note later in their work that

> where a climate of trust prevails, virtue and character are likely to be prized and emphasized in many human relationships. . . . However,

---

[29] Tom L. Beauchamp and James F. Childress, *Principles of Biomedical Ethics*, 7th ed. (New York: Oxford University Press, 2009), 20.

[30] Ibid., 37.

[31] Ibid.

virtue theory works less well for certain other forms of moral encounter, especially where trust, intimacy, familiarity, and the like have not been established. When strangers meet, character often plays a less significant role than principles, rules, and institutional policies.[32]

Despite the nod to virtue (and the increasing attention they pay to virtue in their text from earlier editions than the current one), the driving force of Beauchamp and Childress's methodology is "principles, rules, and institutional policies." The bulk of their text is devoted to the four basic principles and the deductions from them—in short, they present ethics as, if not entirely framable in lawlike dicta, largely reducible to the language of strangers.

The traditions of epikeia and probabilism indicate the centrality of the role of deft agents who use rules well. In other words, Beauchamp and Childress recognize the need for weighing and balancing of norms in their principle-based ethics, but it is the person who possesses epikeia and skepticism who can do that well. To be an excellent practitioner both in the science and the ethics of medicine, even if medical ethics is framed in principlist terms, a physician must possess the virtues of epikeia and skepticism, especially in the practice of probabilism.[33]

Finally, these traditions reveal that Catholic moral tradition is not afraid of doubt—in fact, if my inference about skepticism and prudence is correct, then to be a virtuous person requires skepticism and its practices. Neither is it true, as those overly influenced by the platonic version of epikeia might think, that epikeia is a concession to human imperfection and sin, and probabilism a dodge away from the requirements of Christian morality. Indeed, casuistry and probabilism reflect that one of the requisites of a truly humane medical ethics requires not assuming always that the ethics of strangers is more adequate than the ethics of friends. Only then can the particularities of our humanity be engaged as morally valuable:

> We do need to recognize that a morality based entirely on general rules and principles is tyrannical and disproportioned, and that only

---

[32] Ibid., 382.

[33] This in turn indicates, perhaps, the need for a more developed methodology for a renewed casuistry in medical ethics, an important topic which exceeds my reach in this paper. For a starting point, see Albert R. Jonsen, "Casuistry as Methodology in Clinical Ethics, *Theoretical Medicine* 12, no. 4 (December 1991): 295–307, in which he explores morphology, taxonomy, and kinetics as tools for a casuistic methodology. Scientific casuistry is already central to medical practice—when doctors together review their current cases on rounds, or review morbidity and mortality reports, their discussions are a casuistry of evaluating new cases in light of established practices (rounds) or reflecting on lessons learned when things haven't gone well.

those who make equitable allowances for subtle individual differences have a proper feeling for the deeper demands of ethics.[34]

The aim of conscience is truth, and this aim can be achieved only if we
both assiduously seek truth and also exercise a prudent degree of epistemological rigor in what we admit is true. In this essay I have explored the virtue of
epikeia and the tradition of probabilism, both rooted deep in Catholic ethics,
but underregarded in medical milieus. The ways medical practitioners are
currently trained in internship and residency—essentially by mentorship—is
a rich ground for moral as well as scientific formation, but much of medical
ethics is relegated instead to a calculation of principles. Medical ethics is
construed as an ethics of strangers, not of intimates, a problematic stance both
when one considers the intimacy of the mentoring of physicians in medical
training contexts and the intimate intersections of life, death, flourishing, and
meaning that are part and parcel of the matter of the most significant medical
decisions made by patients with their doctors. In a time in which medical
ethics is predominantly regarded in terms of principles, a return to an appreciation of these "virtues of doubt" can help us address emerging issues, but also
help us appreciate the contours of medical practice and the limits of medical
expertise. An ethics of virtue that emphasizes epikeia and the practice of probabilism can help practitioners and patients alike navigate well in roiled and
murky waters.

---

[34] Stephen Toulmin, "The Tyranny of Principles," *Hastings Center Report* 11, no. 6
(December 1981): 39.

Does a Catholic Health Care Organization Have an Institutional Conscience?

Thomas A. Nairn, OFM

For decades scholars have been discussing the notion of whether health care organizations have an institutional conscience. As early as 1979, Edmund Pellegrino spoke of institutional ethics and described hospitals as moral agents.[1] In the 1990s, Daniel Sulmasy went further to suggest that as moral agents, health care institutions do have consciences:

> Conscience is a fundamental moral commitment on the part of a moral agent to moral integrity, involving a commitment to uphold fundamental moral precepts and moral identity and, based upon these fundamental moral commitments, to make use of reason, emotion, and will to arrive at proper moral judgments and to act on these judgments. Health care institutions seem fully capable of this.[2]

Following Sulmasy's lead, several ethicists have continued to develop in a positive way the notion of institutional conscience.[3]

In recent years, however, the concept of institutional conscience (along with the related notions of institutional conscience clauses and institutional conscientious refusal) has come under strong criticism. Some have suggested that institutional conscientious refusal to perform certain procedures is harmful to "women in need of reproductive health services, as well as the practitioners who are prohibited from providing this essential care."[4] For

---

[1] See Edmund D. Pellegrino, *Humanism and the Physician* (Knoxville: University of Tennessee Press, 1979), 141–52.

[2] Daniel Sulmasy, "Institutional Conscience and Moral Pluralism in Health Care," *New Theology Review* 10, no. 4 (November 1997): 11.

[3] For a recent example, see Elliott Louis Bedford, "The Concept of Institutional Conscience," *National Catholic Bioethics Quarterly* 12, no. 3 (Autumn 2012): 409–20. Bedford refers to several other essays analyzing institutional conscience.

[4] American Civil Liberties Union, *Health Care Denied: Patients and Physicians Speak Out about Catholic Hospitals and the Threat to Women's Health and Lives* (May

others, the criticism has been more philosophical. Spencer Durland grounds the notion of conscience in autonomy and maintains that the notion of institutional conscience "undercuts the affirmative aspect of individual conscience by requiring physicians to refrain from acting in accord with their clinical morality or prevailing best practices."[5] Michael Rie suggests that living in a secular pluralist society imposes important limits on the moral agency of faith-based medical centers.[6] Elizabeth Sepper suggests that hospitals are pluralistic by their very nature and that therefore generally accepted medical standards and not narrow religious reasoning by the institution ought to govern relationships between providers and patients.[7]

Although most of these criticisms have been made from a legal or philosophical point of view, there has also been criticism from within the Catholic theological tradition itself. Daniel Finn, for example, acknowledges that conscience requires subjectivity. He therefore maintains that organizations should simply be considered social structures which influence the consciences of members of the organization. Although institutions can be considered moral agents, they do not exercise conscience.[8]

Many analyses of institutional conscience place the notion primarily within a context of conflict of consciences, individual and institutional, where the institutional conscience always seems to override that of the individual.[9] This sort of analysis seems to conflate several related but necessarily distinct elements—the meaning of conscience, both individual and possibly institutional; the manner in which such institutional conscience functions or ought to function; the possible limits to the exercise of conscience in a pluralistic society; and the influence of both the Church and the law. This essay will suggest that by keeping these issues distinct one may understand better what authors may mean by institutional conscience and whether this notion is useful for Catholic health care at the present time.

2016), 25. See also *Merger Watch, Miscarriage of Medicine: The Growth of Catholic Hospitals and the Threat to Reproductive Health Care* (December 2013), 1.

[5] Spencer L. Durland, "The Case against Institutional Conscience," *Notre Dame Law Review* 86, no. 4 (2011): 1659.

[6] Michael A. Rie, "Defining the Limits of Institutional Moral Agency in Health Care: A Response to Kevin Wildes," *Journal of Medicine and Philosophy* 16, no. 2 (1991): 221–24.

[7] Elizabeth Sepper, "Taking Conscience Seriously," *Virginia Law Review* 98 (2012): 1501–75.

[8] Daniel K. Finn, "Can an Organization Have a Conscience? Contributions from Social Science to Catholic Social Thought" in *Conscience and Catholicism: Rights, Responsibilities, and Institutional Responses*, ed. David E. DeCosse and Kristin E. Heyer (Maryknoll, NY: Orbis Books, 2015), 167–81.

[9] For example, Spencer Durland claims that "in every Catholic hospital lurks the possibility of conflict between institutional and individual conscience" (Durland, "Case against Institutional Conscience," 1661).

To this end, I investigate three related but distinct questions: (1) What is the traditional Catholic understanding of conscience, and how does this notion relate to what some authors have called the institutional conscience of a Catholic health care organization? (2) Does the notion of an institutional conscience help in the understanding of how Catholic health care relates to the larger Church, to the medical profession, and to the larger society? And (3) Can the notion of institutional conscience or some related notion provide a way to negotiate the tensions in which Catholic health care finds itself?

Conscience and the Question of the
Validity of Institutional Conscience

Understandings of Personal Conscience, Secular and Christian

In trying to understand whether there is any validity to the notion of an institutional conscience, one immediately encounters a definitional difficulty. There are different understandings of the term "conscience" depending on whether one is approaching the issue from the legal point of view or from that of Catholic theology.[10] Even within Catholic moral theology there are different, often conflicting, understandings of conscience.[11]

As the term has been used in the law of the United States, "the right of conscience is rooted in autonomy."[12] Legal respect for claims of conscience is usually based not on the truth or falsity of the claim itself but rather on the sincerity and integrity of the one making the claim:

> As a number of scholars have argued, an individual's moral integrity offers the most compelling moral basis for respecting her conscience. In a liberal pluralistic society, the objective truth or falsity of an individual's moral commitments cannot form the justification for determining when to accommodate conscience. Instead, "the moral weight of an individual's conscience-based objection can be grounded in the value of moral integrity and self-respect as well as the significant harm associated with self-betrayal and the loss of self-respect."[13]

---

[10] Part of the argument of this essay is that both of these definitions are necessary. Much of the argument of this essay will concern itself with the Catholic definition. However, as the argument moves toward pluralism and US law, it will move to the second definition.

[11] For the diversity of magisterial and theological statements concerning conscience, see Charles E. Curran, ed., *Conscience: Readings in Moral Theology 14* (Mahwah, NJ: Paulist Press, 2004).

[12] Durland, "Case against Institutional Conscience," 1658.

[13] Sepper, "Taking Conscience Seriously," 1529. Sepper is quoting from Mark R. Wicclair, "Conscience Objection in Medicine," *Bioethics* 14 (2000): 214.

Similarly, Daniel Sulmasy quotes the American Congress of Obstetrics and Gynecologists as defining conscience as "the private, constant, ethically attuned part of the human character."[14] Thus the legal definition understands conscience as a private and autonomous faculty of the individual, grounded in the integrity of the individual, and not in the truth of the content of the claim of conscience.

A different notion of conscience guides the Catholic moral tradition and therefore Catholic health care. Although this understanding of conscience has many similarities with its secular counterpart, there are also differences. The Second Vatican Council has described "conscience" as the person's "most secret core and . . . sanctuary" where one is alone with God. To this extent, it sounds like the legal definition. However, the Council continues:

> By conscience in a wonderful way, that law is made known which is fulfilled in the love of God and of one's neighbor. Through loyalty to conscience Christians are joined to other people in the search for truth and for the right solution to so many moral problems which arise both in the life of individuals and from social relations. Hence, the more a correct conscience prevails, the more do persons and groups turn aside from blind choice and try to be guided by the objective standards of moral conduct.[15]

Although the Catholic moral tradition notes that the activity of conscience occurs in the secret core of one's person, where one is alone with God, the tradition does not maintain that the activity of conscience is simply private. From at least the Middle Ages, Catholic moral theology has considered conscience to be not some sort of inaccessible intuition based on the sincerity of one's subjective beliefs but rather a "dictate or command of reason."[16] For example, the thirteenth-century theologian, the Franciscan Bonaventure of Bagnorea, maintained that "conscience is like God's herald and messenger; it does not command things on its own authority, but commands them as coming from God's authority, like a herald when he proclaims the edicts of the king."[17] His contemporary, Thomas Aquinas, described conscience as "an act in which the first principles of practical reason are applied to . . . specific

---

[14] Daniel Sulmasy, "What Is Conscience and Why Is Respect for It So Important?" *Theoretical Medical Bioethics* 29 (2008): 135. Sulmasy is quoting from ACOG Committee, "The Limits of Conscientious Refusal in Reproductive Medicine," *Obstetrics and Gynecology* 110 (November 2007): 1203–8.

[15] Second Vatican Council, *Pastoral Constitution on the Church in the Modern World*, 16.

[16] Thomas Aquinas, *Summa Theologiae*, q. 19, a. 5, resp.

[17] Bonaventure, *Commentary on the Sentences,* II *Sent*, d. 39, a. 1, q. 3, ad 3.

situations, particular cases and complex circumstances . . . assisted by [the virtue of prudence]."[18]

Both Thomas and Bonaventure understood that the authority of conscience comes from God. This did not mean, however, that they considered that the dictates of conscience were always correct. For both theologians, error can enter the process of making decisions of conscience in any of three ways: from a defect of reason (ignorance), from misguided affections, or from weakness or obstinacy of will.[19]

Of these three possibilities, the most nuanced treatment dealt with ignorance. If ignorance is willful or the result of negligence, then the conscience is culpable or blameworthy.[20] However, the Catholic theological tradition, following Thomas Aquinas, has recognized that ignorance often does not arise from willful negligence. The Second Vatican Council emphasized: "Conscience frequently errs from invincible ignorance without losing its dignity."[21] Even a mistaken conscience binds the individual. In Catholic morality, to act against one's conscience is always wrong, since conscience is that sanctuary where one is alone before God. Thomas adds a further nuance here, however, explaining the manner in which such an invincibly ignorant conscience binds:

> Conscience is said to bind in so far as one sins if one does not follow one's conscience, but not in the sense that one acts correctly if one does follow it. . . . Conscience is not said to bind in the sense that what one does according to such a conscience will be good, but in the sense that in not following it one will sin. . . . A correct conscience and a false conscience bind in different ways. The correct conscience binds absolutely and for an intrinsic reason; the false binds in a qualified way and for an extrinsic reason.[22]

Contemporary Catholic moral theology has retrieved this tradition in a more personalistic manner. Examples of this retrieval can be found elsewhere in this volume, especially in the essays of Ron Hamel, Roberto Dell'Oro, Anne Patrick, and John Paris. A few other definitions of conscience may also be helpful here. Sidney Callahan defines conscience as "that personal

---

[18] Robert Smith, *Conscience and Catholicism: The Nature and Function of Conscience in Contemporary Roman Catholic Moral Theology* (Lanham, MD: University Press of America, 1998), 18. See Thomas Aquinas, *Summa Theologiae* I, q. 79, a. 13.

[19] See Thomas Aquinas, *De veritate*, q. 16, a. 3. See also Bonaventure, II *Sent*, d. 39, a. 2, q. 2, con.

[20] Thomas Aquinas *ST*, I-II, q. 19, a. 6, ad 3. See also I-II, q. 76, a. 2

[21] *Pastoral Constitution on the Church in the Modern World*, 16.

[22] Thomas Aquinas, *De veritate*, q. 17, a. 4.

activity that is uniquely characterized by going beyond analysis and exploration to morally committing ourselves to what we avow we ought to do,
or what we avow ought to be done."[23] Similarly, Walter Conn suggests that
conscience is "the actively involved personal agent struggling to reach a
concrete understanding and practical judgment as to what course of action he
or she should take to respond in a creative and fully human way to the values
in this particular situation."[24] Recently Pope Francis has used this personalistic understanding of conscience to encourage pastors to demonstrate a deep
respect for the consciences of the faithful:

> We also find it hard to make room for the consciences of the faithful,
> who very often respond as best they can to the Gospel amid their
> limitations, and are capable of carrying out their own discernment in
> complex situations. We have been called to form consciences, not to
> replace them.[25]

In all of these examples, one can see the Catholic understanding, going
back to Thomas and Bonaventure, that conscience is not simply an intuition
but rather a reasoned judgment regarding what one must do in the complex
circumstances of life. Others may help form one's conscience, but their judgments cannot replace conscience. It remains deeply personal and yet attends
to objective reality. Persons of conscience (1) commit themselves to an
appropriate purpose in life and to the values stemming from that purpose, (2)
understand that these values are not autonomously chosen but rather transcend
the person (for Christians by coming from God), and (3) have determined
that they will live according to that purpose and commit themselves to those
values by acting in particular ways in the concrete circumstances of life.[26]
The activity of conscience must result in action. Finally, being a person of
conscience does not necessarily ensure the moral correctness of one's action.
In the end, there needs to be a good amount of both maturity and humility
when one deals with conscience in order to be relatively sure that what one
is hearing is indeed the "herald and messenger of God" and not simply one's
own desires or biases. This mix of maturity, humility, and faith becomes the
basis for Christian discernment.

---

[23] Sidney Callahan, *In Good Conscience: Reason and Emotion in Moral Decision Making* (San Francisco: Harper San Francisco, 1991), 23.

[24] Walter Conn, *Christian Conversion: A Developmental Interpretation of Autonomy and Surrender* (Eugene, OR: Wipf and Stock, 2006), 93.

[25] Pope Francis, *Amoris Laetitia*, 37.

[26] Thomas Nairn, "Institutional Conscience Revisited: Catholic Institutions and Christian Ethics," *New Theology Review* 14, no. 2 (May 2001): 41.

Can One Speak of Institutional Conscience?

With this background in mind, what can one say regarding institutional conscience? Those who acknowledge the validity of the notion of institutional conscience explain that a Catholic institution is not simply an aggregate of disparate persons but rather a community with a particular purpose and an enduring ethical culture.[27] As with the conscience of an individual, institutional conscience is seen as guiding the ordinary activities of the Catholic health care facility or system as the organization responds in the best way it can to complex issues amid specific limitations. It may be helpful to return to Sulmasy's description of the moral workings of a Catholic health care organization:

> Morally speaking, health care institutions do seem to possess all the features that one would attribute to moral agents. They make decisions, and, as institutions, are worthy of praise or blame for those decisions. They act intentionally. They "have structures by which in certain contexts acts by persons will *count* as acts by the organization." Both the members of the organization and the society at large acknowledge the validity of these structures.[28]

Granted these similarities, one must nevertheless acknowledge that when speaking of the conscience of an organization, one is using the term "conscience" in an analogical sense—institutional conscience is in some ways similar to, but in many ways different from, what one ordinarily means when using the term "conscience." At issue is the question whether the differences so outweigh the similarities as to render the idea of an institutional conscience meaningless or at least problematic.

There are similarities. Both uses of the term suggest moral agency, commitment to particular values, recognition of moral responsibilities, and a decision-making process that results in action.[29] A Catholic institution would also acknowledge that it does not simply create the values to which it is committed. Rather these values come from beyond the institution and give meaning to its mission. For Catholic health care in the United States, these value commitments are understood as part of a heritage originating with the founders of the institution, usually religious women. At the same time the institution also recognizes itself as a ministry of the Catholic Church. The stated purpose of Catholic health care is to continue the healing mission of Jesus by bringing alive the Gospel vision of justice and peace, fostering

---

[27] See Sulmasy, "Institutional Conscience and Moral Pluralism," 7.

[28] Ibid. Sulmasy quotes Michael D. Smith, "The Virtuous Organization," *Journal of Medicine and Philosophy* 7 (1982): 35–42.

[29] See Nairn, "Institutional Conscience Revisited," 42.

healing, and acting with compassion—especially for those who are poor, underserved, and most vulnerable.[30]

Nevertheless the two concepts also have important differences. One major difference is that a Catholic institution is composed of different individuals, many of whom fully support the values of the institution and many others who do not. It is even likely that the institution will have among its employees those who strongly disagree with the institution's values but for one reason or another find being part of the institution beneficial. A Catholic health care institution also serves patients or residents who may or may not espouse the values of the institution. It is likely that most patients or residents may not have any idea about what the institution actually stands for.

There is another aspect of the Catholic understanding of conscience that appears to be lacking in explanations of institutional conscience. If we return to the definitions that were part of the previous section, we see that the activity of conscience deals with what persons of faith must do here and now in the complex circumstances of life. Thomas Aquinas maintained that conscience is "an act in which the first principles of practical reason are applied to . . . specific situations, particular cases and complex circumstances."[31] Sidney Callahan and Walter Conn similarly emphasize the importance of what must be done here and now, given the circumstances and one's real possibilities and limitations. The Catechism of the Catholic Church similarly acknowledges that conscience is "a judgment of reason whereby the human person recognizes the moral quality of a concrete act that he is about to perform, is in the process of performing, or has already completed."[32] Most descriptions of institutional conscience, however, tend to remain on the level of institutional policy. Part of the recent criticism of the function of institutional conscience is that it seems overly rigid and not adaptable to the concrete circumstances that present themselves in health care.

There is another similarity, however, that arises from this criticism. Like the conscience of individuals, institutional conscience may fail; it may even be willfully wrong. Sulmasy explains:

> Like individuals, institutions can fail conscientiously through faulty reasoning, misplaced emotions, or poor judgment. In doing so, a hospital would join the ranks of other human institutions struggling for integrity in the midst of all the ambiguity of the moral world. Institutions can also fail to act upon their own conscientious judgments,

---

[30] See "The Shared Statement of Identity for the Catholic Health Ministry," https://www.chausa.org/.

[31] See Thomas Aquinas, *Summa Theologiae* I, q. 79, a. 13.

[32] *Catechism of the Catholic Church*, 1778.

either through reasoning by expediency, or by being overwhelmed by emotions such as panic or greed, or by weakness of the will. This is how institutions are caught in the web of evil in the world.[33]

Institutions can fall into many of the same traps in dealing with the questions of conscience as do individuals. "Conscience" can become a least common denominator among the members of the institution, or it can become a public relations gimmick, with mission statements placed in prominent areas of an institution but never internalized in the persons who are part of the institution. As an individual of conscience must engage in moral discernment to ensure that one's conscience is true, so too members of a Catholic health care institution constantly need to engage in discernment to ensure that the institution remains true to its mission and that the institution's structures, including policies and procedures, facilitate its mission and do not undermine it.

Nevertheless, the question remains whether this ongoing discernment by members of a Catholic health care organization is evidence of the existence of an institutional conscience. Given the similarities and differences discussed above, it may be helpful to return to the description given by Daniel Finn at the beginning of this essay. Finn suggests that, properly speaking, one should not speak of an organization having a conscience. Rather, using the insights of critical-realist sociology, he suggests that an organization is a kind of a social structure, that is, "a system of human relations among social positions that exist prior to any one person's taking on one of those positions [which have] causal power through their generation of restrictions, enablements, and incentives."[34] Organizations do not technically act on their own but only through the actions of the individuals within the institution. Yet as a social structure, by means of a mission statement, value statements, policies and procedures, a health care organization influences the judgments and actions of administrators, employees, physicians, and patients. It restricts or enables particular actions. Whether one calls this "institutional conscience" or not, it remains important to understand this influence of institutions on the lives of the individuals who come in varying degrees of contact with them.

Social Structures, Catholic Health Care, and a Pluralist Society

If it is appropriate to see institutions as social structures that influence individuals by means of restrictions, enablements, and incentives, what are the implications of this notion for Catholic health care? First of all, one must

---

[33] Sulmasy, "What Is Conscience?" 144.
[34] Finn, "Can an Organization Have a Conscience?" 180.

acknowledge that as a social structure, Catholic health care itself is embedded in at least three other important social structures, the Catholic Church, the US legal system, and the professional health care community expressed in medical standards and leading practices of care, each of which has its own structures of restrictions, enablements, and incentives.

Catholic Church

Catholic health care recognizes itself as a ministry of the Catholic Church, which recognition in turn entails adherence to the *Ethical and Religious Directives for Catholic Health Care Services* (ERDs).[35] The ERDs articulate a rich spiritual and theological understanding of the healing of the whole person—body, mind, emotions, and spirit—that has been a hallmark of Catholic health care, but they also contain specific prohibitions against direct abortion, contraception, and sterilization, which have become the focus of much debate within the professional health care community.

The ERDs and the Catholic social tradition form the context for Catholic health care's self-understanding. This is more than adequately demonstrated in "The Shared Statement of Identity for the Catholic Health Ministry,"[36] developed by representatives of health care institutions that constitute the Catholic Health Association of the United States. Based on this shared statement, one may speak of the social and ecclesial responsibilities of Catholic health care: If the purpose of Catholic health care is to "continue the saving mission of Christ," how are patients and employees treated? How are the monies allotted to charity care determined? Could one tell that the institution is Catholic by looking at its budget? Does the institution's senior leadership facilitate the achieving of the institution's values or obstruct such achievement? Many who do not share the Catholic faith could nevertheless see the value of these questions, by which the social structure of the Catholic Church influences Catholic health care. This same structure, following the tradition of Catholic moral theology, also influences Catholic health care in its actions regarding abortion, contraception, sterilization, and care for persons at the end of life, actions that may conflict with the values and expectations of others.

United States Law

One way in which the US legal system has influenced Catholic health care has been through the enacting of certain conscience protections for

---

[35] United States Conference of Catholic Bishops, *Ethical and Religious Directives for Catholic Health Care Services*, 5th ed. (Washington, DC: USCCB Publications, 2009).

[36] "Shared Statement of Identity for the Catholic Health Ministry," https://www.chausa.org.

health care providers. Although conscientious objection to war has had a long history within the United States, conscience clauses exempting individuals and health care institutions from certain medical procedures began to appear in the 1970s. After the Supreme Court decision in *Roe v. Wade*, a number of states and the federal government enacted conscience protections for health care providers who refused to perform abortions because it was against their conscience. Often these protections also extended to hospitals as well. Such "conscience clauses" have usually explicitly covered abortion, contraception, sterilization, and physician-assisted suicide in those states where this is legal.

On the federal level, the first conscience clause enacted into law was the 1973 Church Amendment, a reaction to *Roe v. Wade*. The amendment states that public officials may not require individuals or hospitals that receive public funds to perform abortion or sterilization procedures if it would be contrary to their religious beliefs or moral convictions. The Weldon Amendment added further protection. This amendment was part of the appropriation for the Department of Health and Human Services in 2005 and has been readopted in each year's subsequent HHS appropriations act. It prohibits the funding of any federal agency or program, or state or local government, that discriminates against a health care entity that does not provide or refer for abortions. A "health care entity" may be a physician, a hospital, a provider-sponsored organization, a health insurance plan, or "any other kind of health care facility, organization, or plan."[37]

It seems here that the second, legal definition of conscience—a definition linked to sincerity—discussed above comes into play. The principal question for the government at present seems to be not whether a particular claim of conscience is true but whether it is a sincerely held belief. Conscience clauses seem to be an answer to the question whether or not it is in the interest of the state to encourage the form and extent of pluralism that has characterized the United States in recent years or to discourage it. The 1993 Religious Freedom Restoration Act (RFRA) legislated that "sincerely held religious beliefs" must be accommodated. It further stipulated that the government "shall not substantially burden a person's exercise of religion even if the burden results from a rule of general applicability" unless there is a compelling interest and it is done in the least restrictive way in which to further the government interest. The major test here was whether the belief was sincerely held and not whether the government agreed with the content of the belief.

Conscience clauses and the conscientious refusal of health care institutions to perform procedures that the institution deems as against its moral principles have come under great scrutiny by organizations such as the ACLU

---

[37] For a brief history of conscience clauses, see Holly Fernandez Lynch, *Conflicts of Conscience in Health Care: An Institutional Compromise* (Cambridge, MA: MIT Press, 2008), 19–24.

and Merger Watch.[38] These organizations are calling for a severe limitation of such conscience clauses. It is unclear at the present time how this will be resolved in the future.

Medical Standards and Leading Practices of Medical Care

Given the current controversies, the question of the validity of conscience clauses has arisen from within the medical community itself. Several authors maintain that the accepted standard of care should be the only criterion for judging whether a physician should engage in any particular medical procedure, including those deemed immoral by the Catholic Church. Durand, for example, maintains that although conscience clauses protect a physician's moral right to refuse to recommend or perform medical procedures against his or her moral principles, they fail "in affirmatively providing medically indicated care as dictated by her clinical morality."[39] Thus conscience protection for the physician is achieved at the cost of what is seen by the author as appropriate medical treatment for the patient. Similarly, Sepper observes that "only when an institution refuses to deliver legal care does the law recognize 'institutional conscience.'"[40] Although Mark Wicclair generally acknowledges the importance of conscience clauses, he also concludes that "depending on the circumstances, fulfilling [medical] obligations can require acting against a provider's conscience."[41] This controversy will only get more intense, as the debate around the so-called contraception mandate has shown.

In a pluralistic society, moral collisions between the social structure of Catholic health care and other social structures are inevitable. Many critics contend that Catholic health care institutions simply negate the consciences of those such institutions are meant to serve—patients, physicians, and employees, especially the consciences of "willing providers" of the procedures that the Catholic Church (another social structure) deems morally objectionable.[42] Since in a pluralistic society there is no way to adjudicate among such competing claims, this would seem to create an ethical impasse.

What Is a Catholic Health Care Institution to Do?

It is a relatively narrow range of issues that have been the basis for conflicts regarding whether and how the prohibitions of Catholic health care

---

[38] ACLU, *Health Care Denied*, 25.

[39] Durand, "Case against Institutional Conscience," 1658.

[40] Sepper, "Taking Conscience Seriously," 1514.

[41] Mark R. Wicclair, *Conscientious Objection in Health Care: An Ethical Analysis* (New York: Cambridge University Press, 2011), 133.

[42] See, e.g., Sepper, "Taking Conscience Seriously," 1513–14.

should be respected by the medical profession and the larger society. As these Catholic institutional practices are increasingly being exercised in a pluralistic society, society itself experiences a wide divergence of ideas regarding what is accepted as appropriate moral behavior and also a wide divergence in what constitutes acceptable medical standards. Sulmasy observes:

> Conscientious persons will disagree about a wide range of moral issues. . . . As we approach the application of our moral principles and rules to particular cases, we also have less certainty. This is not to say that there are no correct answers to these questions. Rather, given the imperfections of our moral knowledge and reasoning, we must acknowledge that disagreements are inevitable.[43]

Several authors have spoken of the American ideal of a tolerant society,[44] recalling Locke's suggestion that "respect for conscience is at the root of the concept of tolerance." Sulmasy suggests, "Tolerance is a sign of respect for the other person to whom we are connected, not a consequence of our inherent disconnectedness."[45] Catholic health care obviously wants others to be tolerant of its religious-based prohibitions. Yet if Catholic health care demands toleration by the larger society, it seems necessary that it must also respect the conscientious judgments of its own employees, physicians, and patients. Such respect does not entail that a Catholic hospital perform any procedure that it is asked to perform, especially those that it understands to be immoral, but it does mean that those in leadership positions in the institution will explain the moral positions of the institution as clearly and respectfully as possible. Such leaders will also offer their explanations with a humility that does not speak down to their interlocutors.

Given the pluralism of the United States, Catholic health care institutions also need to be transparent. They must be clear about their policies to patients, physicians, and employees. They will also explain *why* these policies are in effect and how the policies relate not only to the mission and values of the Catholic institution but to the goals of medicine. Part of such transparency is the education and formation of employees. A Catholic health care facility will educate its employees as far as it is able regarding not only the Catholic moral position but also the nuances of the Catholic position.

Critics who object to various institutional policies of Catholic health care often relate a litany of horror stories about Catholic hospitals putting patients

---

[43] Sulmasy, "What Is Conscience?" 144.

[44] See, e.g., Nathaniel J. Brown, "Pluralism and Institutional Conscience," *Health Care Ethics USA* (2009): 6.

[45] Sulmasy, "What Is Conscience?" 145.

at risk—for example, stories about emergency medical situations affecting pregnant patients who were not given appropriate treatment or about hospitals that refused emergency contraception to victims of sexual assault.[46] To the extent that such situations have occurred, it has not been *because* of the ERDs but rather because of a misinterpretation or misapplication of them. Ron Hamel has demonstrated, through a careful examination of several emergency situations affecting pregnant patients, that adherence to the ERDs does not conflict with good medical practice.[47] Similarly, the ERDs are explicit in explaining that "a female who has been raped should be able to defend herself against a potential conception from the sexual assault."[48] It is not in the interest of either Catholic health care or the Catholic Church for a Catholic health care institution to somehow be more restrictive than the teaching of the Church itself.

Often transparency and clarity regarding the actual position of the Catholic Church and consequently Catholic health care will help resolve apparent conflict. Often it will not. The way in which Catholic health care continues to negotiate the tensions and conflicts occasioned by the larger social structures of Church, government, and health care professionalism in which it is embedded may very well occasion significant changes in Catholic health care itself. Already one Catholic health care system has been dissolved and replaced by a successor organization that is no longer a formal ministry of the Catholic Church.[49] It is conceivable that many Catholic health care facilities will continue to object strenuously to what they see as inappropriate secular intrusions on their religious freedom and accept the consequences of such refusal. Others may acknowledge the medical or institutional necessity of performing certain prohibited procedures, for example sterilizations, at least in well-defined circumstances, for the good of the patient. They may see this as a pastoral application of moral principles. Still others may contemplate moving away from certain medical specialties all together because they are unable to find a balance within these competing demands of conflicting social structures.

---

[46] See, e.g., ACLU, *Health,* or Wicclair, *Conscientious Objection in Health Care,* 152–66.

[47] These situations include treatment of ectopic pregnancies, miscarriage, and pre-term premature rupture of membranes. See Ron Hamel, "Early Pregnancy Complications and the ERDs," *Health Care Ethics, USA* 22, no. 1 (Winter 2014): 1–13.

[48] See, e.g., Wicclair, *Conscientious Objection in Health Care,* 152–66. For a nuanced Catholic approach to such situations see Ron Hamel, "Emergency Contraception," *Health Care Ethics, USA* 16, no. 2 (Spring 2008): 12–13, and Ron Hamel, "Early Pregnancy Complications and the ERDs," *Health Care Ethics, USA* 22, no. 1 (Winter 2014): 1–13.

[49] See Carol Bayley, "From Catholic Healthcare West to Dignity Health: Conflicts of Conscience in American Catholic Health Care," in *Conscience and Catholicism: Rights, Responsibilities, and Institutional Responses,* ed. DeCosse and Heyer, 139–51.

Whether or not one chooses to label the phenomenon "institutional conscience," Catholic health care institutions are social structures that influence the behaviors of those who are part of them, whether they are employees, physicians, or patients. They do this by means of a series of restrictions, enablements, or incentives. Yet Catholic health care in turn is influenced by other social structures that restrict, enable, and incentivize, most notably the Catholic Church, US law, and the medical or health care profession. Catholic health care entities have negotiated tensions among these social structures in various ways in the past with a variety of consequences. It remains to be seen how Catholic health care will continue to negotiate these tensions in the future.

CATHOLIC PUBLIC WITNESS ON HEALTH CARE REFORM

Toward a More Capacious Model of Conscience

Kristin E. Heyer

Pope Francis has prophetically summoned a bold revolution of tenderness in this Year of Mercy, yet the institutional church's public witness in the United States context remains focused, in large measure, on preventing cooperation in a discrete range of evil acts. Recent public witness surrounding the implementation of the Patient Protection and Affordable Care Act (ACA), for example, risks giving the impression that a Catholic understanding of conscience is one of exclusivist refuge, rather than one communal in character, intellectually accessible, and shaped in dialogue. Notions of conscience that reduce it to cleaning the slate or conformity in obedience to the hierarchy alone can give disproportionate weight to complicity with evil, eclipse significant dimensions of responsibility, and disempower discernment. Surveying the function of conscience in the church's public witness around health care reform in recent years illuminates the need for more adequate models that expand notions of sin and responsibility and focus attention not only on what "dirties our hands" but also on what clouds our discernment or dulls our conscience altogether.

Long a stalwart—indeed countercultural—advocate for universal health care as a human right, in recent years the US institutional church's loudest public voice on health care has been its opposition to the ACA's passage and then its contraceptive mandate. Ecclesial public witness contesting the ACA's provisions has prioritized protection of institutional religious liberty over support for expanding health care.[1] In pastoral outreach, postcard campaigns,

---

[1] My remarks concerning institutional ecclesial political witness on health care in this essay refer to the expressed priorities of the United States Conference of Catholic Bishops, not the myriad ways in which Catholic health care is advocated and operationalized in the US context (including the significant work of the Catholic Health Association). For many lay Catholics as well as those outside the tradition, the pastoral priorities and political advocacy of the hierarchy primarily inform their perceptions of the voice and activity of the US Catholic Church.

political advocacy, and legal recourse, this focus on what the United States Conference of Catholic Bishops (USCCB) deems a substantial religious burden (whether notifying employees about alternative means of reimbursement should they elect contraceptive coverage or, more recently, notifying the government that a religious nonprofit will not be participating in the contraceptive plan) has characterized its primary engagement of the health care law's provisions.[2] Framed in terms of religious liberty infringements, concern for Catholic employers and employees' potential cooperation with evil has dominated involvement at the expense of attention to the demands of the common good amid pluralism. Independent of the relative merit of a complicity-based burden on religious exercise claim, this public witness has obscured the tradition's commitment both to health care as a human right and to a capacious understanding of conscience.

Many have suggested that the objections and rhetoric seem to rest on a misreading of the Department of Health and Human Services' rules, which, particularly in light of the Obama administration's accommodations to further distance objecting employers from contraceptive coverage in response to concerns raised, do not meaningfully threaten the religious freedom of employees who accept Catholic teaching on contraceptive use.[3] In the latest version of "Forming Consciences for Faithful Citizenship," the bishops' treatment of health care prioritizes the value of "subsidiarity" (presumably a reference to Catholic agencies' freedom from government regulation on such matters) to that of meeting "the needs of the poor and uninsured, especially born and unborn children, pregnant women, immigrants and other vulnerable populations." This is followed by an assertion of employers and family-owned businesses' right to provide health care without "compromising their moral or religious convictions" and individuals' right "to purchase health care that accords with their faith."[4] Achieving universal health care should not justify compelling religious nonprofits to deliver morally objectionable services. Hence concerns about shifting burdens or the proximity of cooperation may

---

[2] See the USCCB February/March 2013 "Life, Marriage and Liberty" national bulletin insert, available at http://www.usccb.org. By contrast the Catholic Health Association's "health care in the pulpit toolkit" came to my attention only in researching this essay, not in ecclesial or other settings.

[3] As Georgetown law professor Marty Lederman cautions, misinformation gives Catholics in the pews and the wider public the misconception that "HHS is preparing to require employees to subsidize, if not use, contraception, even when they have religious objections to doing so." See Cathleen Kaveny, "Marty Lederman on the USCCB on the Latest Proposed Accommodation," *dotCommonweal* (September 20, 2013), available at https://www.commonwealmagazine.org.

[4] USCCB, "Forming Consciences for Faithful Citizenship: A Call to Political Responsibility from the Catholic Bishops of the United States," November 2015, available at http://www.usccb.org.

not be insignificant, but disproportionate attention to such a misplaced moral analysis has distorted the focus of the institutional church's public voice and inhibited its efforts to form consciences of the faithful.

Lost in these emphases have been not only understandings of religious liberty properly contextualized by commitments to public morality and justice, but also the significance of a Catholic commitment to universal health care access. Those ministering in Catholic health care witness firsthand the impact and stakes of insufficient access: too often early and avoidable deaths due to delayed medical treatment or family crises due to insurmountable expenses. Indeed, prior to the passage of the ACA, more than 20,000 Americans died annually from manageable illnesses because they were unable to pay for treatment, and a 2009 study estimated 44,789 Americans died annually due to lack of health insurance.[5] Hence the opportunity to witness to the significance of health care as human right has been largely squandered in the service of opposition to perceived undue burdens related to contraceptive coverage. From the time ACA provisions took effect until May 2015, 14.1 million adults gained health insurance coverage and the uninsured rate dropped 20.3 percent to 13.2 percent. Medicaid expansion states have witnessed a decline in the number of uninsured by nearly 40 percent compared to 10 percent in the states that have not expanded, with gains concentrated among low- and middle-income population groups.[6] Advancing such gains in light of persistent coverage gaps and underinsurance within the United States makes significant claims on our collective conscience that get drowned out when, in positions of insured or economic privilege, we give disproportionate attention to complicity with evil. Cathleen Kaveny has written about the "emerging prophetic" meaning of intrinsically evil acts more broadly and has rightly contested efforts that co-opt a technical, moral meaning of "intrinsic evil" for rhetorical purposes.[7]

Finally, the effect of such disproportionate witness may itself cause a stumbling block in terms of the technical theological sense of "scandal." Lisa Fullam has employed the case of condom use in serodiscordant couples to underscore how courting scandal is always a "double-edged sword." She explains, "Those who oppose condom use in such couples on grounds of scandal court the opposite scandal. People might think that the church is

---

[5] T. R. Reid, *The Healing of America: A Global Quest for Better, Cheaper, and Fairer Health Care*, 2nd ed., with a new afterword (New York: Penguin Press, 2010), 1–2; Andrew P. Wilper et al., "Health Insurance and Mortality in US Adults," *American Journal of Public Health* 99, no. 12 (2009): 2289–95.

[6] Office of the Assistant Secretary for Planning and Evaluation, US Department of Health and Human Services, "Health Insurance Coverage and the Affordable Care Act" web resource (May 5, 2015), available at https://aspe.hhs.gov.

[7] Cathleen Kaveny, *Law's Virtues: Fostering Autonomy and Solidarity in American Society* (Washington, DC: Georgetown University Press, 2012).

more concerned with sustaining its public stance on contraception than it is about the welfare of people in danger of HIV infection."[8] The same risk has emerged in the institutional church's public witness related to health care reform and contraceptive mandates—it gives the impression that the church cares more about complicity than it does about expanding health care access for vulnerable populations. This undermines its long-standing commitment to the common good in a pluralistic society. As Fullam concludes, "Opposite scandal is still scandal—it still leads people to a misunderstanding of moral truth, generally by refusing to grant moral weight to the real complexity of our lives, individually and socially."[9] This was not Jesus' primary mode, and we encounter in Pope Francis a consistent emphasis on a church as a "field hospital," concerned less with avoiding dirty hands than with healing wounds. These distinct emphases reveal particular assumptions about authority, agency, and different conceptions of the scope and charge of conscience. In some ways recent rhetoric regarding the ACA's implementation continues the assumptions and dynamics at play in the debate over its passage, to which I now turn.

ACA and the Conciliar Vision of Conscience

Related questions of conscience in Catholicism's public witness came to the fore in the health care reform debate of 2010. Without delving into the details of the Patient Protection and Affordable Care Act or its subsequent revisions, a brief overview of how conscience and authority functioned in the dramatic political battle over passage of the ACA offers insights into these persistent tensions.[10] The later version of the ACA was ultimately opposed by the US Bishops Conference (USCCB) and supported by the Catholic Health Association (CHA), Network social justice lobby, and some congregations of women's religious.[11] In the wake of their support of the

---

[8] Lisa Fullam's "Giving Scandal" in *America* (November 1, 2010) (responding to M. Cathleen Kaveny's "Catholics as Citizens" appearing in the same issue).

[9] Ibid.

[10] A fuller elaboration of different Catholic interpretations of the Affordable Care Act's passage appears in Kristin E. Heyer, "Reservoirs of Hope: Catholic Women's Witness," in *Women, Wisdom, Witness: Engaging Contexts in Conversation*, ed. Rosemary P. Carbine and Kathleen J. Dolphin (Collegeville, MN: Liturgical Press, 2012), 219–36.

[11] As the Senate version of the bill moved to the House for consideration, where pro-life critics charged it allowed for abortion funding, CHA president Carol Keehan broke with the United States bishops' opposition and issued a statement adding CHA's support to the bill. As Keehan indicated, she had become convinced that abortion coverage language in the Senate version could be resolved, as mechanisms were in place to isolate coverage from government-regulated health care markets, and that the legislation presented a historic opportunity to extend the human right of universal and affordable health care to millions of Americans. See Sister Carol Keehan, DC, "The Time Is Now for Health Care Reform," March 15, 2010, available at http://www.chausa.org.

health care reform bill, the motives and competencies of certain groups of women religious were impugned, with the USCCB issuing an official statement charging those who differed from the bishops' interpretation of the health care bill with causing "confusion and a wound to Catholic unity."[12] Archbishop Charles Chaput accused the "self-described 'Catholic' groups" of committing "a serious disservice to justice, to the church, and to the ethical needs of the American people by undercutting the leadership and witness of their own bishops."[13]

The focus in this fallout centered on the nature and limits of the bishops' authority on matters of faith, morals, law, and policy.[14] Important distinctions were revisited, such as the application of universal moral teachings and specific moral principles to concrete policies. Particular strategic applications of principles are more fluid in character, and hence our grasp is more tentative than our knowledge of principles.[15] In the case of the divergence of some women religious from the bishops on health care reform, the disagreement occurred nearly entirely at the level of prudential judgments about technical legislative language, not over the morality or legality of abortion per se.[16] By contrast Cardinal Francis George, then president of the bishops' conference, cast the matter less in terms of prudential judgment than in terms of the very nature of the church and its legitimate spokes(men).

Whereas an understanding of conscience as conformity to the teaching of the hierarchy remains in tension with the shift to a more personalist model at Vatican II, the discernment of Catholic groups at the health care reform moment demonstrated a response to the call to actively discern responsibility in light of the gift and challenge of God's law of love. As CHA president Sister Carol Keehan, DC, put it, "This was a bill that, for the first time in the lives of 32 million Americans, gave them a chance to have decent health insurance. . . . That was a heavy burden on my conscience, and on our

---

[12] Chairmen of USCCB committees on Pro-Life Activities, Immigration and Domestic Justice, Peace and Human Development, "Setting the Record Straight," May 21, 2010, available at http://www.usccb.org.

[13] Archbishop Chaput, "A Bad Bill and How We Got It," *Denver Catholic Register*, March 24, 2010.

[14] See Thomas Weinandy, OFM, Cap, "The Bishops and the Right Exercise of Authority," available at http://www.usccb.org; John Allen, "Health Care: Transcript of Cardinal George June 16 NCR Interview," *National Catholic Reporter*, June 22, 2010, available at http://ncronline.org; Daniel Finn, "Uncertainty Principle: The Bishops, Health Care & Prudence," *Commonweal*, February 11, 2011, https://www.commonweal-magazine.org.

[15] See Charles E. Curran, *Catholic Moral Tradition Today: A Synthesis* (Washington, DC: Georgetown University Press, 1999), 152n71.

[16] Richard R. Gaillardetz, "The Limits of Authority: When Bishops Speak about Health Care Policy, Catholics Should Listen, but Don't Have to Agree," *Commonweal*, June 30, 2010.

organizational conscience. . . . We did not differ on the moral question, or the teaching authority of the bishops."[17]

Gaudium et Spes characterizes conscience as that "secret core and sanctuary of a person, where they are alone with God whose voice echoes in their depths."[18] This "encounter with the divine basis of moral obligation is mediated through [a person's] agency, and hence through the spirit, reason, affections and relationships that constitute human agency."[19] The primacy of the human person is evident in the document's treatment of conscience, particularly in contrast to earlier emphases on moral norms as objective sources of morality. Moral manuals guided priests in the confessional where matters of conscience were assessed, resolved, and absolved from the sixteenth century to roughly the 1960s. The focus of concern was conforming to rigors of church teaching more often than to facing the challenges of the world, and confessors functioned as physicians of soul or psychiatric caregivers for sinners unable to discern and execute right moral conduct. For Bernhard Häring (secretary of the editorial committee that drafted *Gaudium et Spes*), the approach to the problem had a higher estimation of human goodness and a lower estimation of the virtue of obedience, at least understood in the singular terms of complying with church teaching. As Häring put it, conscience is rooted in freedom as the possibility of responding to God's call to do God's will, the power to do good.[20]

This conciliar understanding of conscience entails the capacity and willingness to pursue the truth about doing the right thing in concrete, complicated circumstances rather than having all the answers. Its personalist theology of conscience appreciates the contingent and contextual character of moral discernment.[21] Understanding conscientious discernment as inclusive of multiple sources of moral wisdom—including the riches of scripture, the wisdom of the Catholic community over the centuries, natural law, insights of church officials and theologians, moral exemplars, as well as the reflective experiences of those immersed in on-the-ground ministries or in the details of legislative analysis—calls for a more complex and proactive endeavor than assumptions that restrict such sources to the teaching authority of the

---

[17] John L. Allen Jr., "Minding the Gap between the Bishops and Catholic Health Care," *National Catholic Reporter*, June 16, 2010, available at http://ncronline.org.

[18] *Gaudium et Spes*, 16.

[19] David E. DeCosse, "Conscience Issue Separates Catholic Moral Camps," *National Catholic Reporter*, November 10, 2009.

[20] James F. Keenan, SJ, "Vatican II and Theological Ethics," *Theological Studies* 74 (2013): 165–66.

[21] Linda Hogan, "Marriage Equality, Conscience, and the Catholic Tradition," in *Conscience and Catholicism: Rights, Responsibilities, & Institutional Responses*, ed. David E. DeCosse and Kristin E. Heyer (Maryknoll, NY: Orbis Books, 2014), 89.

hierarchy alone.[22] That said, the council does not absolutize conscience, but accords it "its proper dignity, within a healthy moral ecology."[23] Thus tensions between understanding freedom as the human person's most precious gift and the church as the only reliable interpreter of moral law persist amid fears not only that appeals to conscience too readily offer Catholics an easy "entrance to the cafeteria," but also, as in the health care reform case, amid fears that divergence from the conclusions of clearly established authorities confuses and gives scandal._

Contemporary understandings of conscience and authority are also affected by the recognition that God's Spirit is bestowed on the entire people of God. Anne Patrick has made a distinction between an understanding of obedience as primarily submission, such that conformity with official teaching and interpretation of moral obligation rests with authority figures, and an understanding that emphasizes hearing rather than submission (the Latin root of obedience being "*ob audire*," "hearing toward"); consequently, obedient discipleship entails "listening with care for clues to the divine will" rather than submitting to the voice of authority per se.[24] Genuinely wrestling with the tradition and its demands seems more reflective of the conciliar invitation than are impositions of control via litmus tests, loyalty oaths, or culture war standoffs. Even in the divisive health care reform deliberations in which not every member of the Catholic community arrived at identical conclusions regarding how to best protect the same values, the public reasoning and communal conscience formation arguably influenced pending policy to better reflect and protect such values, as indicated by the executive order ensuring no federal funds would be spent on abortion.[25]

With respect to the subsequent debates, Lisa Sowle Cahill has analogously cautioned that, because individual and institutional conscience and religious liberty exist in a social context, "Catholics must weigh not only whether a [conscientious] objection is a sincerely held religious conviction, but also consider claims in light of the common good." These claims might include the importance of nondiscrimination; what type of contraception is considered a basic health care benefit; what are reasonable alternatives of access to contraception and other aspects of what is considered basic care.

---

[22] DeCosse, "Conscience Issue Separates Catholic Moral Camps."

[23] Thomas Massaro, SJ, "The Role of Conscience in Catholic Participation in Politics since Vatican II," in *The Church in the Modern World: Fifty Years after* Gaudium et Spes, ed. Erin Brigham (Lanham, MD: Lexington, 2015), 71.

[24] Anne E. Patrick, SNJM, *Liberating Conscience: Feminist Explorations in Catholic Moral Theology* (New York: Continuum, 1997), 103–4.

[25] Executive Order 13533, "Patient Protection and Affordable Care Act's Consistency with Long-standing Restrictions on the Use of Federal Funds for Abortion," March 24, 2010, available at http://www.whitehouse.gov.

To bypass this complex discernment not only impoverishes conscience and short-circuits prudence but also gives "the impression that Catholic moral and political positions are simply products of irrational religious dogma rather than rooted in a natural law tradition."[26] Certainly, the conscience is marked by both frailty and sacredness in the Catholic tradition, and a misinformed conscience can lead one (and others) astray. Yet recent approaches by many Catholic bishops and others suggest, for example, that employees at large Catholic institutions like hospitals and universities may not to be trusted to discern what is best for them, burdened as they are assumed to be with an utterly fragile conscience facing an encroaching culture of death.

In several encounters Pope Francis has articulated anew the doctrine of the primacy of conscience and a recovery of the relational and transcendent context for conscience in sync with a person's sanctuary where God's voice echoes.[27] In his interview with Jesuit journalists he indicated: "One must affirm Christ, the church, the moral law, what is immediately before us to be done. But one must always hold those goods in tension with the '*Deus semper maior*, the always-greater God, and the pursuit of the ever-greater glory of God.'"[28] The conciliar understanding of conscience he echoes prompts reflections about where and how the church encourages and facilitates lay discernment. Rhetoric by Catholic opponents of the ACA about how "coercive" government mandates regarding contraception threaten the capacity of parents to conduct proper moral formation of their children around issues of sexuality casts doubt on whether conscientious discernment by laity is perceived as a threat or a gift.[29]

Signals from Pope Francis

Under Francis's papacy we detect a renewed emphasis on the messy and communal nature of the search for truth, whether in his desire that shepherds take on the smell of sheep and his own boundary-crossing examples or calls for cultures of accompaniment and encounter. He has struck chords of dialogue, discernment, and frontier, suggesting that our gaze should

---

[26] Lisa Sowle Cahill, "Contraception and Conscience: A Symposium on Religious Liberty, Women's Health and the HHS Rule on Provision of Birth Control Coverage for Employees," Georgetown Law, September 14, 2012, available at https://www.youtube.com.

[27] See David DeCosse, "The Primacy of Conscience, Vatican II, and Pope Francis: The Opportunity to Renew a Tradition," in *From Vatican II to Pope Francis: Charting a Catholic Future*, ed. Paul Crowley (Maryknoll, NY: Orbis Books, 2014), 156–69.

[28] Antonio Spadaro, "A Big Heart Open to God: The Exclusive Interview with Pope Francis," *America*, September 30, 2013.

[29] In "Faithful Citizenship" the bishops decry "contraceptive and abortion mandates" that endanger not only the rights of conscience but parents' right "to guide the moral formation of their children" (no. 71).

remain "well fixed upon Christ, always . . . prophetic and dynamic towards the future," lowering defenses and building bridges to heal the rift between gospel and culture.[30] His embrace of "a poor church for the poor" and the need to heal the world from structural sin invites heightened attention to social dimensions of conscience.

Pope Francis has repeatedly attuned our focus to structures and attitudes that harm people and planet alike. Whether on Lampedusa or in *Laudato Si'*, he has underscored pervasive, totalizing worldviews that conceal, from anesthetizing soap bubbles of indifference to a technocratic paradigm. He summons listeners to conversion from such mind-sets that inhibit moral growth, underscoring the significance of attending to the way social sin impedes conscience formation—beyond discrete complicities, narrowing our very field of vision. For various levels of social sin intersect in complex manners: Pervasive, internalized ideologies make us susceptible to myths; operative understandings influence our actions or inaction. When bias hides or skews values, it becomes more difficult to choose authentic values over those that prevail in society. Such intersections with respect to the global economy have been of particular concern to Pope Francis. He warns that our "economy of exclusion and inequality kills," challenging not only the reductive market ethos dominating economic policies but also its desensitizing effects. Whereas in the US context much progress has been made toward coverage, the ACA may leave more than 20 million citizens uncovered, and currently more than 31 million remain "underinsured" and vulnerable to medical debt.[31] Along with its state-of-the-art medical technologies the United States has the highest avoidable mortality rate among industrialized countries and highest infant mortality rate among wealthy nations.[32] Persistent disparities and barriers to adequate coverage foster the deadly exclusion Francis decries and yet fail to register with frequency or urgency in local debates about conscience in health care.

In March 2016 the Vatican opened a health clinic offering free medical treatment to those unable to afford basic care.[33] Pope Francis's example and

---

[30] "Pope Francis: Lower Defences and Open Doors," Vatican news reporting on Pope Francis's comments during his audience with personnel from *La Civilta Cattolica*, June 14, 2013. Available at http://www.news.va.

[31] Statistics from Reid, *Healing of America*, 244–51 and S. R. Collins et al., *The Problem of Underinsurance and How Rising Deductibles Will Make It Worse* (Commonwealth Fund, 2015), www.commonwealthfund.org, as cited by Gerald J. Beyer, "Solidarity Strives to Mend Broken World," *Health Progress*, July–August 2015.

[32] Reid, *Healing of America*, 2, 32. See also Marian F. MacDorman et al., "International Comparisons of Infant Mortality and Related Factors: United States and Europe, 2010," National Vital Statistics Reports 63, no. 5 (2014): 1–6, as cited by Beyer, "Solidarity Strives to Mend Broken World."

[33] Ann Schneible, "Vatican Gives Free Health Care to Rome's Poor," *Catholic News Agency*, March 1, 2016.

summons caution that preoccupation with safeguarding against risks impedes a culture of encounter and our ongoing conversion by the suffering and resilience of those in need. His preference for a street-bound over a risk-averse and "self-referential" church challenges Catholics to consider how disproportionate emphasis on not dirtying our hands can shrink the scope of the concerns of conscience and avert our gaze from those excluded or harmed by structural violence.

"Resocializing" Conscience:
Toward a More Capacious Model

Hence, as these health care examples reveal, contemporary appeals to conscience too often function as "conversation stoppers," contributing to impasses in ecclesial and civic dialogue and impeding our shared public responsibilities. When truncated notions of conscience are invoked in public religious discourse, they can serve more as litmus tests than as invitations to communal discernment and growth. Conscience claims in the US church's public witness have recently functioned to narrow its range of concern and obscure significant dynamics; when churches focus on conscience exemptions, or primarily on the issue of institutional cooperation with evil, their witness to the common good may be undermined. Whereas the church advocates on a wide range of social issues, prominent understandings of conscience as an identity marker can risk elevating conformity and scandal avoidance above pursuit of the good. As Linda Hogan rightly argues, more contextual and communal understandings of conscience not only "[articulate] a more comprehensive understanding of the nature of moral truth and how human beings come to discern that truth," but also move discourse from appealing to conscience as trump cards to "more meaningful exchange about why certain of our views are so deeply held, what fundamental values they express and why they are of such elementary significance."[34] In such exchanges, often with real people outside our confined circles, conscience can more readily be confronted with the challenge of its own limited perspective and impoverished formation.

Understandings and invocations of conscience must also take account of the complexities of pursuing the good amid structures that harm and internalized ideologies that conceal. Bypassing the impact of structural constraints and harmful ideologies on the exercise of conscience threatens to undermine formation and to constrain the fidelity and effectiveness of churches' public moral witness. A more adequate understanding of conscience in light of such influences would enhance moral agency for those influenced significantly by

---

[34] Hogan, "Marriage Equality, Conscience, and the Catholic Tradition," 85.

social forces that constrain and obscure alike; significantly enrich conscience formation practices; and strengthen churches' public witness.

A Christian relational anthropology has contributed to a more personalist understanding of conscience in recent decades. Yet a moral anthropology marked not only by relational agency but also by the complexities of sin— pride, insecurity, ignorance, group egotism—should ground analyses of the interlocking forces at play in conscience formation. The impact of social sin is seldom accounted for in discussions of conscience formation or churches' public witness in the US context. Cursory searches for conscience topics in medical and health care ethics predominantly surface research treating conscientious objections of providers, institutional complicity in evil, end-of-life issues, and emergency contraception. Dominant notions of conscience presume freely acting agents, and yet impediments may extend beyond moral subjectivism, culpable ignorance, moral confusion, or even moral injury to include ideologies that distort our field of vision. Failing to adequately attend to such cultural forces in considerations of conscience risks shrinking the scope of moral concern. If a person's dignity as a free and responsible agent remains central to Vatican II's understanding of conscience as "sanctuary," then probing subtle and overt ways in which humans lack genuine freedom remains critical to the tasks of the formation and exercise of conscience. These dynamics are too seldom reflected in the church's moral formation or public witness.

The medical anthropologist Paul Farmer has long argued that contemporary medical ethics obscures obscene disparities in health and well-being because the field remains primarily rooted in theoretical ("experience-distant") disciplines like philosophy and quandary ethics. Attention to important matters such as brain death, end-of-life care, and organ transplantation risk neglecting the roles poverty, racism, and lack of insurance play in health and well-being.[35] Christian ethicists have echoed this concern that "compared to the quandary structure of standard medical ethics—the beneficent and maleficent aims of medical technology brought against the individual patient's sacred autonomy," Christian health care and bioethics necessarily take up a vastly more complicated perspective (e.g., patients are not individuals but defined by webs of interdependent relationships, health as inclusive beyond medical needs).[36] Farmer's insights about the need to "resocialize" the way we perceive ethical dilemmas in medicine (lest its debates, he has warned, remain a "slick ruse" to distract us from easily avoidable and thus "stupid

---

[35] Paul Farmer, *Pathologies of Power: Health, Human Rights, and the New War on the Poor* (Berkeley: University of California Press, 2003), chap. 6.

[36] Joel Shuman and Brian Volck, "A Body without Borders," in *Reclaiming the Body: Christians and the Faithful Use of Modern Medicine* (Grand Rapids, MI: Brazos Press, 2006), 98.

deaths") are instructive for the function of conscience in Catholic reflection more broadly. Attending to the full social complexity does justice to both the Catholic tradition of conscience and the range of factors compromising health and well-being.

Given the impact of economic inequality and other social factors on health access and outcomes, a reductive understanding of conscience obscures relevant concerns. Shawnee Daniels-Sykes's essay in this volume sheds light on persistent racial disparities in US health, in terms of disproportionate insurance rates, mortality rates, access to clinical trials (due to presumed noncompliance), and other negative health consequences of stigma and racial prejudice.[37] One's citizenship status also impedes health care access (including under the ACA's provisions). Understanding health care not only as a human right but as a demand of the common good helps focus attention on those still excluded from viable access to affordable health care, as public health is diminished when members are left out. If health care is affected not only by individual choices of patients and providers but also social contexts of poverty, racism, violence, gender inequities, and resource access, then theological responses must better attend to social dimensions of sin and of conscience alike. As James Keenan has recently admonished, the virtue of solidarity "arises as the guarantor of a socially formed, vigilant, and responsive conscience," given "widespread complacency."[38]

Attending to the presence and call of God amid the world's complex health care and political dilemmas certainly requires assiduous discernment, yet discernment undertaken in a spirit of courage and hope rather than fear or cynicism. As John Hardt has put it, "We ought not to set up an illusory hope for maintaining an inauthentic moral purity when neither our world nor God's work allow for it."[39] Disproportionate focus on avoiding scandal can occlude the primary call to pursue the good, to love. Prevalent understandings of conscience in the institutional church's public witness risk diminishing its scope of concern, the sources relevant for conscience formation and discernment, and the moral agency of the laity. A personalist model of conscience leavened by Pope Francis's example and greater attentiveness to complex social dynamics invites a more capacious understanding, promising salubrious effects for human flourishing and for the church's public witness alike.

---

[37] See also Beyer, "Solidarity Strives to Mend Broken World," and Peter A. Clark, "Prejudice and the Medical Profession: A Five-Year Update," *Journal of Law, Medicine & Ethics* 37, no. 1 (2009): 119; Peter A. Clark and Sam Schadt, "Mercy Health Promoter: A Paradigm for Just Health Care," *Medical Science Monitor: International Medical Journal of Experimental and Clinical Research* 19 (2013): 815.

[38] James F. Keenan, SJ, "Redeeming Conscience," *Theological Studies* 76, no. 1 (March 2015): 143.

[39] John J. Hardt, "Some Thoughts on Conscience in the Delivery of Catholic Health Care," *Health Care Ethics USA* (2008): 4.

THE ROLE OF CONSCIENCE IN THE DELIVERY OF HEALTH CARE

John J. Paris, SJ, and M. Patrick Moore Jr.

"Conscience" is a word often used but little understood. It has a rich and complex history, one that has been explored and analyzed for centuries.[1] Before examining that concept and applying it to two recent federal court cases involving conscientious objection and health care delivery, we want to look at two Academy Award–winning films from 2007 and 2008, *No Country for Old Men*[2] and *There Will Be Blood*,[3] to set the scene for an understanding of conscience. Then we examine a film from 2015, *The Woman in Gold*,[4] for an additional insight into conscience. From this exploration of conscience in film, we then consider a fundamental understanding of conscience, the relationship of conscience and community, and the freedom and authenticity of conscience. Seeing these constitutive—and often overlooked—aspects of conscience will allow us to see the problematic religious and Catholic approach to conscience in the federal court cases on health care delivery at issue here.

Conscience and Contemporary Film

In *No Country for Old Men*, a cold-blooded psychopath ruthlessly hunts down a local who stumbles upon a drug deal gone bad and takes off with a satchel filled with $2 million. Throughout the film the psychopath dispassionately uses a bolt rifle to murder nearly every rival, bystander, and even his employer. In the film violence is wanton, random, and ruthless. It is of no consequence to the perpetrator. There is no remorse, no pity. There is no human response but rather an utter disdain for those who get in the psychopath's way.

---

[1] For two examples, see Douglas C. Langston, *Conscience and Other Virtues: From Bonaventure to MacIntyre* (University Park: Pennsylvania State University Press, 2001), and David E. DeCosse and Kristin E. Heyer, *Conscience and Catholicism: Rights, Responsibilities, and Institutional Responses* (Maryknoll, NY: Orbis Books, 2015).

[2] Joel Coen, dir., *No Country for Old Men* (Paramount, 2008).

[3] Paul T. Anderson, dir., *There Will Be Blood* (Paramount, 2007).

[4] Simon Curtis, dir., *The Woman in Gold* (Weinstein Company, 2015).

There Will Be Blood is equally dark and nihilistic. The protagonist, Daniel Plainview, adopts the orphaned son of a worker who was killed in an accident. Plainview does this, not as an act of kindness, but to play up sympathy for his adopted son. Plainview's only goal is greed. When the boy loses his hearing from a dynamite blast and is no longer of help to Plainview, he promptly sends the boy off to a boarding school for the deaf. As the story jumps ahead, Plainview kills a man impersonating his brother. The adopted son, now a man, is no longer of any benefit, so Plainview disowns him with the cold pronouncement, "You have none of me in you; you are just a bastard in a basket."

Neither protagonist in the two films exhibits the slightest regret. One has no sense of right or wrong. The other is driven by such insatiable greed that he is blind to anything but wealth. No relationships, no reflection, no regrets mark either man's life.

Both lack what we would call "conscience"—a sense of right and wrong. More important, conscience implies a capacity to reflect on the meaning and purpose of one's life. It calls to a sense of purpose moved by values other than self-interest. "Let conscience be your guide" is a frequently articulated moral maxim. What does it mean? What does it demand of us? We know we stand for certain things. We struggle over deciding what to do. We feel pangs of conscience when we do something wrong. Conscience is our capacity for making such a discernment.

Before delving into the meaning of conscience we will examine another film, *The Woman in Gold*, a 2015 movie starring Oscar-winning Helen Mirren as Maria Altmann, a wealthy Jewish woman in pre-Nazi Vienna, whose aunt, Adele Bloch-Bauer, was the subject of Gustav Klimt's lavish portrait now known as the *Woman in Gold*. That portrait along with all the family's wealth was looted by the Nazis in 1938. In the 1950s, Maria Altmann began a long legal battle against the Austrian government to reclaim the portrait. The government, which considered the portrait an Austrian National Treasure, offered a rich payment to Maria if she would leave the portrait at Vienna's Belvedere Gallery. She declined. The issue, she stated, was not about money; it was about "doing the right thing."

After a United States Supreme Court ruling in Maria's favor,[5] the Austrian Restitution Board returned the portrait to Maria, who subsequently sold it to an Estée Lauder heir for $108 million with the proviso that the portrait be on permanent display at the Neue Galerie in New York City. Maria donated the money she received from the sale of the portrait to charity. As she puts it in the film, "It was not about money. It was about principle. It was about doing the right thing."

---

[5] Republic of Austria v. Altman, 541 US 677 (2004).

Conscience:
Philosophical and Theological Roots

With these examples in mind, let us explore the meaning of "moral conscience." We will begin by distinguishing conscience from what it is not. It is not the superego of psychology, that is, the ego of parents or another authority figure imposed on us.[6] It is not a censor or an imposed sense of guilt, a fear of punishment, or a fear of withdrawal of love.

Conscience is the difference between "shoulds" and "wants" as a source of behavior. "Shoulds" belong to someone else (superego). "Wants"— what my truest self would want to do—belong to us. They are personalized and internalized values as well as acquired virtues. The superego acts out of obligation and obedience. Conscience acts out of responsible freedom. Conscience involves the awareness that we are moral beings, that is, we have a freedom that is oriented not to arbitrariness, but to what is objectively good and right.

Various philosophies, worldviews, ideologies, and religions have attempted to give a theoretical explanation for this phenomenon of conscience.[7] A Catholic theological explanation points to the character of the human person as one who is created in the image and likeness of God, or as it was expressed in the older Latin texts, the *Imago Dei*. Catholic theology thus understands two aspects of conscience: We are to act in accordance with what fundamental conscience experiences: being good, behaving rightly, and being responsible for one's actions. We also may fall short of the goal.

We see the first aspect of this theological understanding of human character in Tim Russert's biography of his father, *Big Russ*, when his dad refused to take money in exchange for listing someone for a sanitation super-intendent position. In his father's words, "This is who I am." That is, to take a bribe or to give someone a job based solely on "connections" violated the deepest convictions of his personality. Another example of acting in accord with one's fundamental character is that of John McCain, the son and grandson of four-star admirals, who, when shot down and captured during the Vietnam War, refused his captor's propaganda offer of an early release. As McCain put it, "That is not who I am."[8] He remained a prisoner true to his conscience until the war ended nearly six years after his capture. To McCain, to take advantage of his family's social status in order to be treated differently

---

[6] John Glaser, "Conscience and Superego: A Key Distinction," *Theological Studies* 32 (1971): 30–47.

[7] Ninian Smart, *The World's Religions: Old Traditions and Modern Transformations* (Cambridge: Cambridge University Press, 1968).

[8] John McCain and Mark Salter, *Faith of My Fathers* (New York: Random House, 1999).

from any other prisoner was not only unacceptable; it was offensive to his sense of his identity.

Conscience is rooted in the Hebrew Bible's notion of the "heart." The heart is perceived as the center for feelings and reason and the source of decisions. The hope of the Old Testament prophets was that the people would receive a new heart so they would live out the grace of God's covenant. That hope is found in Ezekiel's words spoken to the Israelites, "I will give you a new heart and a new spirit I will put in you. I will remove the heart of stone from your flesh and give you a heart of flesh."[9] It is also seen in Jeremiah's proclamation spoken in the name of God, "I will give them a heart to know that I am the LORD, and they shall be my people and I will be their God."[10] In the New Testament Paul weaves together Greek and Hebrew thought to speak of conscience as our fundamental awareness of the difference between good and evil. It is a guide to loving decisions and a judge for discerning ways that are unbecoming of a Christian.

As we learned in Vatican II's *Pastoral Constitution on the Church in the Modern World (Gaudium et Spes)*, "Conscience is the most secret core and sanctuary of a man. There he is alone with God, whose voice echoes in his depths." Vatican II's *Declaration on Religious Freedom (Dignitatis Humanae)* reiterates the message that "in all his activities man is bound to follow his conscience faithfully in order that he may come to God, for whom he was created."[11] The dimensions of conscience involve capacity, process, and judgment. Except for infants, the brain damaged or the deranged, such as the psychopath in *No Country for Old Men,* this capacity is ingrained in all as a foundation of human nature.

Aquinas understood fundamental conscience as a certain and infallible insight into first principles: Do what is good. Do not act arbitrarily toward one's neighbor.[12] It is not possible, however, to state with equal clarity what such principles or norms intend to say about concrete behavior in the larger human world. That is the role of the second factor: process. The prophets, scripture, tradition, and wise and prudent mentors provide insights. The context of this resolution is not unambiguously the "voice of God." Nor does this process of "seeking" and "finding" exclude the possibility of error. What we have in process is a human's attempt to give concrete substance to the absolute requirement of the fundamental conscience.

The third factor in conscience is that of judgment. It is the process of discernment and reflection that leads to the practical assessment that takes

---

[9] Ezekiel 36:26.

[10] Jeremiah 24:7.

[11] Vatican II, *Declaration on Religious Freedom (Dignitatis Humanae)*, December 7, 1965. www.vatican.va.

[12] *Summa Theologiae* I q, 79, a 13.

place in one's heart where we are alone with God—"*solus cum Solo.*" This does not mean "*solus cum seipso*"—alone with oneself. As John Paul II notes in his encyclical *Veritatis Splendor*, "It is the judgment which applies to a concrete situation the rational conviction that one must love, do good and avoid evil."[13] As we learned from John McCain's experience as a POW, conscience is not a whim, not self-interest, not fear of disapproval. It is, rather, the moral conviction that this is the right thing to do.

Conscience, Personhood, and Community

A contemporary approach to conscience focuses on an integrated whole person, one who is a thinking, feeling, intuiting, and willing individual. It is not a surrogate for individual freedom against authority or a law unto itself. Nor is it the teacher of moral doctrine. That is the role of authority. Discerning what is right is an ongoing lifetime task. Moral knowledge is not individual, but social, in nature. It is learned within communities that influence us. Conscience, though always made for oneself, is not formed by oneself. We are too limited in experience and knowledge, and we are too accustomed to failure, lapses, and missing the mark to recognize moral truths all by ourselves. We need to consult the established sources of wisdom.

This proves true in the secular as well as the spiritual life. As Justice Paul Liacos of the Massachusetts Supreme Judicial Court remarked in a landmark end-of-life court opinion in *Saikewicz*, "The law frequently lags behind technology. We need to consult philosophy, theology and the traditions of medicine for insight and understanding of what we ought to do."[14] As humans we consult family, friends, colleagues, and experts in the field. We also analyze and test our stories, norms, and laws to determine if they correspond to our moral expectations. For example, a report in 2008 by Mark Boucek and colleagues in the *New England Journal of Medicine* proposed that transplant teams could legitimately declare the death of an infant 75 seconds after cessation of cardiocirculatory functions (asystole).[15] This abbreviated "waiting" period was proposed by the authors "to reduce the risk of injury [to the desired organs] from warm ischemia." That recommendation occasioned widespread criticism.

An unprecedented three other articles and a video roundtable discussion by prominent bioethicists critiquing the report were published in the same

---

[13] John Paul II, *Veritatis Splendor*, no. 59. August 6, 1993. w2.vatican.va.

[14] Superintendent of Belchertown State School v. Saikewicz, 373 Mass. 728, 370 NE 2d 417 (1977).

[15] Mark M. Boucek, Christine Mashburn, Susan M. Dunn, et al., "Pediatric Heart Transplantation after Declaration of Cardiocirculatory Death," *New England Journal of Medicine* 359 (2008): 709–14.

issue of the *Journal*. In one of those essays James Bernat, a neurologist at Dartmouth Medical School, was highly critical of the shortened time between asystole and the declaration of death.[16] He insisted that such a deviation from the standard five-minute protocol proposed by the National Institute of Medicine or the shorter two-minute recommendation by the Society of Critical Care Medicine, was unwarranted.[17] Standards in matters of life and death, particularly those involving children, he argued, should be based not simply on an attempt to increase the supply of vital organs, but on the best interests of the donor patient. The boundaries in such cases, he argued, should be "based on scientific data and accepted principles." Whatever standard is adopted, he stated, should be "demarcated conservatively to maintain public confidence in the integrity of the transplantation enterprise." Bernat concluded his critique with the prediction that whatever prudent boundaries are established, they will exclude "death determination at 75 seconds of asystole."

Conscience: Freedom, Rectitude, and Tests of Authenticity

Conscience and personal character demand that we ask not only "What should I do?" but "What sort of person ought I become?" They also involve the realization that conscience can err. We can miss or distort some facts, we can be mistaken in judgment, and we can be directed by passion rather than reason. To act in conscience requires some degree of knowledge, freedom, and capacity to care for others and a willingness to commit oneself to moral values. It requires not just information or data but experience and reflection.

Freedom is the ability to direct one's actions according to one's self-chosen goals. It is not a license to do whatever we want. It is the freedom of wanting to do what we ought to do because it is the right thing to do. What is missing in the psychopath in *No Country for Old Men* is not the knowledge of right and wrong, but a caring commitment to do the right thing. The psychopath has no empathy. We see that when he tells the store clerk to flip a coin and call "heads or tails" to determine whether the clerk lives or dies.

Is there a test of genuineness or authenticity of a decision purportedly taken in conscience? As we see in the case of the conscientious objectors to war, or in the actions of civil rights activists such as Martin Luther King Jr., the test of authenticity is the willingness of the one concerned to pay the price for challenging the status quo.

---

[16] James L. Bernat, "The Boundaries of Organ Donation after Circulatory Death," *New England Journal of Medicine* 359 (2008): 669–71.

[17] James L. Bernat, Anthony M. D'Allesandro, Friedrich K. Port, et al., "Report of a National Conference on Donation after Cardiac Death," *American Journal of Transplantation* 6 (2006): 281–91.

Conscientious objection is not simply refusing to join the military or protesting the impact of a law. It is deliberately refusing to obey—and accepting the penalty that follows—so that the community might reflect on what produces a willingness to undergo such suffering. The hope of the objector is that such reflection will cause the community to modify its policies. Examples abound in history. In Sophocles' *Antigone* we find the protagonist refusing to follow King Creon's dictate that no one is to bury the body of her brother who had fought against the king.[18] For disobeying Creon's decree, Antigone was sealed alive in a cave.

Martin Luther issued his "Here I stand; I can do no other" denunciation of corruption in the sale of indulgences by the popes. He was promptly excommunicated.[19] Thomas More refused to sign the Oath of Supremacy by which Henry VIII proclaimed himself head of the Church of England and annulled his marriage to Catherine of Aragon. For this, More was removed as Lord Chancellor, convicted of treason, and beheaded.[20] The price for these actions was high: imprisonment, excommunication, death. This is what is meant by "bound in conscience."

There is a long history on conflict of conscience and even conflict of conscience with the Church. Thomas Aquinas in his *Commentary on the Sentences* responded that "we ought to die excommunicated rather than violate our conscience."[21] Aquinas understood the problem well. If we are not bound to what our conscience dictates is right, then we would be free to follow any whim as morally correct. If you know your position is erroneous, that is, wrong, conscience could not dictate doing it. As Aquinas puts it, in the end if there is a conflict between conscience and Church, we are absolutely not free to violate our conscience. That does not necessarily mean we are right. It is easy to get things wrong. It means you must follow what your conscience—correctly or incorrectly—indicates is the right thing to do.

The erroneous conscience is discussed at length in James Keenan's insightful *Moral Wisdom*.[22] There he notes that Bernard of Clairvaux (1090–1153) started with the belief that ignorance was the root of sin. For him actions contrary to law were bad. His contemporary, Peter Abelard, focused on the role of consent. For Abelard consent determines good and bad actions. In his view, if we are in error, but do not consent, there is no sin. In Abelard's thinking whatever happened out of ignorance ought not be

---

[18] Sophocles, *Antigone*, trans. Michael Townsend (Scranton: Chandler Publishing,1962).

[19] Roland Bainton, *Here I Stand: A Life of Martin Luther* (New York: Penguin, 1995).

[20] Robert Bolt, *A Man for All Seasons* (London: Bloomsbury, 2013).

[21] Aquinas, *Scriptum super libros Sententiarum,* IV, 38. 2. 4q. a3.

[22] James F. Keenan, *Moral Wisdom: Lessons and Texts from the Catholic Tradition,* 2nd ed. (New York: Sheed and Ward, 2010).

ascribed as blameworthy. For example, you arrived home and were met at the door by your wife who says, "I have something to tell you. But before you say anything, you should know 'He did it out of love.'" Keenan asks, "Are these comforting words? Or words of warning?" Acting out of love or conscience is not a guarantee of right acting. If our conduct stemmed from erroneous conscience, we may have been loving. But because we were in error, what we did was wrong.

What if a person follows an erroneous conscience? Aquinas questions the sincerity and the striving of the act. Could the individual, with effort, have known otherwise? If the answer is "yes," the person was responsible for the erroneous conscience. If the answer is "no," the person is not. He did not do "good" but Thomas holds him "excused." He is neither good nor bad. He is simply "excused" from blame. In his survey of Catholic moralists' attitude on erroneous conscience, Keenan continues with Alphonsus Liguori, the patron saint of moral theologians. Liguori held that if a person acted out of charity when committing error then he is not only excused, but is a good person.

Today people are regularly praised for following their conscience without any concern for the resultant activity. The common response in today's society is "Who am I to impose my values on him?" That attitude is what Benedict XVI describes as "the apotheosis of subjectivity."[23] To avoid a wholly subjective approach to issues, we need to know the general rules, assess the circumstances, evaluate the contingencies, anticipate the consequence and more importantly anticipate the response to the consequences. To get things wrong, we need to err on only one of these factors.

In contrast to the psychopath in *No Country for Old Men* who has no sense of right or wrong, or the one so blinded by greed in *There Will Be Blood* that he no longer sees right from wrong, we have insights—ranging from the Old Testament story of David and Bathsheba to the actions of Chuck Colson and the Committee to Re-Elect (President Nixon)—as guides to right and wrong behavior. King David when overcome with lust for Bathsheba arranged for the death of her husband. He thought he had successfully covered up his moral failings until confronted by Nathan, the prophet who asked him to judge the actions of the wealthy man who took the only lamb of a poor shepherd. David declared, "The man who did this deserves to die." Nathan said in reply, "Thou art the man."[24] Colson, when working at the Committee to Re-Elect declared, "I'd walk over my own grandmother to ensure the re-election of President Richard M. Nixon."[25] Later, when in jail for his involvement

---

[23] Benedict XVI, *On Conscience* (San Francisco: Ignatius Press, 2007).

[24] 2 Samuel 12:1–6.

[25] Michael Dobbs, "Charles Colson, Nixon's 'Dirty Tricks' Man Dies at 80," *Washington Post*, April 21, 2012, 1.

in the Watergate break-in, Colson had the opportunity to reflect on his actions. He concluded, "I lost my moral compass."[26]

Similar sentiments were expressed by Aleksandr Solzhenitsyn in *The Gulag Archipelago* when, in reflecting on his treatment of his fellow prisoners in the gulag, he observed, "That is what shoulder boards (symbols of officer rank) do to human beings." "And where," he inquired of himself, "have all the exhortations of grandmother standing before the icon gone?"[27]

Conscience and the Delivery of Health Care

How do the demands of conscience play out in today's world of health care delivery? It is not merely a plea for mercy by someone such as fallen former lobbyist Jack Abramoff, who when facing years of prison for corruption, laments he has "fallen into an abyss." Rather, such demands are what the moral theologians label "antecedent conscience," the "inner voice" that directs an individual as to what he or she should or should not do.

Then comes the question, can we keep ourselves morally pure? Is such a reality possible? An insight into that question can be found in J. D. Salinger's classic *The Catcher in the Rye*, which reminds us that no matter how intent Holden Caulfield was to keep his younger sister from losing her innocence, there are just too many graffiti-filled walls in New York City to succeed in doing so.[28]

Early examples of opposition to participation in an "evil" act centered on conscientious objection to war.[29] Contemporary disputes involving conscientious objection focus on the highly divisive issues of abortion, embryonic stem cell research, physician assisted suicide, participation in emergency room response to rape, administration of Plan B, and the general questions of when and under what circumstances may a health care provider opt out of providing a service the provider discerns to be a violation of his or her own moral code.

Two recent court cases—*Stormans v. Wiesman*[30] and *Little Sisters of the Poor v. Burwell*[31]—illustrate the contemporary dilemma of conscientious objection in health care. In the first a pharmacist in the state of Washington refused to fill a prescription for Plan B contraception despite state law requiring pharmacists to fill all lawful prescriptions. The federal trial court

---

[26] Jonathan Aitkin, "Remembering Charles Colson: A Man Transformed," *Christianity Today*, April 21, 2012, 6.

[27] Alexander Solzhenitsyn, *Gulag Archipelago* (New York: Harper and Row, 1973), 164.

[28] J. D. Salinger, *The Catcher in the Rye* (Boston: Little, Brown, 1951).

[29] Michael Walzer, *Just and Unjust Wars* (New York: Basic Books, 1977).

[30] Stormans v. Selecky, 586 F. 3d 1109 (2009).

[31] Little Sisters of the Poor v. Burwell, 799 F.3d 1151 (10th Cir 2015).

accepted the plaintiff's view that "the overriding objective of the regulation was, to the degree possible, to eliminate moral and religious objections from the business of dispensing medication."[32] The Hobson's choice for a pharmacist who objected to Plan B was to dispense a drug that in the pharmacist's religious belief ends a life or leave the profession in the state of Washington. The state argued to no avail at the trial court that it had a compelling interest in ensuring ready access to prescriptions and combating gender discrimination. It further argued that the issue did not involve an individual claim of conscience.

The Federal District Court ruled in favor of the plaintiffs and issued a preliminary injunction barring the state of Washington from enforcing regulations against any pharmacy or pharmacist who refers patients to a nearby source for Plan B. The Ninth Circuit Court of Appeals reversed the lower court's decision. In an opinion issued on July 23, 2015, that addressed some additional appellate issues, the Ninth Circuit reaffirmed that reversal.[33] In its opinion the Ninth Circuit Court of Appeals opined that the rules promulgated by the Washington Pharmacy Quality Assurance Commission were facially neutral, advanced secular state interests in patient safety, and were not selectively enforced. Because the rules were neutral and generally applicable, a review to determine whether they were supported by rational basis rather than a more constitutionally exacting review applied.

More important, the Ninth Circuit panel declined to recognize a fundamental right that protected the religious conscience of a pharmacist who viewed Plan B as an abortifacient. It was unconvinced that the right to own, operate, or work at a licensed professional business free from regulations requiring the business to engage in activities that one sincerely believes lead to the taking of human life was so rooted in conscience and the nation's tradition as to be ranked as fundamental. (Slip opinion at 43.) The plaintiffs petitioned the United States Supreme Court to review the Ninth Circuit's ruling. In June 2016 the Supreme Court declined to review the case.

The second of the two contemporary legal cases with a claim to the sanctity of religious conscience is the Little Sisters of the Poor case.[34] Though the legal questions in the case are somewhat arcane, the central issue in the case is whether the Obama administration's "accommodation of religious conscience"—that allows a religious group to file an affidavit objecting to the provision and be free from any further involvement in the coverage of insurance for contraceptives—provides sufficient protection for religious conscience. The

---

[32] Stormans, Inc. v. Selecky (Now Wiesman), 854 F. Supp. 2d 925 (WD Wash. 2012).

[33] Stormans, Inc. v. Wiesman, 794 F.3d 1064 (2015), 2015 US App. Lexis 12692 (9th Cir 2015).

[34] Nigel Duara, "Court Rules against Little Sisters of the Poor in Contraceptive Coverage Case," *Los Angeles Times*, July 14, 2015, 7.

Little Sisters of the Poor, whose apostolate is the care of the elderly nursing home patients, argue the very act of signing a form for a religious exemption presents a "substantial burden on their free exercise of religion."

The Tenth Circuit Court of Appeals disagreed. It ruled that the Obama administration's accommodation was sufficient. In its words, "The First Amendment [the free exercise of religion] does not—and cannot—protect organizations from having to make any and all statements 'they wish to avoid.'"[35] Mark Rienzi, a lawyer for the Becket Fund, which presents itself as an organization that protects and promotes free exercise of religion, is representing the Little Sisters in the case. He commented that "judges aren't qualified to tell nuns what the right answers are on questions of moral complicity."[36] He appealed the ruling to the United States Supreme Court, an institution composed of judges not moral theologians where the focus is not the character of "religious conscience," but constitutional law. After hearing the case in March 2016, the court issued no decision on the merits but sent the case back for further argument in the lower courts.

As longtime commentator on religious freedom Richard Garnett has noted, "It is not clear that there actually is in American constitutional law a commitment to, or even room for, the *libertas ecclesiae* principle richly understood."[37] By that he means that the free exercise of churches and religious organizations from state regulation has historically been limited to property disputes, employment of ministers, and doctrinal disputes. Other commentators on the issue such as Michael Moreland raise the further question of "whether specific exemptions for Catholic hospitals and social service agencies raise the prospect of religious gerrymander, such as the exemption for Amish children for high school education[38] or the exemption for religious based animal sacrifice in the *Lukumi* case."[39]

Concern over the contraceptive drug benefit does not seem to be taken seriously by the general public or, indeed, by most Catholics. A recent Gallup Poll found that "82 percent of Catholics in the United States say birth control is morally acceptable, a figure that is close to the 87 percent of all Americans and 90 percent of non-Catholics polled."[40] Furthermore, the traditional Catholic principle of *cooperatio* sometimes, even if reluctantly, permits compliance, with state requirements. The classic distinctions between direct

---

[35] Little Sisters of the Poor, 794 F.3d 1204.

[36] Emma Green, "Even Nuns Aren't Exempt from Obamacare's Birth-Control Mandate," *Atlantic*, July 14, 2015, www.theatlantic.com.

[37] R. Garnett, "John Courtney Murray on the 'Freedom of the Church,'" *Journal of Catholic Social Thought* (2007); Notre Dame Legal Studies Paper No. 06-12.

[38] Wisconsin v. Yoder, 406 US 205 (1972).

[39] Church of Lukumi Babalu Aye, Inc. v. City of Hialeah, 502 US 520 (1993).

[40] Gallup News Service, May 3–6, 2017.

versus indirect and formal versus material cooperation are well known in Catholic moral analysis.[41] Direct formal participation—such as performing an abortion—has a far greater degree of moral involvement than the signing of a form requesting a religious exemption. This is true even if the signature may result in a different person providing the drug at a later date.

Claims for conscience, at some point, involve others, and thus sink into a dispute about whether Person A's conscience is infringing on Person B's ability to chart his or her own course. What follows is a morass of disputes about the proper scope of exemptions and supposed burdens on conscience that bear little actual weight in the practical world of health care or the provision of health benefits. The danger of an overemphasis on conscientious objection in health care delivery is lapsing into Pope Benedict XVI's "apotheosis of subjectivity," the elevating of individual conscience into the determiner of morality in every action.

Another issue in the conscientious objection in health care controversy is that of "scandal." Does the action of the individual, even if legal or morally correct, cause scandal among the faithful? If so, the scandal in itself might be a prudent basis for avoiding the action. Aquinas notes that the sin of scandal has not been committed just because one party says, "Your behavior scandalizes me."[42] The Pharisees' protest that they were scandalized by Jesus healing on the Sabbath may have been more pretextual than real. Some might believe an action is sinful or at least is an action that gives the appearance of unacceptable behavior. The action might not in itself be sinful, but it might lead some people to believe it is. For example, a man who is part of an unmarried couple in a nonsexual relationship may on occasion (he missed the last train home) stay overnight at his woman partner's apartment. Some might take this as unacceptable, even scandalous, behavior. Others in a modern urban environment would find nothing untoward in such behavior. In either case, prudence might dictate the avoidance of even the appearance of unacceptable behavior. Another form of nonbinding behavior is the so-called pusillanimous scandal, that is, an action may not be bad or wrong in itself, but it upsets the timid or the fainthearted. The fact that there were those who get the vapors over the thought of Elvis performing on the *Ed Sullivan Show* is not, in itself, a sufficient basis to condemn such a performance as gravely sinful.

To participate in an ordered society one has a moral duty to obey the law—short of cases where rank injustice cries out for disobedience. In such

---

[41] Ronald L. Conte, "Roman Catholic Teaching on Cooperation with Evil," www. amazon.com. See also Cathleen M. Kaveny, "Appropriation of Evil: Cooperation's Mirror Image," *Theological Studies* 61 (2000): 280–313.

[42] John A. McHugh and Charles J. Callan, *Moral Theology: A Complete Course Based on St. Thomas Aquinas and the Best Modern Authors*, vol. 2 (New York: Joseph Wagner, 1958), 571–72.

cases the willingness to undergo the punishment such an action exacts as the price of reforming the community's collective conscience is the mark of authenticity. Filing an affidavit for an exemption from a state-mandated health benefit falls well below that level of moral seriousness. It is not a moral challenge such as that confronting an Antigone or a Thomas More. Nor is it consistent with what those acknowledged as authentic conscientious objectors have endured throughout American tradition to avoid complicity in what they understood to be moral evil. Being a poster child for a political cause does not rise to the level of what Marin Luther King Jr. called "Being a drum major for justice."[43] It has more of the character of what Bonhoeffer labels "cheap grace."[44]

---

[43] Martin Luther King Jr. "The Drum Major Instinct," sermon, Ebenezer Baptist Church, Atlanta, GA. February 4, 1968. This was the last sermon King delivered before being assassinated. http://action.naacp.org.

[44] Dietrich Bonhoeffer, *The Cost of Discipleship* (New York: Macmillan, 1963).

LAW, RELIGION, AND CONSCIENCE IN A PLURALISTIC SOCIETY

The Case of the Little Sisters of the Poor

Cathleen Kaveny

Thirty years ago, the debate about religion, law, and morality in the American public square centered on the enactment of generally applicable laws. The salient issue was whether believers were justified in passing laws that reflected their religiously infused moral commitments on contested matters such as abortion or same-sex marriage. More specifically, the debaters asked whether it is morally acceptable for a politically powerful and religiously committed segment of the population to limit access to abortion or restrict marriage to opposite-sex couples. Or do such restrictive laws impermissibly burden the consciences of those who do not share the relevant religious or moral beliefs?[1]

In our own time, however, the debate has been significantly reoriented. The pressing questions today pertain to *exemptions* from generally applicable laws. The debaters now consider whether believers are justified in claiming relief from a legal framework that they believe to be inconsistent with their religiously infused moral commitments.[2] Contraception, abortion, and same-sex marriage are now endorsed as fundamental rights by the highest law of the land.[3] Is it morally justified for religiously motivated institutions and persons to claim exemptions from legal requirements operationalizing

---

[1] The debate centered on John Rawls's evolving account of public reason, developed in *Political Liberalism*, exp. ed. (New York: Columbia University Press, 2005). Discussion in Catholic circles focused on Mario Cuomo's speech at the University of Notre Dame, "Religious Belief and Public Morality: A Catholic Governor's Perspective" (1984), http://archives.nd.edu.

[2] For a sober and balanced examination of the question, by the dean of law-and-religion scholars, see Kent Greenawalt, *Exemptions: Necessary, Justified, or Misguided?* (Cambridge, MA: Harvard University Press, 2016).

[3] See, e.g., Griswold v. Connecticut, 381 US 479 (1965), Eisenstadt v. Baird, 405 US 438 (1972), Roe v. Wade, 410 US 113 (1973), Planned Parenthood v. Casey, 505 US 833 (1992), and Obergefell v. Hodges, 135 S. Ct. 2071 (2015).

these rights on the grounds that they believe the requirements implicate them in moral wrongdoing?

Viewing the two discussions in terms of American political categories, they can be seen as mirror images of each another. A generation ago, the issue was whether it was fair for politically powerful social conservatives to impose their beliefs about the immorality of abortion and same-sex relations on fellow citizens who did not share their beliefs. In contrast, the issue today is whether it is fair for politically powerful social liberals to impose their beliefs about the moral acceptability of the sexual revolution on those who continue to advocate traditional sexual morality for religious reasons.

This way of understanding the two debates frames both of them in terms of two antagonists—two parties—to a culture war. It asks the question of whether the winners of the culture war can burden the conscience of the losers by holding them to a law that the losers morally cannot accept. Not coincidentally, this way of framing the debate is tailor-made for constitutional litigation, the ultimate American contest between two antagonistic parties.

Claims of conscience, filtered through the First Amendment to the US Constitution, stand at the center of this type of litigation.[4] If religious conservatives had succeeded in outlawing abortion thirty years ago, they doubtless would have faced challenges from their opponents under the Establishment Clause. Secular groups would have joined forces with pro-choice religious groups to argue that the government was impermissibly burdening their consciences with the peculiar moral norms of religious groups to which they did not belong.

In the present day, of course, it is religious conservatives who are invoking constitutional protection for their conscientious moral judgments. They claim that the Free Exercise Clause of the First Amendment and the Religious Freedom Restoration Act of 1993 (RFRA)[5] legitimate their refusal to comply with the contraception mandate enacted by the Department of Health and Human Services in the regulations implementing the Affordable Care Act.[6]

But here is the problem. All litigation involves some form of distortion. The parties to any lawsuit must allow their lawyers to refashion their commit-

---

[4] Scholars regularly point out that there is only one religion clause of the First Amendment, which reads "Congress shall make no law respecting an establishment of religion, or prohibiting the free exercise thereof." Nonetheless, the first part is regularly referred to as the Establishment Clause and the second part is regularly referred to as the Free Exercise Clause.

[5] Religious Freedom Restoration Act of 1993, codified as amended at 42 USC §2000bb–§2000bb-4. RFRA is nothing more and nothing less than a federal statute; it was enacted to restore some of the protections to the free exercise of religion taken away by the Supreme Court's more restrictive reading of the Free Exercise Clause in Employment Division v. Smith, 494 US 872 (1990).

[6] See, e.g., Burwell v. Hobby Lobby Stores, 134 S. Ct. 2751 (2014).

ments and interests to advance their legal cause. Even in a garden-variety lawsuit, it can be disconcerting for clients to see their interests and commitments restricted, refurbished, and hardened for legal combat. When the lawsuit implicates a party's fundamental commitments, however, the process of litigation can significantly damage its moral integrity. This phenomenon is particularly troubling when the litigant has been recruited by legal activists whose loyalties are fundamentally to a cause that the litigant is meant to represent.

Consider, for example, the Little Sisters of the Poor, a group of women religious who have been embroiled as lead plaintiffs in a lawsuit against the Obama administration.[7] They contend that even the most minimal connection to the governmental mandate to provide insurance coverage for contraception burdens their consciences in violation of RFRA. Their lawsuit is managed by the Becket Fund, an activist legal organization theoretically dedicated to advancing the general cause of religious liberty under American law. In practice, however, the Becket Fund has been particularly solicitous of the religious liberty of social conservatives protesting the intrusion of progressive law and policy developments.[8]

After conflicting opinions emerged among the federal appellate courts that addressed the issue, in November 2015 the Supreme Court agreed to hear the case.[9] Rather than issuing a decision, however, the court took the entirely unusual step of vacating the lower court judgments and urging the parties to settle the question themselves.[10] The court directed them to find some way to provide contraception coverage to the Little Sisters' employees without even the slightest involvement of their employer. If such a way can be found, the

---

[7] The briefs, including amicus briefs, are available at SCOTUSblog, "Little Sisters of the Poor Home for the Aged v. Burwell," http://www.scotusblog.com.

[8] The Becket Fund was founded by Kevin Hasson, who, when practicing law at Williams & Connolly in Washington, DC, was part of the legal team that defended the Catholic University of America for firing Charles Curran. Anita Crane, "Kevin Hasson on the Right to Life and Religious Liberty," *CelebrateLife Magazine*, July 1, 2006, http://www.clmagazine.org.

[9] The split was not even: Of the seven circuit courts of appeals that considered the issue of not-for-profit organizations and the contraceptive mandate, only one sided against the government: the US Court of Appeals for the Eighth Circuit. See Lyle Denniston, "Appeals Court Now Split on Birth Control Mandate," SCOTUSblog, September 17, 2015, http://www.scotusblog.com .

[10] "The parties on remand should be afforded an opportunity to arrive at an approach going forward that accommodates petitioners' religious exercise while at the same time ensuring that women covered by petitioners' health plans 'receive full and equal health coverage, including contraceptive coverage'" (citation omitted). Zubik v. Burwell (per curiam), 578 US ___ (2016), slip. op. 4. Some have speculated that the Court took this unusual step because the sudden death of Associate Justice Antonin Scalia presaged a 4–4 tie—which would not have settled the circuit split, but left the appellate court decisions intact.

Little Sisters may well achieve their legal objective. At the same time, the cost that their lawsuit has inflected on their own rich heritage of Catholic moral thinking may be steeper than they bargained for. In this essay, I would like to outline how their legal strategy has occluded key aspects of the Catholic moral tradition, including but not limited to its understanding of the respect due to conscience.

Binary Reductionism

The legal strategy mounted on behalf of the Little Sisters of the Poor tacitly frames the issue at stake in the contraception mandate in terms of a David and Goliath story. The sisters appear as the vulnerable religious victim of the Obama administration, which is in turn cast in the role of a secular bully. This way of framing the situation may be rhetorically appealing, but it is actually quite deceptive. The conflict is not in fact a contest between two private antagonists, because the rights and interests of many other persons and institutions are at stake as well. Moreover, those other parties are not simply unrelated bystanders who might be accidentally harmed by a stray punch thrown by one of the main antagonists. It is not, after all, as if the Little Sisters and the Obama administration are members of rival gangs who finally come to blows on a busy street full of random passersby. Instead, both have role-related obligations that generate legitimate expectations on the part of third parties.

First, the Obama administration is not narrowly advancing its own interests. Instead, it is attempting to implement the Affordable Care Act, a vast and complicated piece of legislation passed by the legislative branch of our government, signed into law by the executive branch, and upheld after constitutional scrutiny by the judicial branch. The Affordable Care Act emphasizes the importance of preventive care for all persons—with no copayment required. It did not specify—nor should it have specified—every particular medical service that should be included under the umbrella of "preventive care." Yet lawmakers generally recognized that women have traditionally been given short shrift with respect to preventive care, and called for the disparity to be addressed.[11] Consequently, the Department of Health and Human Services (DHHS) requested that the Institute of Medicine develop a list of important preventive services for women that should be covered without cost-sharing.[12] The list that was produced included contraceptive

---

[11] US Department of Health and Human Services, "Affordable Care Act Rules on Expanding Access to Preventive Services for Women," August 1, 2011, http://www.hhs.gov.

[12] The rationale for the Institute of Medicine's list of preventive services for women can be found at the National Academies of Sciences, Engineering, Medicine, Health and Medicine Division, "Women's Preventive Services Recommended by IOM to be Covered Under Affordable Care Act," http://www.nationalacademies.org.

coverage. Why? Because the evidence showed that unplanned pregnancies posed significant health challenges to both mothers and babies. Moreover, unlike abortion, the use of contraception is not a morally contested practice in American life. Nor, for that matter, is it generally a morally contested practice among most American Catholics. Although official Roman Catholic teaching rejects the use of contraception as "intrinsically evil," most Catholic Americans do not agree. In fact, Catholic women use contraception at about the same rate as other women in the United States.[13]

So in advocating for the broad accessibility of contraception in health plans, the Obama administration was not advocating its own idiosyncratic interests. It was not waging war with its Catholic citizens, who constitute approximately one quarter of the American population. It was fulfilling its role-related obligations. The executive branch of the American government is charged with implementing and enforcing legislation passed by Congress. In this case, HHS was attempting to implement the Affordable Care Act, which attempted to make a basic package of health care coverage widely available. Contraceptive coverage enhanced the well-being of women and children by helping to ensure that pregnant women were ready to meet the demands that growing a new human life would place on their bodies.

At the same time, it is important to remember that the Affordable Care Act is not the only law that the executive branch is charged with enforcing. RFRA is also a federal statute, which places stringent requirements on federal regulations threatening the free exercise of religion.[14] The Little Sisters of the Poor believe that the HHS contraception mandate as applied to them violates RFRA. Consequently, they (and others) believe that the Obama administration is failing in its duty to execute the laws of the United States, because it is not giving sufficient weight to the requirements of RFRA.

Just like the Obama administration, the Little Sisters of the Poor have a conflicting set of role-related responsibilities that are occluded by the binary character of the lawsuit. It is true, of course, that they are a Catholic religious order that is responsible to the articulation of its charism, which includes fidelity to the teachings of the Roman Catholic Church, as well as to its mission of providing care for the impoverished elderly.[15] At the same time, however, they are also an employer operating in the United States of America, a country in which (sadly) health insurance is very frequently tied to employment. In fact, the national debate over the Affordable Care Act

---

[13] Guttmacher Institute, "Guttmacher Statistic on Catholic Women's Contraceptive Use," February 15, 2012, http://www.guttmacher.org.

[14] Religious Freedom Restoration Act of 1993, codified as amended at 42 USC. §2000bb–§2000bb-4.

[15] According to their website, the order runs almost thirty homes in the United States. Little Sisters of the Poor, US Homes, http://www.littlesistersofthepoor.org.

cemented the ties between employment and health care for the foreseeable future. To put it another way, employees and their families have a reliance interest in obtaining a standard set of benefits through their employer-based health care, a reliance interest that is strengthened by the Affordable Care Act. Furthermore, the Little Sisters are employers that do not insulate themselves from those who think and live differently in a pluralistic society. They operate institutions that they hold open to persons of all faith and of no faith—both with respect to employees and clients.

Although the binary nature of the litigation obscures the multifaceted obligations of each of the parties, the struggle over exemptions gives us insight into the tensions between the parties. The Obama administration attempted, through a series of increasingly broader accommodations for those who objected to the provision of contraceptive coverage, to balance its mutually challenging obligations. The first iteration of the accommodation gave a full exemption to not-for-profit institutions that both employed and served members of the same faith, and operated with the primary purpose of inculcating religious values. No other accommodations were made, although a temporary "safe harbor" was created for other religious institutions that did not qualify for the exemption.[16] Catholic hospitals and institutions of higher learning such as the University of Notre Dame protested the narrowness of the exemption, on the grounds that it failed to respect their particular vocational identity as Catholics, which required them to work with anyone willing to serve the most needy.

But the self-understanding of the religious institution is not the only value at stake. In crafting exemptions, the Obama administration was obligated to consider the health care needs of the employees, not simply the religious commitments of the employers. Granting full exemptions to religious institutions that both employ and serve members of their own faith arguably balanced both concerns. Those who work in a homogeneous and distinctive religious environment would be on notice that all aspects of their employment would likely be governed by Catholic teaching. Moreover, from a practical point of view, many of those attracted to work in such a pervasively Catholic environment might be more likely to support that teaching in its entirety—and perhaps not likely to want to use contraception in the first place. Furthermore, the numbers of such persons would not be enormous, and therefore would not interfere substantially with the public health goals of the law.

Giving full exemptions to Catholic institutions that are fully engaged in our pluralistic society is another matter entirely. Such institutions include many non-Catholics; indeed, they hold themselves out as open to and respectful of persons who are not Roman Catholic, and who therefore do not

---

[16] See *Federal Register*, vol. 77, no. 31 (February 15, 2012), 8725–30.

view the world fully in accordance with the moral framework set forth in the *Catechism of the Catholic Church*. Moreover, for that matter, many Catholics do not fully accept that framework. So the question for the government, therefore, is not only what it means to respect the religious beliefs of an employer, but also whether those religious beliefs should be allowed to affect the health care benefits of employees, many of whom do not share—and cannot be expected to share—their employer's religious beliefs.

In my judgment, the final rule deftly balanced these concerns. Not-for-profit employers that hold themselves out as religious organizations are required only to (1) self-certify to the government that they object to the provision of some or all the covered contraceptives; and (2) provide a copy of that self-certification to the insurer or third party administrator. That third party then contacts the employees and makes contraceptive coverage available to them.[17] It is this final rule, however, that the Little Sisters of the Poor are contesting. They maintain that stating their objection to contraception coverage to the government or a third party payer violates their religiously informed conscience, because it implicates them in the provision of contraception to their employees.

Distortion of Key Moral Concepts

To succeed under RFRA, the Little Sisters of the Poor need to claim, first, that the contraceptive mandate, even with the accommodation, substantially burdens their free exercise of religion. The general practice of the courts thus far has been to accept without question a plaintiff's claim of substantial burden, provided that it is sincere, and turn their scrutiny to the other components of the test, which have to do with the government's need to impose such a burden. This may be a wise prudential decision on the part of the courts, since a more thoroughgoing analysis of the burden would likely require them to enmesh themselves in religious doctrine in violation of the Establishment Clause.

At the same time, there is no reason that fellow Catholics cannot critically examine the arguments put forward by the Little Sisters and their advocates about the normative implications of our common tradition. And such an examination yields troubling results. In my judgment, the arguments advanced on behalf of the Little Sisters undermine the very tradition of Catholic ethical reasoning to which they claim to be committed.

First, I think the Little Sisters' central claim is contributing to the distortion of the venerable tradition of Catholic moral teaching on the issue of

---

[17] *Federal Register*, vol. 78, no. 127 (July 2, 2013), 39870–99. The accommodation was later extended to cover closely held *for-profit* corporations in accordance with the *Hobby Lobby* case.

cooperation with evil. They have argued that it violates their conscience even to sign a paper giving notice of their moral objections to the provision of contraception through the health care plan they sponsor. They maintain that entails morally unacceptable complicity with the use of contraception by their employees and the family members of those employees. Some have gone so far as to claim that counts as formal cooperation with evil.[18] Formal cooperation with evil is always morally impermissible. But formal cooperation with evil requires that the cooperator *intend* the evil that is done by the third party; mere causal connection with that harm is insufficient. To claim that signing a form objecting to providing contraceptive coverage amounts to purposefully furthering the use of contraception by employees is nothing short of nonsensical.

Some might maintain that positions that are adopted for purposes of litigation, even philosophical or theological positions, do not really "count" as interventions in a tradition. They are simply, according to this view, strategic interventions—lawyers (and clients under the direction of their lawyers) say what is necessary to win the case. The statements involved are not to be taken seriously as actual statements of moral or theological beliefs. They are contained safely within the confines of the courtroom, just as the dialogue in a play is contained safely within the confines of the stage.

But this analysis of the impact of the distortions is seriously mistaken. Through their briefs and their lawyers, the Little Sisters and their advocates are actually making a public representation of Catholic moral teaching. They are claiming an exemption from generally applicable law on its basis. To the extent that they are doing so "with fingers crossed," they are provoking skepticism about the possibility of actual moral discernment within the Catholic tradition. More broadly, they are contributing to the widespread cynicism about the possibility of moral reasoning itself. As Alasdair MacIntyre and others have suggested, a growing number of people think that moral claims are simply another tool with which to manipulate others to achieve one's own objectives.[19]

What about the claim that signing the form is impermissible *material* cooperation with evil? While superficially more plausible, it too involves an utter distortion of the tradition. To even rise to a situation involving material cooperation with wrongdoing, one moral agent must make some contribution to the wrongful act of another. Signing the form objecting to providing contraceptive coverage does not in itself make any contribution whatsoever to the use of contraception by employees or their families. To say otherwise would

---

[18] See, e.g., Zubik v. Burwell, Brief of 40 Catholic Theologians and Ethicists as Amici Curiae in support of Petitioners, January 11, 2016, http://www.scotusblog.com.

[19] See, e.g., Alasdair MacIntyre, *After Virtue*, 3rd ed. (Notre Dame, IN: University of Notre Dame Press, 2007), chap. 6.

be to claim that publicly refusing to do evil is cooperation with the evil fore-seeably done by others in one's stead. And this is madness. A bar owner who gives public notice of his refusal to serve underage patrons is not complicit in the foreseeable decision of the more lax proprietor next door to capture the underage business. A conscientious objector who notifies the army of his abhorrence of war is not complicit in the wrongdoing done by the soldier who takes his place.

Moreover, even if signing the form were viewed as some sort of cooper-ation with the wrongful use of contraception, this fact does not mean that it is morally impermissible. If indeed it should count as cooperation, it would fall into the category of (very) remote mediate material cooperation. This sort of cooperation, in the tradition, is justified by proportionate reason. Some instances of cooperation with evil are not only justifiable; they may also be morally required, in light of other obligations. So an engineer can rightly keep the utilities working at a hospital that performs abortions, in order to earn a salary and contribute to the good work done by the hospital.[20] A real weak-ness of the Little Sisters' position, therefore, is that they do not consider what might count as "proportionate reason" to comply with the accommodation.

This weakness, however, is not merely a flaw in its cooperation with evil analysis; it also evidences a myopic view of their moral obligations more generally. This is the second significant distortion in the Little Sisters' public presentation of the Catholic moral tradition. The church's prohibition of the use of contraception has assumed such looming proportions in the Little Sisters' imagination that it has deflected them from the task of considering what other obligations they may have that bear on the decision at hand.

The Little Sisters and their advocates maintain that the Sisters' connection to the provision of contraception creates "scandal," which is a technical term of moral theology and refers to an "attitude or behavior which leads another to do evil."[21] It is highly unlikely that signing a form protesting contraceptive coverage will lead people to believe that the Little Sisters endorse the use of contraception. Yet that does not mean that there is no risk of scandal in this situation, as other contributors to this volume have pointed out. By so empha-sizing their opposition to contraception, the Little Sisters risk occluding other aspects of Catholic Social Teaching, including the universal right to health care. As Pope Francis has pointed out, the church's obsession with abortion, same-sex marriage, and contraception may prove counterproductive. As he

---

[20] A helpful collection of examples from the tradition can be found in Anthony Fisher, OP, "Cooperation in Evil: Understanding the Issues," in *Cooperation, Complicity and Conscience: Problems in Healthcare, Science, Law and Public Policy*, ed. Helen Watt (London: Linacre Centre, 2005), 27–64, and Anthony Fisher, OP, "Co-Operation in Evil," *Catholic Medical Quarterly* 44, no. 2 (February 1994): 15–22.

[21] *Catechism of the Catholic Church*, para. 2284.

stated, "We have to find a new balance . . . otherwise even the moral edifice of the church is likely to fall like a house of cards, losing the freshness and fragrance of the Gospel."[22]

In addition, the Little Sisters and their advocates have failed to consider Catholic teaching on respect for the conscience of others. They do not consider what that teaching might require of them as citizens in a pluralistic society. Nor do they ponder what that teaching might require of them as employers who publicly welcome a diverse workforce.

They are not, however, fully to blame for this omission. Catholic teaching on conscience has nurtured deep roots (see, e.g., Saint Thomas Aquinas on the obligation to follow even an erring conscience)[23] and grown to lofty heights (see, e.g., *Dignitatis Humanae*).[24] Yet much hard, detailed work of discerning what precisely respect for conscience requires of different moral agents in different situations remains to be done.[25] I hope the next section of this essay contributes to the task.

Insufficient Respect for the Conscience of Others

In both religious and secular contexts, we often hear about the importance of respect for the conscience of others. But we do not hear as frequently about the precise requirements of such respect. In my view, these requirements turn on three key factors, the first of which is what precisely we mean by another's *conscience*. The term is very broad; we might well contend that conscience is best understood as a well-developed capacity for moral judgment and that respecting the conscience of others means providing education and equipping others to assess moral situations accurately and to make wise moral choices. In this context, however, we take a more narrow focus: the conscience of another person claiming our respect is his or her conscientious judgment that he or she must or may perform or refrain from performing a particular action.

The second factor focuses on an evaluation of the action in question: Is that action neutral, harmful to the agent, or wrongfully harmful to another party? Needless to say, the call for "respect" for the conscience of another arises most sharply where there is a difference of opinion about how to categorize a particular action. For example, many people who eat meat think it is a morally neutral activity, while others judge that it infringes on the legitimate

---

[22] Laurie Goodstein, "Pope Says Church is 'Obsessed' with Gays, Abortion and Birth Control," *New York Times*, September 20, 2013, A1.

[23] Thomas Aquinas, *Summa Theologica*, I-II, q. 19, art. 5.

[24] Vatican II, *Dignitatis Humanae* (Declaration on Religious Liberty) (1965).

[25] For a critical assessment of the state of the Catholic discussion of conscience, see James F. Keenan, SJ, "Redeeming Conscience," *Theological Studies* 76, no. 1 (March 2015): 129–47.

interests of animals. What does it mean, concretely, for a vegetarian to respect the conscience of a meat eater and vice versa?

Discerning a specific answer to that question in this case, and by extension, in other cases, requires an analysis of roles and relationships between the two parties. This is the third factor at issue in determining what, concretely, respect for the conscience of another—and respect for one's own conscience—requires in a particular case. A morally motivated vegetarian parent might not only make his or her point of view clear, but also flatly refuse to let a rebellious teenage son or daughter bring a pepperoni pizza into the house. In the parent-child relationship, "respect" is consistent with the expression of clear moral direction. A vegetarian seated next to a carnivorous friend might respectfully voice moral opposition—but not go so far as to turn his friend's steak plate upside down. For a vegetarian seated next to a hamburger-eating stranger at a mandatory employment training session, "respect" for that stranger might well mean saying nothing at all.

What does respect for conscience require in the case of Catholic employers of a pluralistic workforce, such as the Little Sisters, a Catholic hospital system, or a Catholic university with respect to the contraception mandate? I would like to suggest that we might make progress in this matter if we focus on two roles such organizations play: the role of employers with respect to the life choices of their employees, and the role of institutional citizens toward the life choices of fellow citizens in a pluralistic society.

Employers and Employees

What is the relationship between an employer and the life choices of an employee? In some cases, of course, an employer has a great deal of legitimate interest in those choices, because it affects corporate identity and integrity. A detox facility may rightly refuse to employ a counselor who regularly uses marijuana, even if it is legal to do so. And an institution that presents itself as pervasively Catholic may not wish to hire anyone whose life undermines the message in any way. Such institutions can and do enter into contractual arrangements with their employees that specify the required and prohibited behavior. But the basis of the regulation is not that the employer is not obliged to respect the employee's moral choices, but rather that the employee's choices directly impinge on the corporate identity of the employer.

In most cases, however, the lifestyle of employees does not directly affect the identity of the employer. Moreover, employers who hold themselves out as welcoming a diverse workforce in a pluralistic society create a set of legitimate expectations in their employees. Such employers are expected to create room for different reasonable conscientious judgments about moral issues as well as religious belief, particularly when those moral issues affect the employee's actions outside the workplace. The leadership of the employer may well see those judgments as morally wrong. But respect for the moral agency of employees requires that the employer leave them a certain range of freedom of action.

Specifically, I am saying that what *respect* for conscience requires in the context of the employer-employee relationship is shaped by the nature of that relationship. An employer is not the parent of an employee and is not responsible for shaping the employee's moral character. The employer is not the friend of an employee and is not responsible for calling the employee to account to shared values. An employee and an employer participate in a mutually beneficial exchange: the employee renders services, for which he or she receives compensation. This is not to say that an employer cannot introduce the employee to its own values in a noncoercive manner. But the means used must be harmonious with the basic nature of the employer-employee relationship.

It is particularly problematic, I think, when an employer places restrictions on the use of compensation earned by the employee. And it is important to remember that both salary and benefits are compensation for services rendered—nothing received by an employee as part of a compensation package is rightly construed as a "gift." One of the reasons that the "paid in scrip for use at the company store" model was problematic had to do with the fact that it gave control over the employee's choices. And many employees were not in a position to bargain for more control over their own lives, because they needed a job. So in my view, an employer who furnishes its employees with drugstore discount cards ought not to place restrictions on the items that can be purchased with it—whether potato chips or condoms. Such restrictions are no more appropriate than employer restrictions on the employee's use of his or her salary.

What about a health care benefit package? Health care coverage is often called a benefit, but the truth is that it is a part of an employee's compensation package. In fact, employer-based health care coverage became increasingly generous over the years because it was advantageous both to employees and to employers; the amount is not considered part of either party's taxable income. But it is a very special type of compensation, in two ways: first, it touches not only on an employee's life outside the office, but on his or her whole identity as an embodied person. Second, health care packages touch on an employee's (and his or her family's) identity as members of the whole community. The contents of mandated benefit packages are not arbitrary; instead, they reflect prudential judgments about what is conducive to the health and flourishing of the whole population. Indeed, the basic justification for not taxing health benefits, like the basic justification for not taxing charitable corporations, is the way in which these activities further the common good, by supporting the health status of individuals and families who make up the community.

It seems to me, therefore, that for employers to respect the consciences of employees requires them to provide a standard benefit package that has received widespread scrutiny and approval. As I noted above, employers are not their employees' parents; nor are they their employees' friends. They are not responsible for harmonizing the physical health and moral virtue of employees and their family members. Respecting the conscientious judgments of employees about health care requires them to stand back from the particular judgments that are made in that context. So it is inappropriate for an employer to refuse to cover, say, HPV virus vaccination, because they believe it encourages sexual promiscuity among teenagers. In my view, it is also inappropriate for most employers to refuse to cover contraception for married or unmarried women—or for religious employers to stand in the way of such coverage. In refusing the accommodation offered them by the Obama administration, the Little Sisters of the Poor fail to give due respect to the consciences of their employees.

Institutional Citizens

In deciding what counts as respect for the consciences of others, the Little Sisters of the Poor need to consider a second set of role-related obligations, which pertain to their identity as an institutional citizen in a pluralistic constitutional democracy. The general issue is when *should* we claim for ourselves —and when *should* we grant to others—exemptions from the generally applicable laws. We tend to think of these issues as matters of judicial adjudication. In the first place, however, they belong to the legislative process. Consequently, they are matters for the virtue of political prudence.

Can we find any overarching concepts to guide the application of political prudence in this case? In my view, we can by mining different aspects of the discussion that took place a generation ago. To be sure, we must be mindful of the different context. John Rawls's idea of "public reason" was meant to channel discussions of the appropriate content of generally applicable laws. It is not particularly helpful in considering the question of conscientious objection to generally applicable laws. Similarly, Mario Cuomo's guiding principle of sufficient consensus, developed most fully in his 1984 speech at the University of Notre Dame, was meant to determine whether there was justification for generally prohibiting practices such as abortion; it offered no help in deciding how to treat those who morally object to such practices in a context in which abortion is already legal. Yet in the thought of both men we find some ideas that can help us address questions today. These ideas are "civic respect" (from Rawls) and the Golden Rule (from Cuomo's speech, found in many religious traditions).

John Rawls maintained that the requirements of public reason are not an end in themselves; their point is to facilitate civic friendship. He writes, "Among individuals with disparate aims and purposes a shared conception of justice establishes the bonds of civic friendship."[26] In Rawls's view, a key element of civic friendship is giving people reasons for restricting their freedom that they not only *understand* but that we can also reasonably expect that they as free and equal persons might reasonably also *accept*. In Cuomo's speech, an important role is played by the Golden Rule: He writes: "I protect my right to be a Catholic by preserving your right to believe as a Jew, a Protestant or non-believer, or as anything else you choose. . . . We know that the price of seeking to force our beliefs on others is that they might someday force theirs on us."[27]

I think that the idea of civic friendship and the ideals of the Golden Rule generate two overarching principles that stand in tension with each other. First, the rule of law is a public good—and perhaps the fundamental public good. Public order depends on a stable, public, reliable interpretation of the law. Each person cannot be the interpreter of the law or the judge of the law in his or her own case. It cannot be comprehensively, privately, reinterpreted without causing chaos. Civic friendship in a pluralistic liberal democracy requires that we commit ourselves to respect for the rule of law, and to calling on our elected officials to maintain it. Consequently, we do not allow animal rights activists who believe that animals are persons whose rights are violated by animal testing to shoot and kill those doing the testing—despite the fact that it is a matter of conscience. We do not allow police officers to make judgments about which crimes to pursue and which lawbreakers to arrest based on their own moral views. This may also be understood as a matter of the Golden Rule. No one in a pluralistic society wants to be subjected to another's idiosyncratic interpretation of the law.

At the same time, there is a countervailing principle to which we hold in pluralistic liberal democracy. Each person is in a radical sense responsible for his or her own actions. No moral agent can totally escape personal responsibility by saying either it was legally permitted or it was legally required. Role-related responsibilities shape personal responsibility but do not swallow it up. The demands of conscience cannot be reducible to the decision to follow the rules of a clan, government, or religion. Our consciences may ask us to call these rules into question—and under some circumstances resist their force. The Golden Rule requires us to recognize the same may be true of other persons as well. Moreover, a long view of civic friendship,

---

[26] John Rawls, *A Theory of Justice* (Cambridge, MA: Harvard University Press, 1971), 5.

[27] Cuomo, "Religious Belief and Public Morality."

which contemplates the need for moral correction and renewal of our political community over time, will make room for citizens to challenge the status quo. We have learned that "I was just following the law" or "I was just following orders" cannot be a complete defense to the commission of atrocities such as in Auschwitz and My Lai. Accommodating the conscientious judgments of those who object to generally applicable law is one way to incorporate a spirit of self-criticism in the process of making law.

Some might say that civic friendship requires almost absolute deference to conscientious decision-making. Yet this cannot be the case—not only because of the need to protect the rule of law, but also because of a nonbinary interpretation of the Golden Rule. In deciding which conscientious objections to accommodate, we need to consider the perspectives of everyone affected by the proposed accommodation—not merely the objector's perspective.

What, concretely, do the ideas of the Golden Rule and civic friendship suggest for the case of the Little Sisters of the Poor? Together, they point to two distinctions that the Little Sisters would have done well to keep in mind before bringing their case. First, there is a distinction between laws which require agents themselves to commit what they believe to be wrongdoing, and laws which require them to be somehow connected to the wrongful acts of other persons. The Golden Rule suggests that the first sort of law is problematic: I do not wish to be forced to perform actions that violate my moral judgment; therefore I should not force others to do the same. But civic friendship in a highly interdependent contemporary pluralistic society means that we will all be contributing to the activities of one another, even activities that we believe are wrongheaded and immoral. Consequently, the law should be more sensitive to accommodate persons who believe they are involved in direct wrongdoing than those who think they are complicit in the wrongdoing of others.

The second distinction is between wrongful activity that harms the agent himself or herself and wrongful activity that harms third parties. As a moral agent in a pluralistic society, I want wide latitude to decide for myself what counts as harmful to me, physically, morally, and spiritually. The Golden Rule suggests that I should give the same latitude to others that I claim for myself. At the same time, civic friendship suggests that we accommodate to the extent we can the objections of persons who believe a law is requiring them to harm another person, particularly a third party. Consequently, the law should be more solicitous of conscientious objection to abortion or euthanasia than contraception or sterilization.[28]

---

[28] There are claims that some contraceptives prevent implantation rather than fertilization, thereby causing a very early abortion. How should such claims be treated? In my view, the answer depends on the best available medical evidence, which now suggests that neither Ella nor Plan B function as abortifacients. See NPR, "Morning-After Pills Don't Cause Abortion, Studies Say," February 22, 2013, http://www.npr.org.

But the Little Sisters of the Poor are protesting an action—the use of contraception—that, even in their view, inflicts direct harm only on those engaged in the act. Furthermore, they are not facing a law that requires their direct involvement in contraception, but only highly remote connection with it. Consequently, in my view, their protests do not accord with the requirements of civic friendship and the Golden Rule.

The Little Sisters of the Poor may well achieve their legal objective in their lawsuit against the Obama administration. Yet the cost that they will pay is substantial, even if their lawyers are working for free. The adversarial nature of the legal process has pressed them to understand both their own obligations and those of the government in a sharp, binary manner. The exigencies of litigation have required them to distort Roman Catholic moral teaching on cooperation with evil and scandal. And the impetus to defend their own rights of conscience has prevented them from helping all of us to discern what sorts of conscience protection are appropriate for everyone in an interdependent and pluralistic constitutional democracy.

ACLU v. CATHOLIC HEALTH CARE

An Inquiry into Disputes over Previability Pregnancy Termination

Lawrence J. Nelson

The American Civil Liberties Union (ACLU) recently pursued at least two major lawsuits that challenge the legal legitimacy of the policy of Catholic health care to not allow direct abortion in its facilities. By "Catholic health care" (CHC) I mean hospitals or other licensed health care facilities as well as systems of health care facilities that are owned and/or operated by entities who identify themselves as Catholic and as a result follow the *Ethical and Religious Directives for Catholic Health Care Services* (the Directives) issued by the United States Conference of Catholic Bishops (USCCB).[1] These lawsuits are related to other contentious litigation over individuals and corporations refusing to provide a heath-related service or product on the grounds that doing so violates their ethical and religious beliefs.[2]

The most provocative suit is *Means v. United States Conference of Catholic Bishops, et al.*,[3] in which the ACLU served as lawyers for a woman claiming the USCCB and other individuals[4] harmed her by being negligent "for promulgating and implementing directives that cause pregnant women who are suffering from a miscarriage to be denied appropriate medical care, including information about their condition and treatment options."[5] The federal judge in this case dismissed the suit because the court lacked personal jurisdiction over

---

[1] The USCCB and the Directives themselves are thus part of Catholic health care for the purposes of this chapter. United States Conference of Catholic Bishops, *Ethical and Religious Directives for Catholic Health Care Services* (Washington, DC: USCCB, 2010).

[2] E.g., Burwell v. Hobby Lobby, 134 S. Ct. 2751 (2014); Zubik v. Burwell, No. 14-1418, US Supreme Court 2016 (consolidating 7 cases challenging the ACA contraceptive mandate bypass provision).

[3] 2015 US Dist. LEXIS 84302 (West. Dist. Mich. 2015); on appeal, Case. No. 15-1779, US Court of Appeals for the Sixth Circuit.

[4] They are three persons associated with the canonical sponsor of the Trinity Health system.

[5] Complaint, Means v. USCCB, et al., No. 1:15-CV-353 (West. Dist. Mich. 2013), 2. Available at https://www.aclu.org.

USCCB and because Michigan law does not recognize a duty to a patient by a sponsor of a hospital system. The federal circuit court has affirmed the district court's decision.

Some two years after filing the suit on behalf of Ms. Tamesha Means, the ACLU itself, on behalf of its members, sued Trinity Health Corporation,[6] which owns and operates eighty-six health care facilities (including the one that treated Ms. Means), claiming that its policy and practice of denying appropriate emergency care to women who suffer from complications of pregnancy (such as miscarriages and ectopic pregnancies) violates both the federal Emergency Medical Treatment and Active Labor Act (EMTALA) and the Rehabilitation Act.[7] This litigation targets the defendants' alleged refusal to provide an abortion to women who experience complications of pregnancy prior to fetal viability when the standard of care may include or possibly require termination to preserve the woman's life or health.

This chapter will offer a survey of the possible merits and demerits of the positions and concerns of both the ACLU and CHC reflected in these disputes over the medical management of pregnancy, rather than any kind of evalua-tion of the legal validity of the allegations, arguments, or evidence on either side. I am more interested in attempting to point out some misunderstandings, misconceptions, or questionable assumptions on both sides and to offer some suggestions of what the ACLU might better learn and appreciate about CHC and of what CHC might take to heart about the problems the ACLU has with the way it serves the general public. In doing this, I should disclose that I sympathize with some of the positions and concerns advanced by both sides. Neither CHC nor the ACLU deserves to be vilified for their views.

In the first section I offer some comments about the views of both the ACLU and CHC on key issues in the controversy over reproductive services that should provide some background context and atmosphere to the main points of contention between them, and in the second section I present an analysis of the ACLU's two lawsuits about the provision of abortion services and the crucial issues they raise. This section includes an introductory assess-ment, both positive and negative, of the views of both sides. Some concluding commentary follows that section.

This one brief chapter cannot possibly address, much less resolve, the many different legal, ethical, religious, and public policy elements raised

---

[6] ACLU v. Trinity Health Corporation and Trinity Health-Michigan, Complaint, No. 15-cv-12611 (East. Dist. Mich. 2015). Available at https://www.aclu.org.

[7] EMTALA, 42 USC §1395dd (2016), requires hospitals to provide "immediate medical attention" as required to stabilize a patient's condition. ACLU claims such medical attention sometimes includes abortion. The Rehabilitation Act, 29 USC §794 (2016), prohibits recipients of federal funds from denying benefits to the disabled. ACLU claims that certain pregnancy complications constitute a disability and that denying treatment for them violates this statute.

by the ACLU lawsuits, especially including the constitutional scope of CHC's free exercise of religion. It does not assume that all Catholic hospitals and staff behave in precisely the same way. It also cannot consider whether some Catholic moral theologians might interpret Catholic doctrine or the Directives differently than is described below. It can, perhaps, identify some of the central issues that must be faced and resolved at some point if CHC can continue to retain its value identity and function fairly and reasonably in a nation full of patients and other citizens who do not share its beliefs and values.

Background

In 2002, the ACLU Reproductive Freedom Project issued a report about reproduction and religious objections to providing certain services. In it the ACLU states that it proceeds "from a long-held position of profound respect for both reproductive right and religious liberty."[8] Unfortunately, this starting point can be contradicted by its own rhetoric. One ACLU lawyer entitled a blog entry critical of a Catholic hospital's refusal to allow a patient to undergo a tubal ligation "How 'Evil' is Getting Your Tubes Tied, Really?"[9] This sarcastic rhetorical question seems to mock the Catholic position on sterilization apparently because it is not widely shared or seems silly. Mockery does not betoken respect.

Another ACLU lawyer commented on this same case: "Patients seeking medical care from public institutions should not have to worry that religious doctrine rather than medical judgment will dictate what care they receive."[10] Although the ACLU has a reasonable concern about what public accommodation laws require of all hospitals, including CHC, it should not use the term "public institution" to describe Catholic hospitals as they are not the same as truly public hospitals like San Francisco General Hospital. Catholic hospitals are seeking to "embody our Savior's concern for the sick. . . . The mystery of Christ casts light on every facet of Catholic health care: to see Christian love as the animating principle of health care; to see healing and compassion as a continuation of Christ's mission."[11]

These religious beliefs truly matter to those individuals who operate Catholic hospitals and to some, perhaps many, who work within them. They

---

[8] ACLU Reproductive Freedom Project, "Religious Refusals and Reproductive Rights," 2002, Preface. Available at https://www.aclu.org.

[9] Ruth Dawson, "How 'Evil' Is Getting Your Tubes Tied, Really?" January 20, 2016. Available at https://www.aclunc.org.

[10] Elizabeth Gill, "Hospital Refuses Pregnancy-Related Care Again Because of Religious Directives," December 29, 2015. Available at https://www.aclu.org.

[11] US Conference of Catholic Bishops, *Ethical and Religious Directives for Catholic Health Care Services*, 5th ed., 2009, 6. Available at http://www.usccb.org.

adhere to core values that are very different from those held by people who operate hospitals owned by the public and (perhaps especially) those who run hospitals in order to make private profit. Clearly the ACLU and many other individuals and organizations do not share these beliefs and values, but this does not somehow invalidate those of the Catholics.

The ACLU frequently employs other language in a seeming effort to convince the public that Catholic hospitals are no different from those that are publicly operated and that these hospitals cannot have any religious character.[12] The ACLU often mentions that Catholic hospitals "receive billions of taxpayer dollars each year . . . [e]ven as [they] impose religious restrictions on the services they provide."[13] However, Congress has enacted laws which state that receipt of federal funds cannot serve as the basis for requiring objecting individuals or institutions to perform abortions or sterilizations.[14] The fact that Catholic hospitals receive Medicare and Medicaid reimbursement for services provided to those beneficiaries (like *every other* hospital in the United States) does not mean that their religious character is somehow inappropriate or illegal. Many secular and religious entities receive government money for services that they provide directly to the government or beneficiaries, but this fact by itself has no necessary implications for their legal right, whether under the Constitution or a statute, to adhere to their particular core religious values and moral commitments.

Finally, the fairness of the ACLU's criticism of CHC over reproductive matters can be questioned. A title to another ACLU blog seems to claim that CHC is literally toxic to pregnant women: "Pregnant? Avoid Alcohol, Caffeine, and Catholic Hospitals."[15] While the merits of the ACLU's opposition to the way the Directives are being applied to the treatment of women who are suffering from certain complications of pregnancy will be discussed below (fairly, I hope), its suggestion that Catholic hospitals can do nothing but harm them and their unborn is unfair and inflammatory.

Likewise, the ACLU seems to have been unfair to CHC in at least one instance when it discussed the latter's service to the poor. In its report "Miscarriage of Medicine," the ACLU states that "Catholic hospitals often

---

[12] Elizabeth Gill and Physicians for Reproductive Health, "Can Government-Funded Hospitals Serving the Public Invoke Religious Directives to Deny Basic Healthcare to Women?" January 25, 2016. Available at https://www.aclunc.org; Dawson, "How Evil."

[13] ACLU and Mergerwatch, "Miscarriage of Medicine: The Growth of Catholic Hospitals and the Threat to Reproductive Health Care," December 2013, 10. Available at https://www.aclu.org.

[14] William Galston and Melissa Rogers, "Health Care Providers' Consciences and Patients' Needs: The Quest for Balance," *Governance Studies at Brookings*, February 23, 1012, 17–20. Available at http://www.brookings.edu.

[15] Brigitte Amiri, "Pregnant? Avoid Alcohol, Caffeine, and Catholic Hospitals," December 8, 2014. Available at https://www.aclu.org.

counter criticisms of their reproductive health restrictions by emphasizing their mission of serving the poor and providing charity care."[16] In support of this assertion, it offers one reference to the promotional materials of one Catholic hospital that "boast[s] of having provided more than $612 million in charity care and community benefits during fiscal 2011."[17] But the "boast" as cited does not offer this sum as a "counter" to criticism, nor can one instance of a "boast" unconnected to reproductive matters justify the assertion that Catholic facilities "often" use their charity care to "counter" criticism. Nowhere in this section of the report (titled "Debunking the Myth: Catholic-Sponsored and -Affiliated Hospitals and Service to the Poor") does the ACLU provide any other evidence of a Catholic hospital using its charity care to offset unfavorable judgments of its practices. Furthermore, the report offers no evidence in support of its assertion that "some" Catholic hospitals claim that they provide more charity care than other types of hospitals.[18]

The ACLU's criticism also reflects its apparent lack of awareness of the millennia-long commitment and practice of Catholicism to provide for the poor. Health care institutions connected to this faith do not provide care to the poor for public relations purposes, but to fulfill a value at the heart of their Gospel and tradition. Pope Francis articulated this view when he observed: "We may not always be able to reflect adequately the beauty of the Gospel, but there is one sign which we should never lack: the option for those who are least, those whom society discards."[19]

On the other side of the controversy, some physicians have reported their personal experiences with pregnant women (often with previable premature rupture of membranes) who have been denied needed medical treatment at Catholic hospitals due to the Directives' ban on direct abortion and who have suffered as a result.[20] A study of obstetrician-gynecologists also described a number of similar reports and concluded: "The case histories . . . indicate that, in some Catholic-owned hospitals, . . . patient safety and patient comfort are compromised by religious mandates that require physicians to act contrary to the current standard of care in miscarriage management."[21] One could reasonably infer from these reports that some participants in CHC (though it

---

[16] ACLU, "Miscarriage of Medicine," 12.

[17] Ibid., n. 44.

[18] Ibid., 12. None of this is to say that the ACLU has made these claims out of whole cloth, only to note the lack of supporting evidence for them.

[19] Pope Francis, *Evangelii Gaudium*, 195.

[20] ACLU, "Health Care Denied: Patients and Physicians Speak Out about Catholic Hospitals and the Threat to Women's Health and Lives," May 2016, 11–13. Available at https://www.aclu.org. It should be noted that the ACLU acknowledges that it took these "physicians at their word" and did not investigate their stories. Ibid., n. 2.

[21] Lori Freedman et al., "When There's a Heartbeat: Miscarriage Management in Catholic-Owned Hospitals," *American Journal of Public Health* 98, no. 10 (2008): 1774, 1778.

is very unclear how numerous they are) express their conscientious objection without sufficient regard for the impact on the patient or what the standard of care legitimately requires of every clinician. This position is in sharp contrast with the ACLU's view: "Patients of all faiths and no faith need reproductive health care. Health professionals of all faiths and no faith *must* make decisions about how to *balance* their personal convictions with their professional obligations to their patients."[22] Nevertheless, several federal laws as well as statutes in over forty states broadly sanction conscientious refusal to provide abortion-related services.[23]

The USCCB supports the Conscience Protection Act of 2016 (CPA) which would grant CHC (and others) legal immunity to refuse to participate in abortion.[24] Specifically, the CPA would prohibit the federal government and any state that receives health-related federal funds from penalizing any provider who does not "perform, refer for, pay for, or otherwise participate in abortion." More important, it provides any person or entity affected by a violation to take legal action to redress the violation. Under current law, the federal statutory provider conscience protections are enforceable only by the federal government itself.[25] As the CPA contains no exceptions, it would permit CHC to refuse to provide an abortion or refer a patient for abortion even if the woman's life or health were thereby endangered.

Strict opposition to providing a service that a sick patient may need and to referring a patient elsewhere for the service is troubling to many. Sources of this trouble can be the concept that professionalism in medicine means putting patients' welfare and interests before one's own. One commentator has argued that professionals should "avoid exploiting their positions to pursue an agenda separate from their profession," and professionals have a collective duty to ensure that their profession "provides nondiscriminatory access to all professional services."[26]

Another critical question is how CHC's objections comport with existing applicable laws and, more generally, with the rule of law itself, that is, the concept that everyone must comply with neutral (nonbiased) and universally applicable laws designed to ensure the public's health, welfare, or safety. The ACLU claims that existing law requires that all providers perform certain

---

[22] ACLU, "Religious Refusals," preface (emphasis added).

[23] Thaddeus Pope, "Legal Briefing: Conscience Clauses and Conscientious Refusal," *Journal of Clinical Ethics* 21, no. 2 (2010): 163–65.

[24] Archbishop Lori and Cardinal Dolan on behalf of the USCCB, letter to members of the House of Representatives, March 31, 2016. Available at http://www.usccb.org.

[25] USCCB Secretariat of Pro-Life Activities, "Why We Need the Health Care Conscience Rights Act," September 8, 2015. Available at http://www.usccb.org.

[26] Alto Charo, "The Celestial Fire of Conscience—Refusing to Deliver Medical Care," *New England Journal of Medicine* 352, no. 24 (2005): 2471, 2473.

medical interventions or information to pregnant women in some clinical situations and that the First Amendment's guarantee of free exercise does not forbid enforcement of these laws. The USCCB denies that these laws require provision of these interventions, asserts that conscience protection laws exempt them, and holds that free exercise forbids their enforcement.

What is at stake, then, is how CHC, with its particular religious beliefs, can operate within law that does not disfavor religion and that is generally applicable.

> Conscientious scruples have not, in the course of the long struggle for religious toleration, relieved the individual from obedience to a general law not aimed at the promotion or restriction of religious beliefs. The mere possession of religious convictions which contradict the relevant concerns of a political society does not relieve the citizen from the discharge of political responsibilities.[27]

Put differently, may CHC act upon its particular beliefs and values and remain within the nation's rule of law? As the opinion in *Reynolds v. United States* asks, "Can a man excuse his practices [contrary to the law] because of his religious belief? To permit this would be to make the professed doctrines of religious belief superior to the law of the land, and in effect to permit every citizen to become a law unto himself. Government [and the rule of law] could exist only in name under such circumstances."[28] The USCCB can be understood to deny the tension between religious practice and the legitimate reach of the rule of law that must govern evenhandedly. For example, the USCCB denies any conflict with EMTALA (Emergency Medical Treatment and Active Labor Act): "[EMTALA] does not require that *abortion* be the stabilizing treatment [required by that law] in any case" and "EMTALA requires care for the pregnant woman and her unborn child, without second-guessing . . . providers' judgments as to what treatment is most appropriate."[29]

Some in CHC perceive no conflict between their facilities providing high quality care to patients and the Directives. The USCCB notes that although Catholic facilities "are guided by an ethical code forbidding *all* direct abortion . . . , data show that they provide the finest and most effective medical care in the country."[30] In response to the ACLU's suit, Trinity Health declared "The

---

[27] Employment Division v. Smith, 494 US 872, 878–79 (1990) (internal quotation marks and citations omitted).

[28] Reynolds v. United States, 98 US 145, 166–67 (1879).

[29] USCCB Secretariat of Pro-Life Activities, "Conscience Protection on Abortion: No Threat to Life," March 31, 2016. Available at http://www.usccb.org.

[30] Ibid.

. . . Directives are entirely consistent with high-quality health care."[31] The plausibility of these claims will be explored below.

Finally, the "conscience without consequences"[32] question can be addressed to CHC: Are you seeking to exercise your conscience without regard for the consequences of your actions on your patients, especially those who do not share your religious beliefs, and on the larger community's commitment to the rule of law? The discussion below indicates that CHC should not be able to answer this with an unqualified "no."

Termination of Pregnancy:
Means v. USCCB and *ACLU v. Trinity Health*

The main question the ACLU raises in both *Means* and *Trinity Health* is whether the application of the Directives can result in medical management of pregnant women that violates the accepted standard of care. "Standard of care" is predominantly a legal term that identifies the conduct of a "reasonable and prudent physician [or other provider], whose conduct is then described by the profession [or other provider group] itself."[33] "This objective tort standard does at least require physicians [or other providers] to deliver a basically uniform minimum standard (quality) of care."[34] The standard of care can also be thought of, in the health care context, as treatment that is "medically necessary" or "medically indicated" to preserve the patient's life or health.

A malpractice lawsuit for damages would be successful, then, if the plaintiff could prove by a preponderance of the evidence that the physician or provider failed to provide the requisite quality of care and the patient suffered harm as a result. Typically, expert witnesses are needed to identify the standard of care, and they do so by referring to relevant peer-reviewed publications, statements by professional organizations that articulate the standard, and other authoritative sources of proper practice. These ACLU lawsuits are claiming that application of the Directives can result in a refusal to provide a standard of care service, including disclosure of information, that may be fairly characterized as bad medical practice.

I will provide a somewhat detailed account of what allegedly happened to Ms. Means so that we have a case with particular facts and circumstances to consider. After all, pregnancy only happens to individual women with an individual story.

---

[31] Steve Ertelt, "ACLU Files Lawsuit to Force Catholic Hospital Network to Do Abortions," December 18, 2015. Available at http://www.lifenews.com.

[32] Charo, "Celestial Fire," 2471.

[33] Haavi Morreim, "Stratified Scarcity: Redefining the Standard of Care," *Law, Medicine and Health Care* 17, no. 4 (1989): 356, 357.

[34] Ibid.

According to the complaint filed by Ms. Means's ACLU lawyers,[35] the following describes the basic facts of her interactions with Mercy Health Partners hospital (MHP) in Michigan in 2010. Means sought emergency care at MHP on December 1 because she was experiencing contractions. MHP performed an ultrasound which showed that she was at 18 weeks of gestation, that her fetus had a heartbeat, and that she had a low amniotic fluid index. MHP diagnosed[36] her with preterm premature rupture of membrane (PROM) and informed her that her fetus was not yet viable.

The patient was given pain medication and told to return eight days later for her regularly scheduled prenatal visit. She returned home under the impression that there was a chance her fetus could become viable and she could continue her pregnancy. In fact her condition usually results in fetal death either in utero or shortly after birth.

Ms. Means returned to MHP in the early morning of the following day with symptoms of pain (10 on a 10-point scale), bleeding, and a temperature of 100.4.[37] The attending physicians suspected she had chorioamnionitis, a bacterial infection affecting the fetal membranes and amniotic fluid. After her fever reduced, she was again sent home and advised to return if her fever rose or her contractions became unbearably painful.

Ms. Means returned to MHP later that same day with regular contractions and severe pain. While MHP was in the process of discharging her again, she began to deliver spontaneously and underwent a breech birth. Her baby died a few hours later. The placental pathology report indicated that Ms. Means had acute chorioamnionitis and acute funisitis (inflammation of the umbilical cord) at the time of birth. On none of these visits did MHP inform her of the serious risks to her health if she continued the pregnancy, of the hospital's policy forbidding termination on its premises, of the extremely low likelihood that the fetus could survive, or of the option of terminating her pregnancy at a different hospital. Her complaint alleges that if she had known all of this, she would have terminated her pregnancy.

The patient claimed that the standard of medical care required MHP to disclose all of this and to "provide appropriate medical care" to her. MHP did none of this "because it was a Catholic hospital that adheres to Defendant USCCB's Directives." Her lawsuit lays blame on the USCCB and other

---

[35] These facts will be taken as true here, for purposes of argument only, as they were by the federal District Court, although they may or may not actually be so.

[36] A hospital cannot diagnose any patient; generally only licensed physicians may. I am assuming that a physician employed by or on the medical staff of MHP actually made the diagnosis described here.

[37] This temperature is considered abnormal in pregnancy. A. Nita et al., "Diagnosis and Management of Clinical Chorioamnionitis," *Clinical Perinatology* 37, no. 2 (2010): 339, 341.

defendants for imposing the Directives on MHP and all clinicians who work there. She alleged that the negligence of the USCCB in imposing the Directives on MHP resulted in her enduring severe pain, mental pain and anguish, and a riskier and more painful breech delivery and asked the court to award her compensatory and punitive damages. Allegedly the MHP Vice President of Mission Services admitted to a third party that MHP's decision not to induce labor was proper because the Directives prohibited induction in this situation.[38]

Did MHP comply with the proper standard of care? The patient was suffering (literally) from chorioamnionitis and preterm PROM, conditions typically "followed by the prompt onset of spontaneous labor and delivery."[39] With the cusp of fetal viability apparently being 22 weeks of gestation,[40] the patient's child had no chance of survival. The medical literature demonstrates that PROM does pose risks to the woman.

> Significant maternal complications that occur after previable PROM include intraamniotic infection, endometritis [inflammation of the living tissues of the uterus], abruptio placentae [premature separation of the placenta from the uterus], and retained placenta. Although it occurs infrequently, life-threatening maternal infection may complicate management. . . . Maternal sepsis is reported in approximately 1 percent of cases, and isolated maternal deaths due to infection have been reported.[41]

Another article also lists wound infection, pelvic abscess, bacteremia, and postpartum hemorrhage as maternal complications of chorioamnionitis and notes that "fortunately . . . septic shock, disseminated intravascular coagulation [abnormal blood clots inside blood vessels which can lead to massive internal bleeding], adult respiratory distress syndrome [fluid collects in the lungs making it difficult or impossible to breathe], and maternal death are only rarely encountered."[42]

---

[38] The hospital itself could not terminate the patient's pregnancy by inducing labor; only a physician could. I am assuming both that the attending physician chose not to offer termination and chose not to disclose the information in question and that the hospital would not allow the termination or the disclosure as a result of the Directives.

[39] Practice Bulletin of the American College of Obstetricians and Gynecologists, "Premature Rupture of Membranes," no. 160, interim update, January 2016, 1.

[40] Matthew Rysavy et al., "Between-Hospital Variation in Treatment and Outcomes in Extremely Preterm Infants," *New England Journal of Medicine* 372, no. 19 (2015): 1801, 1802. ("Active intervention for infants born before 22 weeks of gestation is not generally recommended"); Hugh MacDonald and the Committee on Fetus and Newborn, "Perinatal Care at the Threshold of Viability," *Pediatrics* 110, no. 5 (2002): 1024 (no mention of survival before 23 weeks).

[41] ACOG Practice Bulletin 160, 2 (internal reference omitted).

[42] Nita, "Clinical Chorioamnionitis," 6.

The long-term consequences of the listed complications "can include infertility, recurrent miscarriage . . . , pelvic pain, dysmenorrhea, mental health conditions, and even death."[43] In short, the patient's medical conditions are associated with "serious maternal health risks,"[44] or as put by other commentators, "Preterm PROM before fetal viability . . . carries significant maternal morbidity."[45]

On her second visit to MHP, the attending physicians thought Ms. Means had chorioamnionitis, a condition that is among the "indications for delivery," and bleeding which "should raise concern for abruptio placentae and also should prompt consideration of delivery."[46] The ACLU complaint contends that on none of her visits did MHP or her physicians inform her that inducing delivery was a medically indicated option for her condition, that she faced serious risks if she continued her pregnancy, that MHP would not deliver her due to its adherence to the Directives but another hospital could, or of the extremely low likelihood that the fetus would survive given her condition. However, according to ACOG (the American Congress of Obstetricians and Gynecologists), the standard of care required these disclosures: "Women presenting with PROM before neonatal viability *should be counseled* regarding the risks and benefits of expectant management versus immediate delivery. Counseling *should include* a realistic appraisal of neonatal outcomes. *Immediate delivery should be offered.*"[47]

A consensus document of ACOG and the Society for Maternal-Fetal Medicine concurs that such disclosure must be made even when providers "have objections to discussing or providing [termination]."[48]

However, it appears that MHP would not offer "immediate delivery" because doing so would constitute a prohibited direct abortion. Directive 45 states that "abortion (that is, the directly intended termination of pregnancy before viability . . .) is never permitted."[49] Effecting delivery of a woman with preterm PROM like Ms. Means can reasonably be interpreted as a "directly intended termination of pregnancy," albeit for reasons of protecting the woman's health when her fetus cannot survive in any event. But the facts that

---

[43] Means v. USCCB et al., Brief of *Amici Curiae* Obstetricians-Gynecologists in Support of Plaintiff-Appellant and Reversal, Case. No. 15-1779, US Court of Appeals for the Sixth Circuit, 8.

[44] Ibid., 8–9.

[45] Thaddeus Waters and Brian Mercer, "The Management of Preterm Premature Rupture of the Membranes Near the Limit of Fetal Viability," *American Journal of Obstetrics and Gynecology* 201, no. 3 (2009): 230, 237.

[46] ACOG Practice Bulletin 160, 3.

[47] Ibid., 7 (emphasis added).

[48] ACOG/SMFM Obstetric Care Consensus, "Periviable Birth," *American Journal of Obstetrics and Gynecology* 213, no. 5 (2015): 608.

[49] USCCB, Directives, no. 45.

termination in this situation may avoid risks to her life or health and that her fetus has no prospect of surviving outside the womb appear not to have decisive moral relevance to the USCCB: "One may never directly kill an innocent human being, *no matter what the reason*."[50]

The Directives permit medical interventions that will result in the death of the fetus under certain circumstances: "Operations, treatments, and medications that have as their direct purpose the cure of a proportionately serious pathological condition of a pregnant woman are permitted when they cannot be safely postponed until the unborn child is viable, even if they will result in the death of the unborn child."[51] An example of a medical intervention permitted by Directive 47 is surgery to remove a pregnant woman's cancerous uterus. This surgery "*directly* addresses the health problem of the woman, i.e., the organ that is malfunctioning. . . . The surgery does not directly target the life of the unborn child."[52] It appears that MHP interpreted the Directives to forbid both delivering the patient as that would be a direct abortion and referring her to another hospital for delivery or informing her of this as an option because this would be illicit "material cooperation" in a direct abortion which is impermissible under Directive 45 even if the termination is performed by a third party.

In sum, if the assessment of the standard of care for medical management of a woman with preterm PROM offered above is reasonable and MHP is to conform to it, then it follows that it at least had the obligation to fully inform her that delivery/termination of her pregnancy was a medically recognized option, that she faced risks if she did not end her pregnancy, and that other hospitals could perform the delivery. Without this information, the patient was simply unable to determine the best course of medical action for her and to avoid the risks posed by her medical problems. The application of the well-established ethical and legal principle of informed consent seems to require no less. She cannot be expected to diagnose herself or know what the standard of care treatment is for someone given that diagnosis.

Consequently, the ACLU is in principle right: MHP did not provide the patient with important information she needed to make the right treatment decision for her as required by the standard of care. Whether the USCCB and the other individuals sued by the ACLU can be held legally liable for this is a different matter beyond the scope of this chapter. However, in addition to disclosure of pertinent medical information, the ACLU also claims that "the standard of medical care required MHP to . . . provide appropriate medical care," which in this case, if chosen by the patient, presumably would be termi-

---

[50] USCCB, "The Distinction between Direct Abortion and Legitimate Medical Procedures," June 23, 2010, 3 (emphasis added). Available at http://www.usccb.org.

[51] USCCB, Directives, no. 47.

[52] USCCB, "Distinction," 3.

nation, an act that the USCCB considers to be morally the same as directly killing Ms. Means herself.[53]

Although *ACLU v. Trinity Health* raises the same basic issues as *Means v. USCCB*, it does so in a different manner. The legal theory of liability in *Means* is grounded in the alleged negligence of the USCCB and a few individuals. The legal theory of liability in *Trinity Health* is based on a hospital system's allegedly violating two specific federal statutes, EMTALA and the Rehabilitation Act. In *Means,* the ACLU acted only as the lawyers for an individual plaintiff who supposedly was harmed by the defendants. In *Trinity Health*, the ACLU is the plaintiff suing on behalf of its members.

The gravamen of this lawsuit is clear: Trinity has a "policy and practice of denying appropriate emergency care to women suffering pregnancy complications, including miscarriages," in violation of the statutes. But its complaint gives no facts about any individual woman's case: it claims only that Trinity "repeatedly and systematically failed to provide women suffering from pregnancy complications—including at least one of Plaintiffs' members—with the emergency care required" by the statutes.[54]

Ectopic pregnancy (one in which the embryo implants outside the womb and cannot survive to viability) is another complication of early pregnancy, in addition to previability miscarriage, that the ACLU presumably wishes to target in this lawsuit and that poses a challenge for CHC. Some 2 percent of all pregnancies are ectopic, and 97 percent of these are in the Fallopian tube; they are associated with "significant maternal mortality and morbidity. . . . Hemorrhage from [them] remains the leading cause of pregnancy-related death during the first trimester in the United States."[55] Ectopic pregnancy is a life-threatening condition. "The pregnancy cannot continue to birth (term). The developing cells must be removed to save the mother's life. You will need emergency medical help if the area of the ectopic pregnancy breaks open (ruptures). Rupture can lead to bleeding and shock, an emergency condition."[56]

The allegation in the ACLU suit against the Trinity system that is of interest for present purposes is based on EMTALA (Emergency Medical Treatment and Active Labor Act).[57] This statute states that hospitals receiving Medicare funds and having an emergency department "must stabilize any

---

[53] Ibid., 4 ("[No reason] can . . . justify the deliberate killing of an innocent human being.")

[54] *ACLU v. Trinity Health*, Complaint, 2.

[55] Angel Foster et al., "Do Religious Restrictions Influence Ectopic Pregnancy Management? A National Qualitative Study," *Women's Health Issues* 21, no. 2 (2011): 104.

[56] US National Library of Medicine, "Ectopic Pregnancy." Available at https://www.nlm.nih.gov.

[57] It is simply too unclear whether pregnancy and its complications constitute a "disability" under the Rehabilitation Act, not to mention that the ACLU points to no particular person with a recognized disability wrongly treated by Trinity.

individual determined to have an emergency medical condition" and "may not transfer (which includes discharge) any individual with an emergency medical condition who has not been stabilized" unless certain conditions are met.[58] EMTALA defines an emergency medical condition as "a medical condition manifesting itself by acute symptoms of sufficient severity (including severe pain) such that the absence of immediate medical attention could reasonably be expected to result in placing the health of the individual . . . in serious jeopardy, [cause] serious impairment to bodily functions, or serious dysfunction to any bodily organ or part."[59]

To stabilize means "to provide such medical treatment . . . as may be necessary to assure, within reasonable medical probability, that no material deterioration of the condition is likely to result from or occur during the transfer of the individual from a facility."[60] Although it is unknown if the single ACLU member who had complications of pregnancy and was denied emergency care was Ms. Means or someone else, I will use the facts of her case to see if it appears that EMTALA may have been violated.

Did she have an "emergency medical condition"? She reportedly had symptoms at least on her second visit to MHP that signal she did: severe pain, bleeding, and an elevated temperature, all indicative of chorioamnionitis and (given the length of gestation) preterm PROM. She was diagnosed with these conditions at that time, and the list of related health risks documented above provide prima facie support for the conclusion that the "absence of immediate medical attention could reasonably be expected to result in placing the health of the individual . . . in serious jeopardy." Specifically, the ACOG (American Congress of Obstetricians and Gynecologists) standards state that "immediate delivery" should be offered to the patient, and this intervention reasonably constitutes a (though apparently not the only) "stabilizing" treatment that would prevent "material deterioration" from occurring. Consequently, it is not unreasonable to conclude that EMTALA may have been violated in the case of Tamesha Means—putting to the side whether any federal or state provider conscience protection law might trump EMTALA.

Aside from the undisclosed cases alluded to by the ACLU's complaint, evidence exists that women presenting to Catholic hospitals with symptoms of pregnancy complications, such as miscarriage and ectopic pregnancies, were denied information about, and access to, possible treatments. A report by the National Women's Law Center concludes that a study done by Ibis Reproductive Health[61] "is consistent with anecdotal accounts that provide

---

[58] 42 USC §1395dd(b & c).

[59] 42 USC §1395dd(e)(1)(A).

[60] 42 USC §1395dd(e)(3)(A).

[61] Angel Foster et al., "Assessing Hospital Policies & Practices Regarding Ectopic Pregnancy & Miscarriage Management: Results of a National Qualitative Study," Ibis Reproductive Health, 2009. Available at http://www.ibisreproductivehealth.org.

strong evidence that some hospitals and health care providers have interpreted the *Directives* to prohibit prompt, medically-indicated treatment of miscarriage and ectopic pregnancy, placing women's lives and health at additional and unnecessary risk."[62] A study by Angel Foster and others found that information and treatment options for ectopic pregnancy were limited at some Catholic facilities.

> These findings raise concerns about the degree to which some institutions operating under the *Directives* are providing women with ectopic pregnancies with complete information about, and timely access to, the full range of treatment options. The restrictions on methotrexate . . . suggest that some facilities may not be adhering to widely recognized standards of care and that women may be managed expectantly or with a salpingectomy without being fully informed of the risks and benefits associated with these and other treatment modalities.[63]

Another study found that physicians working in Catholic hospitals around the country "disclosed experiences of being barred from completing emergency uterine evacuation while fetal heart tones were present, even when medically indicated."[64] These authors concur with ACOG and the other medical authorities cited above regarding termination of pregnancy as sometimes being a standard of care intervention.

According to the generally accepted standards of care in miscarriage management, "abortion is medically indicated under certain circumstances in the presence of fetal heart tones. Such cases include first-trimester septic or inevitable miscarriage, previable premature rupture of membranes, and situations in which continuation of the pregnancy significantly threatens the life or health of the woman."[65] A report made public by a former Michigan county public health official claimed that Mercy Health Partners, the hospital that attended Ms. Means, "forc[ed] five different women between August 2009 and December 2010 to undergo dangerous miscarriages by giving them no other option."[66]

Based on the foregoing, it appears that EMTALA can be violated if a physician or hospital does not disclose the full range of standard of care

---

[62] National Women's Law Center, "Below the Radar: Health Care Providers' Religious Refusals Can Endanger Pregnant Women's Lives and Health," January 2011, 3–4. Available at http://nwlc.org.

[63] Foster, "Religious Restrictions," 108.

[64] Freedman, "Miscarriage Management," 1777.

[65] Ibid., 1775.

[66] Molly Redden, "Abortion Ban Linked to Dangerous Miscarriages at Catholic Hospital, Report Claims," *Guardian*, February 18, 2016. Available at http://www.theguardian.com.

treatment options and fails either to render treatment to the patient or to refer her in a timely manner to other providers who will. Again, the ACLU appears to be right in principle.

One commentator on the ACLU's litigation claims that the organization has a "passion for abortion" and "hatred for Catholicism" and considers "unborn children and the Catholic Church" two of its enemies.[67] I certainly hope none of this is true of the ACLU (or anyone else), yet it is not above criticism of the rhetoric it directs at CHC and Catholic beliefs. Spokespersons for CHC have criticized a recent ACLU report about CHC merger activity[68] as "grossly unfair, distorted and dishonest," displaying "sloppy research and reasoning," and constituting a "vendetta" aimed at forcing CHC "to adopt secular rather than Catholic values, especially in the area of what they call reproductive care."[69]

However, by suing the USCCB for negligence in the *Means* litigation and *not* MHP or the physicians who allegedly actually treated her improperly, the ACLU is employing a strategy that, if successful, could affect CHC in all states that assign policymakers a duty of reasonable care in formulating hospital policy. The same is true for the *Trinity* litigation as the federal laws at issue apply to all hospitals. The ACLU *is* challenging CHC's management of pregnancy complications across the board.

CHC should honestly confront the quality of care problems it apparently has, if the analysis above is valid, with its management of ectopic pregnancy and previability PROM, the standard of care, and the stabilization duty under EMTALA. Although I understand the prohibition against some forms of cooperation with evil, it is hard to defend on a human and secular moral level the refusal to disclose vital clinical information to sick women who do not share Catholic beliefs and are doomed to lose their unborn anyway. No one should have a strict legal duty to participate in a non-emergency abortion, but that is not what the ACLU aims to do in the *Means* and *Trinity* lawsuits. Nonetheless, moral agents owe some deference to the sincere judgment of others, out of respect for them, that unborn humans have high moral status, even if that judgment is not widely shared or is not recognized in the law. ACLU policy and practice could show more of this deference and respect.

The ACLU currently has another lawsuit against Dignity Health for its refusal to allow a postpartum, non-emergency tubal ligation. In it, the ACLU alleges that California law, primarily its public accommodation statute,

---

[67] Bill Donohue, "ACLU's Catholic Hospital Fixation." Available at http://www.catholicleague.org.

[68] ACLU, "Health Care Denied."

[69] Mark Zimmerman, "Critics Blast Report on Catholic Hospitals as 'Distorted, Inaccurate,'" *Crux*, May 14, 2016. Available at http://www.cruxnow.com.

requires Dignity to allow such procedures on its premises.[70] The complaint itself acknowledges that some sterilizations are allowed by Dignity and that the plaintiff's own physician doesn't understand which are and are not allowed. Consequently, it is possible that physicians don't understand the Directives well or that the hospital is not educating them sufficiently on this matter. In any event, obstetricians at Dignity's hospitals should know that some, but not all, sterilization procedures violate the Directives.[71] They should discuss this with their patients at an early prenatal visit and make alternative arrangements as needed—which may well impose some hardship on patients, such as travel to a different hospital. But some price has to be paid by someone to allow sincere believers to follow their moral convictions. The ACLU appears not to appreciate this, although it does seem wrong to allow this price to be serious risk to the life or health of someone who has not voluntarily and knowingly assumed that risk.

The USCCB has chided the ACLU for failing to document a case in which the exercise of conscientious refusal has "prevented a woman from obtaining emergency treatment needed to save her life."[72] Apparently this is true in the United States, but a woman in Ireland did die from septicemia after she was denied an emergency abortion due to the Catholic prohibition when she was having a miscarriage.[73] If the pregnant woman at an Arizona Catholic hospital had not been given an abortion when she was critically ill with severe pulmonary hypertension, right-sided heart failure, and cardiogenic shock, she also might well have died.[74]

Many unknowns haunt the intersection and collision of CHC, the law, the standard of care, and women suffering the complications of pregnancy. The Supreme Court has yet to hold that the constitutionally protected free exercise of religion allows believers who have a duty to care for someone else also to have the right to refuse to help when doing so results in harm. The constitutionality of federal conscience protection laws have not yet been vigorously tested, and they do not clearly shield objectors from participation in an emergency abortion. If they did, the USCCB would not be lobbying diligently for passage of the CPA. Consequently, a legal accommodation or solution to the

---

[70] First Amended Complaint for Declaratory and Injunctive Relief and Nominal Damages, No. 15-549626, Superior Court of the State of California for the County of San Francisco, 2016.

[71] USCCB, Directives, #53. "Direct sterilization . . . is not permitted. . . . Procedures that induce sterility are permitted when their direct effect is the cure or alleviation of a present and serious pathology and a simpler treatment is not available."

[72] USCCB, "Conscience Protection," 1.

[73] Associated Press, "Irish Jury Finds Poor Care in Death of Woman Denied Abortion," *New York Times*, April 19, 2013. Available at http://www.nytimes.com.

[74] M. Therese Lysaught, "Moral Analysis of Procedure at Phoenix Hospital," *Origins* 40, no. 33 (2011): 537.

conflict of religious conviction and the safe and effective provision of treatment to patients in need will be tricky to come by.

One in six patients in the United States is cared for in a Catholic hospital, CHC hosts nearly 20 million emergency visits per year, and evidence exists that religious hospitals have significantly better results than for-profit and government hospitals on patient safety, length of stay, and patient satisfaction.[75] This is important, good, and useful service that should continue and be publicly supported. Yet the ACLU is rightly calling attention to a troublesome lacuna in this service with respect to women experiencing certain serious complications of their pregnancies. These are women who matter, who are being cared for by religious institutions and people who matter. A just reconciliation of women's reproductive rights and interests with the religious liberty of CHC may not be realized in short order, but the ACLU and CHC should work diligently toward it.

---

[75] Catholic Health Association, "Catholic Health Care in the United States," January 2016. Available at https://www.chausa.org.

Forming Conscience in an Age of Radical Biomedical Discovery

Kevin T. FitzGerald, SJ

Human history is replete with examples of individuals and communities wrestling with sudden and significant advances in medicine and biotechnology. These examples spread across the literary, public policy, and professional landscapes, as well as across human history in general. Concretely, as examples one can readily cite the stories of Icarus,[1] Frankenstein,[2] and Dr. Moreau,[3] and the documents referencing Helsinki,[4] Belmont,[5] and Guatemala,[6] as well as the events that took place in Nuremberg,[7] Tuskegee,[8] and Asilomar.[9] Although much has been written in the analysis and explanation of these efforts to determine appropriate uses of biotechnology by individuals and societies, the challenge of developing a "good" conscience (individually or collectively) regarding how best to use (or not) new medical discoveries and biotechnologies often appears to be as formidable now as when humankind began this decision-making process ages ago. Current public debates surrounding reproductive technologies, human embryo research, and genomic sequencing and manipulation indicate how difficult public moral decision-making in the biomedical arena continues to be in our own age.

---

[1] http://www.greekmyths-greekmythology.com.

[2] Mary Shelley, *Frankenstein*, rev. ed. (1831; New York: Barnes and Noble, 2005).

[3] H. G. Wells, *The Island of Dr. Moreau* (1896; New York: Bantam Classics, 1994).

[4] World Medical Association, "Declaration of Helsinki—Ethical Principles for Medical Research Involving Human Subjects," rev. 2013, http://www.wma.net.

[5] "Belmont Report: Ethical Principles and Guidelines for the Protection of Human Subjects of Research," *Report of the National Commission for the Protection of Human Subjects of Biomedical and Behavioral Research* (Washington, DC: Department of Health, Education, and Welfare, 1979).

[6] Presidential Commission for the Study of Bioethical Issues (PCSBI), "'Ethically Impossible' STD Research in Guatemala from 1946 to 1948" (Washington, DC, September 2011).

[7] *Trials of War Criminals before the Nuremberg Military Tribunals under Control Council Law No. 10* (Washington, DC: US Government Printing Office, 1949), 2:181–82.

[8] http://www.tuskegee.edu.

[9] Institute of Medicine, Biomedical Politics, "Asilomar and Recombinant DNA: The End of the Beginning" (Washington, DC: National Academies Press, 1991).

One reason for this difficulty can be a lack of clarity in answering the following question: What does a well-formed conscience look like when making moral decisions regarding the use of medical knowledge and biotechnology? In this chapter I attempt to provide some clarity regarding this question. I argue for the need to develop and implement a process of conscience formation that is adequate to the task of addressing the challenging moral complexities of our rapidly advancing biotechnology in the even more challenging context of our culturally diverse world. Citing the work of several of the scholars involved in this Conscience and Catholicism Project, I propose that much of what we need to develop that adequate conscience formation process already exists within the Catholic moral tradition. I then propose one configuration such a process could take using structures already well developed in the Catholic moral tradition, as well as in the secular world.

In the *Catechism of the Catholic Church* "conscience" is defined as follows:

> A judgment of reason whereby the human person recognizes the moral quality of a concrete act that he is going to perform, is in the process of performing, or has already completed. In all he says and does, man is obliged to follow faithfully what he knows to be just and right. It is by the judgment of his conscience that man perceives and recognizes the prescriptions of the divine law.[10]

Furthermore, the Catechism states that "conscience enables one to assume *responsibility* for the acts performed"[11] and that "man has the right to act in conscience and in freedom so as personally to make moral decisions."[12] With regard to concrete situations the Catechism recognizes that

> man is sometimes confronted by situations that make moral judgments less assured and decision difficult. But he must always seriously seek what is right and good and discern the will of God expressed in divine law.
>
> To this purpose, man strives to interpret the data of experience and the signs of the times assisted by the virtue of prudence, by the advice of competent people, and by the help of the Holy Spirit and his gifts.[13]

---

[10] *Catechism of the Catholic Church* (New York: Image Books, 1995), 1778.
[11] Ibid., 1781.
[12] Ibid., 1782.
[13] Ibid., 1787–88.

These statements from the Catechism may be interpreted as primarily focused on individuals who are determining when their consciences require them to pursue, opt out of, or actively resist certain actions, in this case a particular use of biotechnology. But the documents of the Second Vatican Council remind us that there is also a socially oriented notion of conscience embedded in the Catholic tradition. In its *Pastoral Constitution on the Church in the Modern World*, *Gaudium et Spes*, the church states, "In fidelity to conscience, Christians are joined with the rest of men in the search for truth, and for the genuine solution to the numerous problems which arise in the life of individuals from social relationships. Hence the more right conscience holds sway, the more persons and groups turn aside from blind choice and strive to be guided by the objective norms of morality."[14]

Considering the broad societal impacts biotechnologies have had and will continue to have, one can readily argue for the need to address the role of conscience in decision-making about biotechnological use on both the individual and community levels. This community perspective can be as broad as the entire world, which was the perspective taken in *Gaudium et Spes*.

> Though mankind is stricken with wonder at its own discoveries and its power, it often raises anxious questions about the current trend of the world, about the place and role of man in the universe, about the meaning of its individual and collective strivings, and about the ultimate destiny of reality and of humanity. Hence, giving witness and voice to the faith of the whole people of God gathered together by Christ, this council can provide no more eloquent proof of its solidarity with, as well as its respect and love for, the entire human family with which it is bound up, than by engaging with it in conversation about these various problems.[15]

Still, even if we agree with this concept of conscience at times acting on a global scale, it does not solve the issue of different people, and different groups, who consider themselves to have well-formed consciences—even according to Catholic Catechism standards—having very different perspectives regarding how the biomedical discoveries that come our way should be used and to what ends.

The Catholic Church is not unique in its recognition of the need to engage with the entire world in addressing the challenges of our rapidly developing biotechnology. In light of the diversity of individual and public perspectives in the biomedical research arena, there is a growing acknowledgment

---

[14] *Gaudium et Spes*, 16, http://www.vatican.va.

[15] Ibid., 3.

by the medical research community of the need for extensive and robust public engagement on the issue of the ever-increasing potential of these new biotechnologies to alter individuals, societies, and the world.[16] However, even with this acknowledgment of the need for extensive public engagement by the research community, recent decisions made by influential governmental bodies, professional societies, and special interest groups raise troubling questions regarding how substantive this purported desire for broad public engagement is within the research community. For example, in Washington, DC, from December 1 to December 3, 2015, the US National Academy of Sciences, the US National Academy of Medicine, the Royal Society, and the Chinese Academy of Sciences held a summit on "the scientific, ethical, legal, social, and governance issues associated with human gene editing."[17] Even though over five hundred individuals attended the meeting, little real public engagement occurred during the meeting. Then, even after criticisms of the lack of substantive public engagement in the meeting were widely disseminated,[18] the Human Fertilisation and Embryology Authority of the United Kingdom (HFEA) decided to support the use of the genome editing tool, CRISPR, in an experiment on the genomes of human embryos with merely one day of public comment and a relatively sparse representation of different perspectives on the topic.[19] In addition, the HFEA made their decision public the morning before the Nuffield Council on Bioethics had even closed their designated time period for submission of public comment on this topic.[20] Despite this lack of substantive public engagement, several proclamations were made from researchers involved in this research area as to the comfort and trust the public should have in this highly controversial and contentious research decision by the HFEA.[21]

This lack of substantive public engagement is unfortunately common in the decision-making processes used by various governmental institutions charged with setting policies and guidelines regarding cutting-edge biomedical research. In addition to pressures applied by various interest groups to

---

[16] David Baltimore et al., "A Prudent Path Forward for Genomic Engineering and Germline Gene Modification," *Science* 3 (April 2015): 37.

[17] National Academies of Sciences, Engineering, and Medicine, *International Summit on Human Gene Editing: A Global Discussion* (Washington, DC: National Academies Press, 2016).

[18] For example see Sharon Begley, "Global Summit Opens Door to Controversial Gene-Editing of Human Embryos," *Stat*, December 3, 2015, at https://www.statnews.com, and J. Benjamin Hurlbut, "The Demands of CRISPR's World: Must We Defer to the Experts?" *Ethics and Medics* 41, no. 4 (April 2016): 1–2.

[19] See http://www.hfea.gov.uk.

[20] See http://nuffieldbioethics.org.

[21] Ewen Callaway, "Gene-editing Research in Human Embryos Gains Momentum," *Nature* 532 (April 21, 2016): 289–90.

obtain a particular policy decision, the institutions often operate within a political environment that desires them to pursue and fulfill certain predetermined agendas. Hence, within these institutions there is usually a majority of the policy-making group that have been selected whose consciences fit comfortably within the dominant political environment of the institution. Since the members of these selected groups are relatively similar in their overall perspectives regarding the goods and goals of biomedical research, their policy and guideline decisions often appear to groups outside the biomedical arena to be insensitive to perspectives that run counter to the pro-research biases of the policy-setting group.

This problem of individual and group conscience bias has already been explicated and analyzed well by several authors in this volume and a previous volume connected to this Conscience and Catholicism project.[22] For example, one could take the powerful insight that Bryan Massingale brings to the cultural underpinnings of racial bias and blindness in conscience formation[23] and ask if similar biases exist in the mainstream biomedical research culture with regard to other vulnerable human beings, such as people with intellectual disabilities, or human embryo and fetal research. Obviously, addressing this issue of cultural bias and blindness will be incredibly challenging, since it has been with us from the beginning of human culture. However, in addition, there will also be significant challenges to our ideas of conscience formation raised by the biomedical research itself. The chapter written by Stephen Pope in *Conscience and Catholicism: Rights, Responsibilities, and Institutional Responses* raises a particularly relevant issue of how advances in moral psychology are challenging our concepts of good conscience formation both in its methods and its goals.[24]

Citing the work of psychologist Jonathan Haidt in particular, Pope wrestles with the claim that most of our moral decision-making is based on individual or group moral intuitions and emotions that arise in any given situation. Hence, the role of rational processes in decision-making is primarily to

---

[22] For example, in this volume see the contributions of Roberto Dell'Oro, "Conscience after Vatican II: Theological Premises for a Discussion of Catholic Health Care," and Shawnee Daniels-Sykes, "Conscience, Race, and Health Disparities: Catholicism and the Formation of Conscience in Light of a Black Liberation Bioethics." In the previous volume, David E. DeCosse and Kristin E. Heyer, eds., *Conscience and Catholicism: Rights, Responsibilities, and Institutional Responses* (Maryknoll, NY: Orbis Books, 2015), see James F. Keenan, SJ, "To Follow and to Form over Time: A Phenomenology of Conscience," and William R. O'Neill, SJ, "The Wisdom of Serpents: Conscience, Power, and Politics in the Abortion Controversy."

[23] Bryan Massingale, "Conscience Formation and the Challenge of Unconscious Racial Bias," in DeCosse and Heyer, *Conscience and Catholicism*, 53–68.

[24] Stephen J. Pope, "Conscience, Catholicism, and the New Science of Morality," in DeCosse and Heyer, *Conscience and Catholicism*, 39–52.

justify the decision made based on these nonrational elements or to formulate new approaches to certain situations when the usual decisions in a particular context no longer work. This interpretation of moral decision-making by Haidt and colleagues certainly fits well with the insights and challenges of conscience bias and blindness Massingale describes in his article. Hence, every person and every group of people, whether it be the Catholic Church or the biomedical research community, is challenged by these authors to develop their individual and group consciences in a way that is both honest about one's own limited understanding of the human condition and open to learning from others' different insights and values regarding the goods and goals of human life.

In response to the challenge from Haidt, Pope calls for a "significant culture change within the church at its grassroots."[25] This culture change will mean that

> Christians in the future will need to cultivate adult consciences that can sustain vital faith communities that are not supported by the wider society. The church of the future will have to be one in which thoughtful Christians are free to raise questions and come to different conclusions about non-infallible teachings, not out of an attitude of disobedience, but on the contrary, out of obedience to God as one understands God's will.[26]

However, even if this significant change is accepted (or adapted) and implemented throughout the Catholic Church, there still remains the question: How to know what a well-formed conscience will look like in the secular biomedical arena—with its many diverse groups of stakeholders? Even if Haidt and his colleagues are correct about the major influence of moral instinct and emotion in moral decision-making, the correctness and applicability of their insights will have to be confirmed and addressed through research and reasoning. In fact, even if everyone throughout the world becomes more aware of their moral bias and blindness, there will still remain the need to engage each other in the global public square to determine how we might together best develop and use our biomedical research and treatment advances.

With this brief elucidation of the current state of affairs for ethical decision-making in biomedical policy, I now return to the core issue stated at the beginning of this chapter—the need to develop and implement a process of conscience formation that is adequate to the task of addressing the challenging

---

[25] Ibid., 52.
[26] Ibid.

moral complexities of our rapidly advancing biotechnology in the even more challenging context of our culturally diverse world. Such a conscience formation process will need to be (1) capable of adequately framing complex technical material for ethical analysis and judgment, (2) teachable practically to everyone, and (3) able to foster broad agreement regarding both the goods and goals of our rapidly advancing biomedical knowledge and its technological applications. Hence, good conscience formation in the future, both individual and communal, not only will require awareness of self and group biases but will also require processes that enable constructive moral decision-making among widely variant groups and individuals.

Though this type of individual and communal conscience formation may appear difficult to achieve at first, a review of the history and development of the Catholic moral tradition reveals many resources already in place to help structure a successful process of good conscience formation for both individuals and communities. This should not be surprising since good conscience formation has been a focus of the Catholic moral tradition for some time. Because the focus in this article is on the need for broad public engagement as a part of good moral decision-making in the biotechnology arena, I touch on only a few of the many possible approaches in the Catholic moral tradition that might serve as useful parts for the development of a widely accessible process of conscience formation.

The first requirement of an adequate conscience formation process listed above is the capacity to make sense of complex and rapidly evolving information that arises from both biomedical research and biotechnology development. The example of how research in moral psychology might substantively change our concepts of moral decision-making has already been examined, but, even beyond that, biomedical research findings that challenge our fundamental concepts of health are also coming to the fore.

For example, there is a group of people in Ecuador, all of whom are related, who suffer from Laron Syndrome, a metabolic disorder that significantly stunts their growth (most are shorter than four foot eleven) in addition to causing other physiological challenges. This group of people was carefully studied by researchers for more than twenty years, both to find the cause of the condition and possibly to develop a treatment for it. In 2011, the researchers published their findings, which did uncover the genetic basis of Laron Syndrome. The researchers discovered a single genetic change in the human Growth Hormone Receptor (GHR) gene that resulted in a growth hormone system deficiency, resulting in their short stature, as well as other clinical features.

In addition to this group's deleterious clinical features they also exhibited some amazing positive physical characteristics, most especially an absence of both malignant cancer and type 2 diabetes. In fact, among the members of the group studied for the published article not one individual exhibited type 2 diabetes or malignant tumors, while a control group of other local people to whom they were compared exhibited a 5 percent rate of type 2 diabetes and a 17 percent rate for cancer.[27] This amazing research project revealed a disconcerting reality that may become much more common as genomic research expands around the globe: the fact that apparently simple genetic differences result in extremely complex and confounding physiological interactions that promote both health benefits and disease challenges in the human beings who have these remarkable genomes.

This remarkable research finding has stimulated additional research projects for this condition, and authors of a more recent review article of such metabolic conditions concluded that "numerous studies suggest that GH deficiency early in life is beneficial for healthy aging with likely mechanisms including reduction in cancer incidence and improved stress resistance." However, at the same time, "GH is essential for growth, reproductive fitness, and providing optimal tissue function through life, but at the cost of increased neoplastic disease later in life."[28] This discovery of the complexity of the role of the GHR gene in human biology reveals an intricate balance between health and disease that is intrinsic to the fundamental genetic fabric of our human nature. This intrinsic balance will become an ever-increasing challenge for health care providers as research uncovers more and more of this complex trade-off of health and disease that is so much a part of who we are in our biology as well as our behavior. Hence, not only will health care decision-making be challenged by such biological complexity, but those trying to promote our health will have to address the heightened complexity that will come from combining this convoluted genetic information with information regarding how an individual's genetic makeup interacts with environment, diet, lifestyle, and so on.

Still, even in the midst of this complexity, recent biotechnological advances will offer people the opportunity to manipulate their own, or their children's, genomes in an attempt to shift the balance of a person's health benefits and risks in a chosen direction. In the case of GHR mutations, parents could decide that they want to use genome editing technologies, such as CRISPR,[29] to create a Laron-like mutation in their child's growth hormone receptor so their child would then not have to worry about getting cancer or type 2 diabetes, even if the child's diet, environment, and lifestyle would normally create a relatively high risk for these illnesses.

---

[27] Jaime Guevara-Aguirre et al., "Growth Hormone Receptor Deficiency Is Associated with a Major Reduction in Pro-Aging Signaling, Cancer, and Diabetes in Humans," *Science Translational Medicine* 3 (2011): 70ra13.

[28] J. K. Perry et al., "Growth Hormone and Cancer: An Update on Progress," *Current Opinion in Endocrinology, Diabetes, and Obesity* 20 (2013): 308.

[29] Michael Specter, "The Gene Hackers," *Annals of Science*, November 16, 2015.

Interestingly, in the many talks and classes where I have raised this possibility, I have yet to encounter one person who said that he or she would choose to do such human genetic engineering. The primary reason I have been told by those who reject considering this option is that they do not want their children to be that short. I interpret this response as a clear indication that social values and goals (i.e., taller is always better!) often carry more weight for people in their conscience-based medical decision-making than do physiological facts and risks. This response, again, may represent another example of the challenge the world faces in addressing bias in the moral decision-making process. However, the primary point of the Laron Syndrome example is to illuminate the issue that both the discoveries and treatments generated by new biotechnologies will at times challenge the fundamental conceptual frameworks we use to understand ourselves as human and as healthy. Hence, such findings also can destabilize and confuse public policy deliberations regarding how best to pursue and use biomedical technological developments.

In light of this conceptual challenge to our fundamental ideas of health and humanness, a well-formed conscience for decision-making with respect to biotechnological advance will require a comprehensive and dynamic heuristic framework that can integrate and evaluate the myriad of individual and social issues raised by rapidly advancing biotechnologies—especially those technologies that can alter the biological substratum of any living organism and thereby significantly alter our concepts of health and human nature. This type of heuristic framework can be contrasted with a variety of competing frameworks currently used around the world that instead employ a narrow or reductionistic approach to addressing such ethical issues. The narrowness of these competing approaches is often the result of a choice (explicit or implicit) of prioritizing one set of goods or one type of knowledge over all other types of knowledge or goods.

For example, less comprehensive and integrative heuristic frameworks will give precedence to individual autonomy, or science, or a technological imperative, or economic/financial issues, or even a particular traditional view of human nature grounded in outdated biological information. Regardless of whatever particular type of knowledge, or good, is chosen as favored over all others, the problem of these narrower and less integrative approaches is an inability to adequately integrate rapidly expanding biomedical knowledge with the many other types of knowledge that inform both our understanding of our shared human nature and our goal of becoming healthier—individually and communally.

I have explained the advantages of taking a more dynamic and integrative approach to conceptualizing our notions of health and humanness in earlier works,[30] and other authors in this Catholicism and Conscience

---

[30] Kevin T. FitzGerald, "The Need for a Dynamic and Integrative Vision of the

project also explore some of the richness of the Catholic tradition in this area.[31] Hence, in this chapter I only summarize the key insight of this approach as it pertains to creating a well-formed conscience with regard to twenty-first-century biotechnology.

To truly understand who we are and who we want to become, from the level of individuals to the level of our societies, we need to reflect on all the different fields of inquiry we have that inform our understanding of ourselves—such as philosophy, theology, sociology, psychology, history, literature, the fine arts, economics, law, political science, as well as the natural sciences. This broad scope of reflection also needs to be a balanced reflection. In other words, the different fields of inquiry come to the discussion as partners in this critical endeavor, since the effects of using these new, powerful biotechnologies will be felt in all facets of human existence.

Academic institutions may serve as one arena wherein this broad and balanced interchange of experience, insight, and knowledge can be fostered. However, the breadth and depth of public engagement that will be required to truly develop a comprehensive, dynamic, and integrative framework of human nature and health will necessitate access to and interchange with as broad a spectrum of the public as possible. Those whose voices are most often not heard in the clamor of the public square—the marginalized across our societies—will be particularly key to weaving the rich tapestry of human understanding that will be needed for well-informed consciences to be applied to the biotechnology decision-making process. This intentional inclusion of the marginalized also fits well with the oft-repeated claim of biomedical researchers that the primary goal of their research is to bring new and better treatments and care to people in need.

This inclusive and broad public approach resonates well with the emphasis Pope Francis has placed on the church reaching out to engage those most in need, and to see the richness of the human experience through their experiences:

> For the Church, the option for the poor is primarily a theological category rather than a cultural, sociological, political or philosophical one. God shows the poor "his first mercy." This divine preference has consequences for the faith life of all Christians, since we are called to have "this mind . . . which was in Jesus Christ" (Phil 2:5).

Human for the Ethics of Genetics," in *Genetics, Theology, and Ethics*, ed. Lisa Cahill (New York: Crossroad, 2005).

[31] For example, see the chapters in this volume by Roberto Dell'Oro, "Conscience after Vatican II: Theological Premises for a Discussion of Catholic Health Care," and Lisa Fullam, "Dealing with Doubt: Epikeia, Probabilism, and the Formation of Medical Conscience."

Inspired by this, the Church has made an option for the poor which is understood as a "special form of primacy in the exercise of Christian charity, to which the whole tradition of the Church bears witness." This option—as Benedict XVI has taught—"is implicit in our Christian faith in a God who became poor for us, so as to enrich us with his poverty." This is why I want a Church which is poor and for the poor. They have much to teach us. Not only do they share in the *sensus fidei*, but in their difficulties they know the suffering Christ. We need to let ourselves be evangelized by them. The new evangelization is an invitation to acknowledge the saving power at work in their lives and to put them at the center of the Church's pilgrim way. We are called to find Christ in them, to lend our voice to their causes, but also to be their friends, to listen to them, to speak for them and to embrace the mysterious wisdom which God wishes to share with us through them.[32]

However, even if this critical goal of developing a comprehensive, integrative, and dynamic framework for understanding our human nature and health is achieved and taught globally, this framework will still have to be applied to real world problems that involve varied contexts and values, as well as groups of people with different needs. For example, the current global health challenges of type 2 diabetes and cancer may not be particularly relevant to the needs of the individuals with Laron Syndrome. In addition, even the multitudes of people with type 2 diabetes and cancer will experience varying responses to the same treatments due to their genetic and lifestyle differences. Therefore, any well-formed conscience, individual or group, will need to be able to apply a more general understanding of human nature and health to each specific issue, group or situation—whether their own or another group's. This challenge will require the ability to contextualize appropriately the unique facts of the decision at hand with the overarching goods and goals of the individual or the community in need.

To assist with this facet of the moral decision-making process, one can employ practices that have been used for thousands of years in various religious and cultural traditions to address the specificities of complex and challenging decisions. Many religious traditions include methods for making wise decisions based on a well-informed conscience. In the Christian tradition there is a long history of such decision-making called "discernment."[33] Discernment in the tradition over the past two thousand years includes several

---

[32] Pope Francis, *Evangelii Gaudium*, 198.
[33] Marian Cowan and John Carroll Futrell, *The Spiritual Exercises of St. Ignatius of Loyola: A Handbook for Directors* (Shelton, CT: Le Jacq, 1981), 161–62.

features. First is an inner impulse that an individual or group has that is leading the individual or group to make a decision. This impulse can be made up of passions, thoughts, feelings, desires, and so on. This impulse can also be seen as similar to the nonrational elements involved in moral decision-making identified by Haidt and his colleagues, as discussed above. The impulse is experienced as a sense of being pushed or pulled in a certain direction or course of action. The second feature is to identify the origin or source of the impulse. Whatever issue or problem is creating the impulse to make a decision is the focus of the discernment. Finally, deciding among the various options available to address the issue or problem that has arisen requires elucidating the trajectory or direction of the impulse.[34]

In other words, in a discernment process a person or a group of people attempts to determine the direction a particular course of action will lead that person or group if that course of action is chosen. In working backward along the trajectory of that course of action, the person or group can identify the impulse that is the source of the desire to make a decision. From this determination of both the source and the trajectory of the impulse to choose a particular course of action, the person or group can ascertain whether or not choosing that course of action is truly aligned with the overall goods and goals the individual or group considers foundational to living a good life. If not, the person or group can then seek a different course of action (including inaction) which does conform with what the individual or group claims to be the focus of their existence.[35]

Discernment, then, involves a person or group gathering all the information relevant to the decision at hand. Once the relevant information and the available options are known, the person or group comes to the best moral decision for this particular issue by evaluating how each of the possible options would help that person or group fit this decision into the overall life trajectory that the person or group has already chosen to pursue. People involved in clinical care might recognize the elements of this discernment process as practically the same as those involved in making a good treatment plan for a patient or doing a clinical ethics consultation process well. This similarity is evidence of the generalizability of this discernment process for good decision-making in almost any situation. The usefulness of this discernment process is also a highly probable reason it has become so broadly accepted in different religious and professional traditions.

A practical question that can arise at this point is: How does one determine at what level of societal structure the discernment process should take place—individual, family, community, national, or international? Since

---

[34] Ibid.
[35] Ibid.

a significant amount of information and reflection is required for a good discernment, pursuing a full discernment process on a national scale certainly presents greater difficulties than it does for a small group or individual. In Roman Catholic social justice teaching this issue is addressed by applying the principle of subsidiarity. This principle has been formulated in the following way: "Just as it is wrong to take away from individuals what they can accomplish by their own ability and effort and entrust it to a community, so it is an injury and at the same time both serious evil and a disturbance of right order to assign to a larger and higher society what can be performed successfully by smaller and lower communities."[36]

How might this principle of subsidiarity be applied to the challenges raised by our current biotechnologies? Considering that at this time the discussions regarding the use of CRISPR in human genome editing are taking place on an international level, one could rightly conclude that it needs to remain at that level for the time being until a better global sense of what is an appropriate use of CRISPR, and what is not, is developed. Hence, the HFEA might be encouraged to stay their decision to move ahead with the genome editing of human embryos in order to better participate with other nations, and their biomedical regulatory institutions, in a broad and comprehensive discernment regarding how best for everyone to move forward in this area. However, regarding the use of CRISPR to address a regional or local problem with a particular pathogen—of people, animals, or plants—one could make the argument that a limited discernment might suffice if global guidelines are already in place to help give a context to the local issue being addressed.

Any international discernment of how to proceed with developing a powerful biotechnology would require a reflection on the various trajectories that have been at work up to our present day in the international pursuit of individual and community health. Though this would certainly reveal various conflicting orientations and inconsistencies of application, it will also help clarify how present policies are not commensurate with the often claimed goal of healthy living for both individuals and communities around the world. Addressing these fundamental problems may well delay some answers as to how to proceed with new biotechnologies, but, as is taught within many religious and moral traditions, the best way forward for all is often not the fastest or easiest option.

When addressing national and international public policy discussions, one constantly hears the lament about the diversity of beliefs and values that is encountered when an attempt is made to create broad policies on such controversial issues as human or plant genetic engineering. How might our very diverse world address complex and controversial issues such as these without

---

[36] Pius XI, *Quadragesimo Anno*, 79.

falling into a biotechnical policy gridlock or morass? Building on facets within the Catholic tradition, I have already presented a heuristic framework that facilitates the integration of varied and complex information and insight, along with a discernment process that allows both individuals and communities to better choose among different options which choices fit well with their overall life goals and goods. Now to address this issue of adjudicating among various competing stakeholder groups I turn to an educational methodology that focuses on reasoning skills instead of particular moral codes or ethical principles. Though this methodology is presented in modern, secular educational terminology, I believe those familiar with Ignatian pedagogy will see its influence quite readily.

The impulse for the development of this educational methodology was the requirement by federal funding agencies, such as the National Institutes of Health and the National Science Foundation, that researchers be trained in the responsible conduct of research, so that people from around the world who come to be a part of the biomedical research community in the United States all share a common understanding and practice regarding how biomedical research is to be done responsibly. Though this goal is only a small piece of fostering broad international agreements regarding the goals and goods of cutting-edge biotechnologies, successful educational methods for addressing the goal of fostering responsible conduct in research might then be applied to this larger task.

Of course, having requirements and fulfilling them are two very different realities. To bridge the gap between these two realities, Dr. Rochelle Tractenberg, PhD, and I developed an educational program that is focused on training researchers in the practice of ethical reasoning, rather than focusing on learning ethical theory or policy. Hence, it is designed to be applicable across cultural and societal divides, as well as across the span of a researcher's career, in order to remain relevant and applicable regardless of the pace and place of scientific research and technological development. We summarized our approach in this manner:

> We describe a Mastery Rubric for the design and evaluation of an institutional curriculum in the responsible conduct of research (RCR), motivated by new federal (US) research funding requirements for documenting this training over investigators' careers. A Mastery Rubric outlines the desired knowledge, skills and abilities (KSAs) for a course or curriculum, rather than for an assignment, together with descriptions of a learner's performance and/or capabilities from novice to proficiency, expertise or mastery of the curricular target(s). Our MR encompasses, formalises and provides a roadmap for the institutional implementation of career-spanning training in RCR. The

rubric highlights the KSAs that support learning goal articulation for the targeted content areas; it also promotes assessment that demonstrates development in the target KSAs and encourages reflection and cognitive self-monitoring throughout RCR training over the scientist's career. It represents a flexible, criterion-referenced definition of "success" for both individuals and the institution itself—concretely reflecting the institution's norms and standards with respect to RCR and representing a flexible mechanism for self-monitoring by individuals as well as the institution. A Mastery Rubric for a curriculum in the RCR can be generated using any topical KSA framework.[37]

In essence, this approach is based on the premise that anyone can be taught ethical reasoning, since there are certain KSAs that can be identified and assessed in the development of one's expertise in ethical reasoning from a complete novice through to an accomplished expert. Each person is helped to identify where they are along the spectrum of novice to expert, identify what level of expertise is the desired goal, and to identify what that person needs to do to achieve that level of desired expertise. The curriculum is structured to allow an individual to plug in at whatever level he or she is at, and then move ahead from there. When the individual concludes that she or he has attained the level of expertise desired, the individual has the evidence generated in the course work to demonstrate the individual's KSAs appropriate to that level of expertise. Although we are still early on in our implementation and use of this pedagogical tool, our preliminary results are quite encouraging regarding both the abilities of the students to learn how to begin to reason well in an ethical arena and to identify gaps in their knowledge and ability, and plan how to address those gaps as they move forward with their careers.[38]

Although this pedagogical approach was designed primarily to address the challenge of educating scientists from all corners of the globe in the responsible conduct of research, the adaptable structure of this educational methodology makes it amenable to tackling a much larger task. That task is the challenge everyone faces in developing a well-formed conscience for moral decision-making in the twenty-first-century biotechnology arena. Key to addressing this task will be an educational methodology that fosters the reasoning skills necessary to engage in global public engagement regarding

---

[37] Rochelle Tractenberg and Kevin FitzGerald, "A Mastery Rubric for the Design and Evaluation of an Institutional Curriculum in the Responsible Conduct of Research," *Assessment and Evaluation in Higher Education* 37, no. 8 (December 2012): 1003–21.

[38] Rochelle E. Tractenberg and Kevin T. FitzGerald, "Responsibility in the Conduct of Quantifying Sciences: Preparing Future Practitioners and Certifying Professionals." Presented at the 2014 Joint Statistical Meetings in Boston, Massachusetts. In *JSM Proceedings*, Statistical Education Section (Alexandria, VA: American Statistical Association, 2015), 4296–4309.

how best to pursue our biomedical advances. The MR for ethical reasoning is designed to allow anyone comfortably and confidently to engage others who have very different cultural and societal backgrounds, and even different levels of expertise in ethical reasoning, in deliberations on how best to move forward (or not) with new and powerful biotechnologies. It can also be used to empower the socially marginalized because it can level the field of engagement with powerful groups by giving those on the margins the reasoning tools to present their goals and needs with equal logic, evidence, and clarity.

If we have no common ground on which to reason with one another due to the diversity of goals and goods among the many human communities, then we may well continue the polarized, contentious, fractured, and often paralyzed deliberations we so often encounter today. If we, instead, foster reliable and broadly applicable reasoning skills shared and accepted by all and add to those skills a comprehensive and dynamic heuristic framework for integrating new scientific information and a well-developed process for discernment of best choices for each individual or group, then, perhaps, we will have a foundation from which people anywhere in the world, and any social and medical situation, can make decisions with truly well-formed consciences in an era of promising and perilous biotechnological advance. Though, as part of the Catholic and Conscience project, the conscience-formation process presented in this chapter is grounded in the Catholic moral tradition, this process is designed to be accessible to any person from any culture or tradition. In this way, the conscience-formation process, and the project as a whole, fulfills a primary mandate of the Catholic moral tradition—sharing the gifts we have received with all those who are in need.

Situating the Catholic Opposition to Physician-Assisted Suicide in the Context of the Teachings of Pope Francis on Conscience and Mercy

Gerald Coleman, PSS

It is likely that the next several years will witness aggressive attempts in the United States to advance physician-assisted suicide (PAS), sometimes called medicalized suicide, assistance in dying, or physician-assisted dying (PAD).[1] In 2015 alone, a total of twenty-three states and the District of Columbia have sought to codify the practice of PAS. This unprecedented legislation wave represents more than double the number of PAS bills introduced in any year since 1995 and a sixfold increase relative to 2014.[2] Results from the latest Gallup "Values and Beliefs" survey make it clear that nearly seven of ten people polled in the United States are now favorably disposed to the practice, the highest level in a decade.[3]

This chapter suggests that the phenomenon of PAS is dependent on a radically autonomous view of conscience. In contrast with this, the Catholic point of view, witnessed in the teachings of Pope Francis, situates conscience within the imperatives of compassion and mercy, attitudes that try to bring hope out of hopelessness.

Physician-Assisted Suicide

According to Catholic Church teaching, PAS is a form of euthanasia. Euthanasia can be active (doing something whose direct object is the termination of life, e.g., intentionally administering a lethal dose of pain killers) or passive (the omission or withholding of a drug or therapy with a view toward

---

[1] Lawrence O. Gostin and Anna E. Roberts, "Physician-Assisted Dying: A Turning Point?" *Journal of the American Medical Association* 315, no. 3 (2016): 249–50.

[2] Ryan P. Clodfelter and Eli Y. Adashi, "The Liberty to Die," *Journal of the American Medical Association* 315, no. 3 (2016): 251–52.

[3] http://www.gallup.com.

ending life). Caution should be taken not to confuse legitimate termination of extraordinary or disproportionate means with passive euthanasia. The *Ethical and Religious Directives for Catholic Health Care Services* explain: "A person may forgo extraordinary or disproportionate means of preserving life. Disproportionate means are those that in the patient's judgment do not offer a reasonable hope of benefit or entail an excessive burden, or impose excessive expense on the family or the community" (no. 57).

In the United States, PAS refers to a request by a competent person to seek aid in dying from a physician who prescribes barbiturates whose purpose is to end life. Under present proposals, a person must be able to self-administer this medication.[4] The drugs most commonly prescribed in Washington State and Oregon are secobarbital or pentobarbital in high dosages. The person taking the drug is counseled not to eat for four to five hours beforehand, to take an anti-nausea medication an hour ahead of time, not to take laxatives or ingest acidic beverages such as orange juice, to drink water or soda only at room temperature, and to say goodbyes first and then drink the lethal cocktail all at once. The average time for dying is twenty-five minutes, but in some cases dying has taken up to four days.

The battle over PAS has been shaped over many years in the United States. In the 1990s, Dr. Jack Kevorkian assisted in the deaths of more than a hundred terminally ill people. In 2009, politicians sparred over a provision in the Affordable Care Act concerning end-of-life consultations, called "death panels" by critics, to help control health care costs. Roughly 28 percent, or $170 billion per year of Medicare, is spent on patients' last six months of life.

More recently, the movement toward PAS gained considerable momentum due to two highly publicized cases. The first had to do with Jennifer Glass of San Mateo, California, who was diagnosed with stage 4 lung cancer in 2013. She had a slim chance of surviving five years. Glass's case rallied a group of Democratic lawmakers in the state to actively pursue aid-in-dying legislation. Glass testified that she would fear the end of life less if she had wider choices about how to die. She advocated for the right to obtain from a physician medication that would speed her dying process. In her support, State Senator Bill Monning (D-Carmel) maintained that the core of Glass's request has to do with "respecting dignity and self-determination," and her desire constitutes "a civil right and a human right, deserving of a patient with a terminal diagnosis who faces a death sentence not of their own choosing." Jennifer Glass died of lung cancer at her home on August 11, 2015.[5]

---

[4] See James T. Bretzke, *Handbook of Roman Catholic Moral Terms* (Washington, DC: Georgetown University Press, 2013), 82, 173.

[5] Samantha Weigel, "Right-to-Die Advocate Dies without Reprieve," *San Mateo Daily Journal,* August 14, 2015, 12–13.

The second case concerned Oakland, California, resident Brittany Maynard.[6] In January 2014 she was diagnosed with aggressive stage 4 malignant brain cancer (glioblastoma). In April she learned that she had six months to live. She declined hospice care because "I do not want to live into the end-stage of my illness when the fast-moving tumor will eat deeply into my brain and inflict pain even morphine can't control."

Maynard, her husband, and her mother moved to Portland, Oregon, to gain access to the state's Death with Dignity Act. She decided to end her life on November 1, 2014, through voluntary self-administration of lethal medications costing about $300. She rejected characterizations that she was "choosing" death. Rather, "cancer is ending my life. I am choosing to end it a little sooner and in a lot less pain and suffering." Surrounded by friends and family, she swallowed a fatal dose of barbiturates, and died by assisted suicide at her home in Oregon on November 2.

Statistics from Oregon indicate that the majority of patients requesting PAS were reported as being concerned about "losing autonomy" (91.5 percent), being "less able to engage in activities making life enjoyable" (88.7 percent), "loss of dignity" (79.3 percent), "losing control of bodily functions" (50.1 percent), and being a "burden on family, friends/caretakers" (40 percent). Only 1 in 4 (24.7 percent) even reported "concern about inadequate pain control." Those who oppose PAS believe that the emphasis on autonomy and private choice may likely lead to poorer health care and increased pressure on the sick, the elderly, the disabled, and the traumatically injured to choose PAS. As the concept "a life is not worth living" increases, the idea may likely gain traction that disabilities are a fate worse than death. Such disabled persons can become easy targets for those who advise suicide. Some may feel pressured to no longer be a burden while they have their sense of dignity lessened. In the case of elderly individuals seeking PAS, family pressure is often one of the motivating factors.[7]

Advocates of PAS legislation argue that the scope of the law is "limited" and bears "sufficient controls and safeguards" to avoid misuse. For example, physicians are allowed to prescribe life-ending drugs only to individuals who are deemed mentally competent and expected to die within six months, and two doctors must sign off on the order. In an attempt to set parameters around eligibility for PAS, a person must have a prognosis of six months or less to live. Medical professionals, however, will testify that such predictions are often miscalculated and misjudged and can easily lead a vulnerable patient to deeper anxiety.

---

[6] Nicole Egan, "Inside Story: How Brittany Maynard Became a 'Death with Dignity' Advocate," www.people.com, March 24, 2015.

[7] Margaret Pabst-Battain, "Manipulated Suicide," *Bioethics Quarterly* 2 (1980): 123–134.

Opponents of PAS contend that there is no inherent reason to think that current restrictions on PAS in the United States will not escalate into more generalized aid in dying. PAS has been legalized in the Netherlands since 1981 and has increased at approximately 15 percent per year. It is also becoming easier to qualify for state-legitimated PAS with such non-life-threatening conditions as depression, autism, or blindness. In addition, children aged twelve to fifteen can seek PAS if they have parental permission (and there are current social pressures to lower the age limit still further). There is also an increase in "double euthanasia" where the spouse of someone seeking PAS also requests aid in dying because life will be unbearable without the spouse's partner. In January 2016 the Netherlands government decided to extend to people with dementia who are incompetent to request euthanasia to die by lethal injection if the person requested euthanasia while still competent. The 2014 Netherlands euthanasia statistics state that out of 5,306 euthanasia deaths, 81 people were lethally injected for dementia, and 41 people for psychiatric reasons. A study recently published in the *Journal of the American Medical Association* found that 28 percent of requests for euthanasia in the Netherlands were granted to people who said they were simply "tired of living."[8]

Because PAS assumes a radical, secularized notion of conscience, it places individual autonomy as the ultimate measure of public policy. Since the most frequently cited reason for seeking aid in dying is fear of losing autonomy and dignity, PAS advocates believe they affirm mercy by heeding a patient's request to die. This approach drifts into a kind of subjectivism that leads a person to feel a radical isolation, expecting no help from others. The Catholic tradition, in contrast, understands the dignity of conscience as relational. Human autonomy is situated in relation to others, for example, one's family, medical professionals, and support personnel. Conscience is always oriented to an expectation that one ought to be helped by others. The radically autonomous conscience, however, easily yields to a throwaway culture that disconnects people, especially those who are most vulnerable. Aid-in-dying proponents understand mercy as permission to die alone. In the Catholic tradition, mercy never discards people and always accompanies patients with loving attention, along with spiritual and palliative care.

Granting individuals the right to end their lives ultimately threatens everyone as it implicitly denies the dignity of the dying.[9] Failure to honor this

---

[8] Sue Reid, "The Country Where Death Is Now Just a Lifestyle Choice," *Daily Mail*, January 1, 2015, 4–8.

[9] See Timothy E. Quill, Anthony L. Back, and Susan D. Block, "Responding to Patients Requesting Physician-Assisted Death: Physician Involvement at the Very End of Life," *Journal of the American Medical Association* 315, no. 3 (2016): 245–48.

dignity will lead to poorer care and will likely increase pressure on the elderly and dying to end their lives so that they will no longer be a burden. In other words, the "right to die" can too easily become the "duty to die."[10]

PAS is also the result of a misunderstanding of mercy and compassion derived from assumptions about the radically autonomous nature of human conscience and life. Albert R. Jonsen has pointed out that advocates of PAS see this option as "mercy," for it ends a life of emotional losses as experienced in pain, loneliness, fear, and ennui. Jonsen explains that since the 1970s several organizations such as the Euthanasia Society, Hemlock Society, and Compassion in Dying have consistently urged an examination of the moral and legal questions surrounding assistance in dying. They widely publicized the issue, focusing on prominent examples in Europe where several nations have legalized PAS. However, the emphasis of these organizations on compassion and care leans in a consistently individualistic direction. A person facing death is seen as utterly alone: neither embedded within a world of loving relationships nor as part of a whole network of a health care system with its obligations to heal. Moreover, compassion and care are understood as pertaining only to this individual facing his or her mortality but not as the animating principles and virtues behind what could be a whole social system of palliative care and support in a time of dying. Instead, the very persons who need such compassion and care are offered the option of death. Thus assisted suicide becomes an inexpensive substitute for proper health care. PAS legislation abandons social solidarity with the poor, mentally ill, the sick and fragile, and the lonely.

The Teachings of Pope Francis
on Conscience and Mercy

The teachings of Pope Francis demonstrate a very different understanding of conscience and mercy. Conscience is understood as a personal attribute—but it is also understood as inherently related to others and especially to the vulnerable, sick, and poor. In his 2014 World Day of Peace Message, Pope Francis said: "The many situations of inequality, poverty, and injustice are signs not only of a profound lack of fraternity but also of the absence of a culture of solidarity. New ideologies, characterized by rampant individualism, egocentrism, and materialistic consumerism, weaken social bonds, fueling that 'throw away' mentality which leads to contempt for, and the abandonment of, the weakest and those considered 'useless.'"[11]

---

[10] Wesley Smith, "'Right to Die' Can Become a 'Duty to Die,'" http://www.telegraph.co.uk/comment/personal-view/4736927/Right-to-die-can-become-a-duty-to-die.html.

[11] Pope Francis, 2014 World Message of Peace. Available at http://www.cacatholic.org.

Pope Francis echoes the teaching of Vatican II when he describes conscience as "the interior place for listening to the truth, to goodness, for listening to God; it is the inner place of my relationship with God, the One who speaks to my heart and helps me to discern, to understand the way I must take and, once the decision is made, to go forward, to stay faithful."[12] Here we see the deeply personal nature of conscience in the Catholic moral tradition. In this way, Catholicism shares an interest in the autonomy of conscience with secular liberal culture. But we can also see how on face value, this portrayal of the personal nature of the Catholic conscience could also lead to a type of egoism that translates into subjectivism: Whatever "truth" I discern is "the" truth. However, in *Laudato Si'*, the Pope's 2015 encyclical on the environment, he counsels against overly subjective understandings of conscience and calls each of us to an examination of conscience that seeks conversion of hearts (no. 217). We must detach from personal desires and constantly rethink our standards and goals. We must renounce selfishness in favor of choosing what God truly wants of us, which demands an attentiveness to the poor and the suffering among us and the common good (no. 14). Francis's teaching on conscience, therefore, does not mean a free pass to do whatever we want. Conscience in the Catholic tradition demands a careful navigation among personal listening to God within the sanctuary of our heart, regard for the common good, and a reverential listening to the teachings of the church. In his homily in the chapel of Domus Sanctae Marthae in October 2015, Francis warned us that seeking to become the "master of our consciences" can too easily lead to a muddiness that no longer sees the difference between right and wrong. Conscience, then, requires formation and development.

For Pope Francis, conscience is intimately related to a correct understanding of mercy. On March 13, 2013, when Cardinal Jorge Mario Bergolio received the necessary votes required for election as Successor of Saint Peter, the assistant dean of Cardinals put this question to him: "*Acceptasne electionem de te canonice factam in Summum Pontificem?*" (Do you accept your canonical election as Supreme Pontiff?) The traditional response is "*Accepto.*" Astonishingly, Bergolio responded, "I am a great sinner, trusting in the mercy and patience of God in suffering. I accept."[13] A "potential revolution" was set in motion whereby decisions of conscience must be assessed by the standards of mercy and God's patience.

The pillar of mercy is an integral part of the ecclesiology of Pope Francis and informs the role of individual and corporate conscience in health care. Francis envisions a church open to all, a "work of ministry" which is always welcoming and especially nourishes the weak and the poor. Francis places the

---

[12] "Conscience Means Listening to God," Angelus Address, St. Peter's Square, June 30, 2013.

[13] Cited in Jeffrey A. Krames, *Lead with Humility* (New York: American Management Association, 2015), 37–38.

church in the midst of human suffering and emphasizes the healing ministry of Jesus as the foundation of the church's mission. The church by its very nature must assist all people to experience God's mercy. The face of God is seen in compassion and mercy. Compassion literally means "to suffer together," which gives rise to an active desire to alleviate the suffering of others. Among all major religious traditions, compassion is considered the greatest of virtues. Compassion never tolerates abandonment. Saint Paul's description is perfect: "Praise be to the God and Father of our Lord Jesus Christ, the Father of compassion and the God of comfort, who comforts us in all our troubles, so that we can comfort those in any trouble with the comfort we ourselves received from God" (2 Cor 1:3–4).

In his apostolic exhortation *Evangelii Gaudium* (2013),[14] Francis identifies areas of change that have implications for the whole work of ministry in the church.[15] First, the church must be welcoming, going forth radiating joy, with doors open to the fringes of humanity. The sacraments are not prizes for the perfect, "but a powerful medicine and nourishment for the weak." He envisions the church as a home for all and "not a small chapel that can hold only a small group of selected people. We must not reduce the bosom of the universal church to a nest protecting our mediocrity."[16]

Second, the church must first go to the poor. While the Gospel is for everyone, Francis envisions a church that is bruised, hurting, and dirty because it has been out on the streets, rather than being confined and clinging to its own security, caught up in a web of obsessions and procedures. We must leave behind outmoded structures and habits. Francis explains: "This is why I want a church which is poor and for the poor. They have much to teach us. Not only do they share in the *sensus fidei*, but in their difficulties they know the suffering Christ. We need to let ourselves be evangelized by them" (no. 198).

Third, the church must have a missionary impulse capable of transforming everything, so that the "church's customs can be suitably channeled for the evangelization of today's world rather than for her self-preservation."

These goals shape Francis's ecclesiology, which understands the church as a field hospital.[17] In a 2013 interview with Antonio Spadaro, SJ,[18] Pope

---

[14] Pope Francis, "Evangelii Gaudium," *Origins* 43 (2013): 421–65.

[15] Sr. Doris Gottemoeller, "Anticipating the Changes That Will Touch Us All," *Health Progress* (November–December 2015): 9–15.

[16] Antonio Spadaro, "A Big Heart Open to God," *America*, September 13, 2013, http://americamagazine.org.

[17] Erin Brigham, "The Church as a Field Hospital: The Ecclesiology of Pope Francis," in *Pope Francis and the Future of Catholicism in the United States: The Challenge of Becoming a Church for the Poor,* ed. Erin Brigham, David E. DeCosse, and Michael Duffy (San Francisco: University of San Francisco, 2015), 25–30.

[18] Spadaro, "Big Heart Open to God." See also Pope Francis, *Walking with Jesus* (Chicago: Loyola Press, 2015), 105–11.

Francis said, "I see clearly that the thing the church needs most today is the ability to heal wounds and to warm the hearts of the faithful; it needs nearness, proximity. I see the church as a field hospital after battle. It is useless to ask a seriously injured person if he has high cholesterol and about the level of blood sugar! You have to heal his wounds. Then we can talk about everything else. Heal the wounds, heal the wounds."

This image places the church in the center of human suffering, emphasizing the healing ministry of Jesus as the foundation of the church's mission. Francis wants the church to be a community that accompanies all people on their journey through life, particularly the poor in the midst of their own burdens. The Gospel story of the disciples on the road to Emmaus is the paradigm that invites ministers to act not as distant administrators but as pastors, walking with people and meeting them where they are. Pastors should particularly demonstrate the church's mercy through reconciliation and inclusivity.

The church as a field hospital cannot be insular since it goes to the battlefield where the wounded lie. The nature of emergency care given to the wounded leaves no time to judge the victims for their injuries. In Francis's mobile army surgical hospital (MASH) unit, the church not only takes care of the physically injured but also attends to the wounds of the soul. "The church's ministers must be merciful, take responsibility for the people and accompany them like the good Samaritan, who washes, cleans, and raises up the neighbor. . . . Francis is urging his clergy to offer solace to the soul before anything and everything else. It is always the people and their wounds that come first."[19]

The parable of the Good Samaritan reaches its turning point when it states that the Samaritan "had compassion" on the dying man. The verb expressing compassion (*splanchnizomai*) refers to "bowels," including the heart. The Samaritan does not stop at merely seeing the dying man but becomes involved in his innermost life, and it is such visceral compassion that sets in motion the possibility of saving the dying man. True compassion is not a feeling but an action that results in caring for the other.[20]

Many find Francis's focus on mercy "suspect" and "superficial," a way of being Christian at a reduced cost. However, mercy does not abolish justice but surpasses it. Mercy is "no cheap grace for a kind of clearance sale. Pastoral care and mercy are not contradictory to justice, but are . . . the higher righ-

---

[19] Krames, *Lead with Humility*, 74–76. Mercy was the central theme of Francis's first address as Pope in St. Peter's Square on March 17, 2013. On a flight from Rio de Janeiro to Rome four months later, he told the international media that this is *kairos*, the appointed historical moment for mercy and that the church as mother "must travel this path of mercy and find a form of mercy for all."

[20] See "Compassion for a Stranger," in *The Parables of Mercy*, Pontifical Council for the Promotion of the New Evangelization (Huntington: Our Sunday Visitor, 2015), 23–30.

teousness because behind every individual legal appeal stands not only a case that can be viewed through the lens of a general rule, but rather a human person, . . . a being who possesses unique personal dignity."[21]

Francis is outlining an agenda for a compassionate church, one that heals wounds and follows the path of mercy. Behind every moral and pastoral concern is a human person who must always be the recipient of compassion. Being compassionate and merciful is God's way. It must also be our way. This optic is explored in Francis's 2016 Exhortation *Amoris Laetitia,* "The Joy of Love: On Love in the Family." He explains that too often the church has been on the defensive, "wasting pastoral energy on denouncing a decadent world without being proactive in proposing ways of finding true happiness. . . . Jesus never failed to show compassion and closeness to the frailty of individuals like the Samaritan woman or the woman caught in adultery" (no. 38).

Conscience, Mercy, and the Response of Catholic Health Care to PAS

Pope Francis's teachings on conscience and mercy have profound impli-cations for Catholic health care in the United States as it responds to the call for PAS. "Catholic health care is *in* the world and *for* persons."[22] Catholic health care listens attentively to the world while engaging in a mission to transform the world. One way it does this is through the medium of health care for any and all persons who are sick, regardless of their religious beliefs. Catholic health care brings alive the healing ministry of Christ as a work worthy of the Kingdom of God. A healing ministry that follows this trajectory is necessarily Catholic, a sponsor of health care, and an American institution all at the same time.

Catholic health care is a ministry of the church where all persons must experience compassion and mercy. As Catholic health care carries on the healing mission of Jesus, it commits itself to self-identifying moral beliefs. These core moral principles ground Catholic health care institutions and situate the types of practices that must be done and cannot be done.

Individual conscience demands a careful listening to the voice of God which resides in an individual's "secret core and sanctuary" (*Gaudium et Spes,* no. 16). It is here where a person searches for truth. Truth, however, is not superficially grasped, but necessitates a careful listening to others and to the teaching of the church, whose duty it is to uphold a corporate conscience.

---

[21] Walter Kasper, *The Gospel of the Family* (New York: Paulist Press, 2014), 29.

[22] Brian Hehir made this point in a 1995 speech to the Catholic Health Association. See Daniel P. Sulmasy, "Institutional Conscience and Moral Pluralism in Health Care," *New Theology Review* 10, no. 4 (1997): 5–21. I follow Sulmasy's thinking in this part of the chapter.

In addressing any moral issue, therefore, it is necessary to balance personal conscience, corporate conscience, and the mediating role of mercy.

We live in a world where subjectivism unfortunately plays a dominant role in conscience formation. Sometimes called ethical egoism, this attitude asserts that one's primary moral obligation is to oneself, and selfishness becomes a virtue. This posture truncates all objectivity; truth becomes individualistic; and conscience becomes ego-centered. Subjectivism is the major factor leading to support for physician-assisted suicide.

The *Catechism of the Catholic Church* teaches that "those whose lives are diminished or weakened deserve special respect. Sick or handicapped persons should be helped to lead lives as normal as possible. Whatever its motives and means, direct euthanasia (or assisted suicide) consists in putting an end to the lives of handicapped, sick, or dying persons. It is morally unacceptable. Thus an act or omission which, of itself or by intention, causes death in order to eliminate suffering constitutes a murder gravely contrary to the dignity of the human person and to the respect due to the living God, his Creator. The error of judgment into which one can fall in good faith does not change the nature of this murderous act, which must be forbidden and excluded" (nos. 2276–77).

In part 5, the *Ethical and Religious Directives for Catholic Health Care Services* address care for the seriously ill and dying. The introduction to this section is singularly outstanding in its panoramic overview of how the Catholic moral tradition situates care for those who are ill and dying.

Christ's redemption and saving grace embrace the whole person in his or her illness, suffering, and death. The Catholic health care ministry faces the reality of death with the confidence of faith. In the face of death—for many, a time when hope seems lost—the Church witnesses to her belief that God has created each person for eternal life. Above all, as a witness to its faith, a Catholic health care institution will be a community of respect, love, and support to patients or residents and their families as they face the reality of death. What is hardest to face is the process of dying itself, especially the dependency, the helplessness, and the pain that so often accompany terminal illness. . . . The truth that life is a precious gift from God has profound implications for the question of stewardship over human life. We are not owners of our lives and, hence, do not have absolute power over life. We have a duty to preserve life and to use it for the glory of God, but the duty to preserve life is not absolute, for we may reject life-prolonging procedures that are insufficiently beneficial or excessively burdensome. Suicide and euthanasia are never morally acceptable options. The task of medicine is to care even when it cannot cure. . . . Even the most severely debilitated and helpless patient retains the full dignity of a human person and must receive ordinary and proportionate care.

In light of this theological and moral perspective, two directives are pertinent. Number 60 states that "Catholic health care institutions may never condone or participate in euthanasia or assisted suicide in any way. Dying patients who request euthanasia should receive loving care, psychological and spiritual support, and appropriate remedies for pain and other symptoms so that they can live with dignity until the time of natural death."

Number 24 states: "In compliance with federal law, a Catholic health care institution will make available to patients information about their rights, under the laws of their state, to make an advance directive for their medical treatment. The institution, however, will not honor an advance directive that is contrary to Catholic teaching. If the advance directive conflicts with Catholic teaching, an explanation should be provided as to why the directive cannot be honored."

Because of the church's belief that PAS is contrary to the inherent dignity of all, should an individual in a Catholic health care institution request PAS, or should the person's advance directive or POLST[23] state this desire, the institution cannot honor this request because it is contrary to everything the church cherishes about Jesus' embrace of every person, especially at the point of one's illness, suffering, and death. The church recognizes the darkness that often surrounds the dying process but witnesses to its mission of respecting life as God's gift given for our stewardship. The Catholic institution does not abandon a patient at this critical time but rather accompanies a person to be free of pain and suffering while waiting peacefully for eternal life. Here one sees the interlocking anguish between autonomous conscience and corporate conscience. The latter cannot honor the former if an individual's wishes conflict with an institution's self-defining moral beliefs.

James T. Bretzke states it well: "We must recall the central message of Christianity with regard to our life here on earth. This is not our ultimate home, and thus, as Christian leaders from St. Paul to John Paul II remind us,

---

[23] The POLST paradigm (Physician Orders for Life-Sustaining Treatment) was initiated in 1991 under the leadership of the Center for Ethics and Health Care at the Oregon Health and Science University. POLST was designed to "translate advance directives into a physician order that could be followed by clinicians directly when a patient is too sick to speak for him or herself. It was created for patients for whom, due to advanced illness, frailty, or status of being chronically or critically ill, it was impossible to decide in advance whether or not an intervention in response to a clinical event would carry a 'reasonable hope of benefit' or whether that intervention would entail 'excessive burden.'"

our life here and now is only a penultimate. This means that it is certainly an important aspect of Catholic moral theology to continue to insist on the sanctity of life, but also a dignified death."[24]

The final report of the October 2015 Synod of Bishops emphasizes human dignity. It addresses an "egotistical manner of living," which too often looks upon the elderly as a "burden" (no. 13). The report cites the General Audience of Pope Francis on March 4, 2015: "The elder is not alien. We are that elder: in the near or far future, but inevitably, even if we don't think. And if we don't learn how to treat the elder better, that is how we will all be treated" (no. 17).

In his article "A Church for the Poor," San Diego Bishop Robert W. McElroy writes that "we are called to create a Catholic political conversation that proclaims the greatest problems of our day can only be solved with a vision rooted in the transcendent dignity of the human person. For in the end, the very purpose of Catholic political conversations is to help our nation see human suffering not through the lens of politics but as God sees them."[25]

The magisterium of Pope Francis has made this point incessantly. In *Evangelii Gaudium* Francis wrote: "Just as the commandment 'Thou shalt not kill' sets a clear limit in order to safeguard the value of human life, today we also have to say 'thou shalt not' to an economy of exclusion and inequality. Such an economy kills. Human brings are themselves considered consumer goods to be used and then discarded. We have created a 'throw away' culture" (no. 53). In his "2013 Message to Muslims," Francis stated that "human life, the person, is no longer perceived as a primary value to be respected and protected, especially if poor or disabled, if not yet useful—such as the unborn child—or no longer needed—such as the elderly."

The pope upholds the belief that "every elderly person, even if he is ill, or at the end of his days, bears the face of Christ. They cannot be discarded as 'the culture of waste' suggests! They cannot be thrown away."[26] The human being is at stake. We cannot tolerate a "scrap culture" where persons are seen as disposable and can be discarded as trash. Every individual bears the face of Christ and deserves limitless care.

A radically autonomous view of conscience stands in opposition to a posture of relationality that necessarily embraces compassion and mercy, attitudes that bring hope out of hopelessness. People's lives are not worth-

---

[24] James T. Bretzke, SJ, "A Burden of Means: An Overlooked Aspect of the PVS Debate," *Landas* 18 (2004): 230. See Thomas R. Kopfensteiner, "Protecting a Dignified Death: A Contemporary Challenge for Moral Reasoning," *New Theology Review* 6 (1993): 6–27.

[25] Robert W. McElroy, "A Church for the Poor," *America*, October 21, 2013, 13–16.

[26] See John Coleman, SJ, "Pope Francis and the Consistent Ethic of Life," in *Pope Francis and the Future of Catholicism in the United States*, 22.

less accidents but purposeful and meaningful. Persons are much more than their diagnosis. "Whole Person Care" is informed by consciences rooted in compassion and offers accompaniment through palliative care, prayer, and respect for human dignity. Whole Person Care reminds the frail and sick that they are loved, wanted, worthy, and dignified. PAS undermines these values by reducing persons to their illness and offering not accompaniment but abandonment. Unlike the meaning of mercy in the writings of Pope Francis, PAS supports a description of mercy that leads to merely feeling sorry for dying persons and abandoning them. True mercy, in contrast, translates into doing something positive for dying persons by accompanying them through their final days of life. *Misericordiae Vultus* describes the point clearly: "Mercy is the very foundation of the Church's life. All of her pastoral activity should be caught up in the tenderness she makes present to believers; nothing in her preaching and in her witness to the world can be lacking in mercy. The Church's very credibility is seen in how she shows merciful and compassionate love" (no. 10). In this debate, the human being is at stake.

THE INACCESSIBLE CONSCIENCE

The Case of Unrepresented Patients

Margaret R. McLean

Life's most persistent and urgent question is: "What are you doing for others?"

—Martin Luther King Jr.

Do to others as you would have them do to you.

—Luke 6:31 (NRSV)

Truly I tell you, just as you did it to one of the least of these who are members of my family, you did it to me.

—Matthew 25:40b (NRSV)

The bright red cover caught the eye. Under the *Time* magazine masthead were the glaring white words—HOW TO DIE. Inside, between the eternal bloodbath of Syria and the mojo of Joe Biden, was the gut-wrenching story of the last days of columnist's Joe Klein's mother and father. As is often the case with lifelong companions, Klein's parents, who had met the first day of kindergarten, died within a few weeks of each other. As is also so often the case, their dying began months before, burdened at first by a "flotilla of doctors" and the chaos of fee-for-service medicine; and later, graced by the coordinated care of the salaried staff at Geisinger Medical Center in Danville, PA. As his parents were "fading away," Klein answered dozens of phone calls and shouldered a cascade of medical decisions. He became part of the health care team, consulted by nursing home staff about every medication and every inevitable fall of his increasingly frail parents, becoming a willing "co-conspirator" in "making their passage as comfortable as possible." In her earlier years, his mother had been forthright about her desire for a dignified death, saying with more than a hint of melodrama, "Just pull the plug. Let me die." When it became clear that "Mom was not coming back" from the decline of dementia and refusing to eat, Klein and his brother acted on her wishes and ceased "prolonging the inevitable," deciding to disconnect her feeding tube. A few months later came the decision "to let Dad go" from renal failure. Klein sat by his father's bedside, holding his hand during that final week in the nursing home until "Dad . . . inhaled and sighed and was gone" in a moment of "gorgeous serenity." At the end, Klein reflected, "My parents died serenely, with dignity. When you are a death panel—when the time and manner of their passing is at least partly in your hands—that is the very best you can hope for."[1]

Katy Butler's mother's pumpkin-shaped Japanese teapot graces the cover of her moving memoir, *Knocking on Heaven's Door*. Like Klein, Butler faces the reality of her parents dying in a health care system bent on sustaining life. Butler's long good-bye begins with the struggle to turn off the pacemaker implanted in her "stroke-shattered" father's chest. Her father, a retired university professor, was suffering from dementia as his heart outlived his brain. Butler's years-long, pain-infused good-byes end with her mother dying "the death she chose, not the death [the physicians] had in mind,"[2] dying "well because she was willing to die too soon rather than too late."[3] Butler's mother learned how to die from watching her husband being poked and prodded and living "two years of limbo, two of purgatory and two of hell"[4] with him, the unintended, tragic gift of a health care system built on cure and a pacemaker that would not die. Hours before her mother's death, Butler recalls how her mother would "swirl boiling water into her beloved Japanese iron teapot to warm it, pour it out and add fresh hot water and loose tea, putting on the lid and tucking the pot under the indigo-blue tea cozy she'd sewn herself."[5]

Now imagine an elderly woman who, after collapsing at the corner grocery store, is delivered by ambulance to the emergency room. She is alone and unable to communicate. Now stabilized but unconscious, she is in the intensive care unit, needing procedures that require informed consent. A call to the board and care facility that she calls "home" reveals that no one has phoned or visited her in the last half dozen years. The intensivist is at a loss—

---

[1] Joe Klein, "The Long Goodbye," *Time* 179, no. 23 (June 11, 2012): 18–25.

[2] Katy Butler, *Knocking on Heaven's Door* (New York: Scribner, 2013), 251.

[3] Katy Butler, "The Ultimate End-of-Life Plan," *Wall Street Journal*, September 6, 2013, http://www.wsj.com.

[4] Katy Butler, "What Broke My Father's Heart: How a Pacemaker Wrecked Our Family's Life," *New York Times*, June 18, 2010, http://www.nytimes.com.

[5] Butler, *Knocking*, 249.

there is no one to call; no one to ask about resuscitation, invasive diagnostic tests, or the possibility of a feeding tube. Ideally, in such circumstances, the physician would turn to a surrogate decision-maker—a loving Joe or Katy sitting by her bedside caressing her hand—to make such decisions and to provide informed consent. Ideally, such decision-makers know the patient well—as Klein and Butler each knew their parents—and base decisions about medical treatment on what the patient would decide if able to do so—decisions respecting patient values, preferences, and conscience.

This woman and the thousands of other adults who have lost (or perhaps never had) decision-making capacity and do not have either an advance directive or an identifiable, capable, and willing surrogate to make medical decisions on their behalf are some of the most marginalized and at-risk members of society. American health care in the twenty-first century assumes that patients are autonomous, rational beings capable of making treatment—and other—decisions by relying on their own reasoning, understanding, values, aspirations, conscience, and choices. Failing this, there is an assumption that when a patient is unconscious, confused, suffering from dementia, or otherwise unable to make a reasoned and informed medical decision, a loving family member or caring friend will step in to make decisions in their stead. All well and good when it works, but what happens when there is no Joe or Katy—no surrogate decision-maker, no advocate, no loving family, no caring friend, no court-appointed guardian?

Medical decision-making for these "unrepresented" patients is one of the least recognized and most vexing issues in contemporary health care and bioethics. It challenges the commitment and conscience of health care providers, especially in the Catholic health care system with its dedication to caring for the least of these, for those who are poor and marginalized.

Whereas other chapters in this volume focus on conscience formation, conscientious objection, the rhetoric of conscience, and like matters, this chapter strives to do something different, to ask questions not about what conscience is and does but to consider the ramifications of its absence, of its inaccessibility.

Definitions

An unrepresented patient—often mischaracterized as "unbefriended"—is a patient who lacks decisional capacity and for whom no willing, knowledgeable, and capable surrogate decision-maker can be located. It is worth exploring both elements of this definition in more depth.

Decisional capacity is a fluctuating cognitive ability required for informed consent. Capacity is determined by a physician—usually the attending physician—in relation to a specific medical decision and does not imply an across-the-board ability or inability to make any or all decisions related to health or other matters. It is a prerequisite for required informed consent to medical tests, treatments, and procedures and assures that patients are able to appreciate their diagnosis and prognosis, the recommended medical intervention, possible other options, and the risks, benefits, and likely results of each option. Acute and chronic illness, medication, or unconsciousness may impair the ability to decide and render a patient incapacitated, at least for a time. Recent studies indicate that over one quarter of adult general medical inpatients are incapacitated. Residents of nursing homes and Alzheimer's patients lack capacity 44 percent and 54 percent of the time respectively.[6] Currently, an estimated 5.1 million Americans over age sixty-five have Alzheimer's disease; by 2025 that number will rise to 7.1 million.[7] Approximately 10 percent of people age seventy or above have moderate to severe cognitive impairment, the prevalence increasing with age.[8]

Present at the heart of a person, conscience entails the capacity to reflect on one's life, to discern the difference between good and evil, to act responsibly, and to be and become who God is calling one to be.[9] Incapacitated patients at the time of diagnosis can neither form their conscience nor choose in accordance with conscience as their inability to exercise a "judgment of reason"[10] is the source of their diagnosis of incapacity. God's voice may still echo in the heart, but the person cannot, in medicine's measure of capacity, seemingly hear conscience's voice. Far from an abstract notion, here conscience, defined by its absence, renders incapacitated patients uniquely vulnerable in a health care system that centers on autonomous decision-making.

The second characteristic of unrepresented patients, again, is that they are (mischaracterized as) "unbefriended." "Unbefriended patients" may have friends, even family; what they lack is someone who is both willing and capable of making medical decisions—including end of life decisions—for them. Such patients usually do not have an Advance Directive or a Physician Orders for Life-Sustaining Treatment (POLST) form documenting their medical preferences. The elderly make up the largest portion of this patient population. Twenty-two percent of those over the age of sixty-five currently are or are at risk of becoming "elder orphans," aging alone and unsupported

---

[6] Laura L. Sessums, Hanna Zembrzuska, and Jeffrey L. Jackson, "Does This Patient Have Decision-Making Capacity?" *Journal of the American Medical Association* 306, no. 4 (2011): 420–27.

[7] "2015 Alzheimer's Disease Facts and Figures," www.alz.org.

[8] "Growing Older in America: The Health and Retirement Study" (2007): 20, hrsonline.isr.umich.edu.

[9] United States Catholic Conference, *Catechism of the Catholic Church* (2011), article 6, http://www.usccb.org.

[10] Ibid.

with no one to help care for them when the need arises.[11] Other identifiable populations of incapacitated patients include individuals who are homeless, mentally ill, substance abusers, and those who are chronically socially isolated. These people face enormous challenges in our patient-knows-best health care system.

A Wicked Problem

In the words of the bioethicist Nancy Dubler, quoted by Naomi Karp and Erica Wood in their landmark systematic study of incapacitated older adults, "unbefriended older people are the most vulnerable patients because no one cares deeply if they live or die."[12] Dubler observes that the "single greatest category of problems we encounter [at an academic medical center] are those that address the care of decisionally incapable patients who have been transferred for care from nursing homes and who have no living relative or friend who can be involved in the decision-making process."[13] As a result, decisions about diagnosis and treatment risk being ad hoc, arbitrary, biased, secret, prolonged, and careless. The current shift to seeing patients as more than a diagnosis lying in a bed, of looking deeper to unearth narratives of inadequate housing, mental illness, trauma, grief, and the like that affect patients' ability to become and remain healthy are of little help to those who cannot tell their story and have no narrator to tell it for them. It is precisely because they are alone, unseen, and without a knowable story that they command our greatest care.

In a medical system that relies heavily on patient autonomy, choice, and consent, these patients appear to be "a problem." In fact, although such patients should never be considered *the* problem, medical decision-making for these most vulnerable patients has become a wicked problem[14]—a problem that is difficult, if not impossible, to solve because (1) our knowledge is incomplete as these patients are strangers to us; (2) a large number of people and opinions are involved, including members of the medical team and administrators but notably not the patient; (3) the economic burden is potentially large if the length of stay is prolonged due to the lack of a surrogate and an understanding of what the patient would want; and, (4) medical decisions are often matters of life and death.

---

[11] "Aging Baby Boomers, Childless and Unmarried, at Risk of becoming 'Elder Orphans,'" *EurekaAlert!* (2015), http://www.eurekalert.org.

[12] Naomi Karp and Erica Wood, *Incapacitated and Alone: Health Care Decision-Making for Unbefriended Older People* (Washington, DC: American Bar Association, 2003), 1.

[13] Ibid.

[14] See John Kolko, "Wicked Problems: Problems Worth Solving," Austin Center for Design, (2012), www.ssireview.org.

With its commitment to respecting and protecting human dignity and answering God's call to care for the least of these, Catholic health care should be front and center in tackling this wicked problem. Jesus' love for every person—notably, in this case, those who, having taken leave of their senses, are ostracized and alone—informs and animates Catholic health care. The *Ethical and Religious Directives for Catholic Health Care Services* (ERDs) claim that "particular attention should be given to the health care needs of the poor, the uninsured, and the underinsured."[15] The incapacitated and alone should be added to the list.

The Question of Conscience

Conscience is an increasingly important matter in Catholic health care. Catholic considerations speak of the need to respect conscience as both the seat of selfhood and the capacity to engage in rational decision-making. But what does it mean to respect conscience in patients who suffer from dementia, mental illness, or neurodegenerative disease, those in whom the self is hidden and unknown to us? Adding complexity to this question, consider what might and what should happen when there is no one who can convey patient values, speak of deep commitments of conscience, and make decisions on behalf of those so afflicted. Patients of such extreme vulnerability force us to reconsider the role of conscience in light of its inaccessibility and to construct the decisional frameworks required if we are to live out our commitment to social justice and concern for decisionally incapacitated persons. How can Catholic health care respect the conscience of such persons—no less made in the image of God than a fully rational person embedded in deep relationships—and exercise a preferential option for them? This essay is an effort to provide some perspectives on this vexing question.

Unrepresented patients call for a reawakening of moral imagination and a reconsideration of our go-to notion of conscience as solely an individual matter. In contrast, the concept of conscience envisioned by Catholic health care is grounded in the meaning of its Latin roots—*con-scienta*—a "knowing together" and "is fed by four sources: one's own natural inclination to discern and do the good and avoid evil, the shared experience of the community in which one lives, reality itself and, finally, divine revelation."[16] In medicine's estimation, incapacitated patients have no ability to evaluate reality or to discern good from evil and cannot access "the deposit of faith" shared by

---

[15] United States Conference of Catholic Bishops, *Ethical and Religious Directives for Catholic Health Care Services* (Washington, DC: USCCB Publishing, 2009), 7.

[16] John J. Hardt, "Some Thoughts on Conscience in the Delivery of Catholic Health Care," *Health Care Ethics USA* 16, no. 1 (2008): 2–3.

"a believing community."[17] However, they remain embedded in "the shared experience" of the community in which they live, placing a weighty responsibility on the community to respond to their plight and to care deeply about whether and in what way vulnerable patients live and die.

The Current State of Decision-making for Unrepresented Patients

Consider the following patients:

- Juan is a thirty-year-old homeless Latino man who arrives in the ER with severe burns after being set on fire in a local park. After he is stabilized, he is transferred to the burn unit. He has no identification and, due to the severity of his burns and to his medication, no ability to communicate.

- Deepak is a twenty-year-old student who collapses in a pizza parlor. The cook calls 911, and the young man is taken to the ER by ambulance. Three days later, he remains unconscious in the ICU. His personal effects include a Calgary library card as his only identification.

- After twenty years in a nursing home, ninety-year-old Alzheimer's patient Sara has outlived her husband and her children. She is admitted to the hospital because of a high fever. On exam, she has severe decubitus ulcers and septicemia. She is awake but confused. Her thick chart indicates numerous previous admissions for aspiration pneumonia. There is no advance directive or POLST, and the social work notes indicate a failed search for family and friends. The resident wants to write comfort care orders.

All of these patients have two things in common—they have lost the capacity to make medical decisions and they are alone.

Because our health care system privileges patient autonomy and relies on patient informed consent, incapacitated patients from any subpopulation who have no legally recognized instruction for physicians to follow and do not have a surrogate decision-maker to make decisions on their behalf pose two equally vexing ethical questions:

- *Who* should make decisions for them?
- *How* should medical decisions be made for them?

---

[17] Ibid.

These questions take on heightened valence when the decision needing to be made involves invasive, risky, uncomfortable procedures or life-sustaining interventions, where the decision to withhold or withdraw medical intervention may result in death.

In general, in emergency situations such as after a crushing motor vehicle accident or massive stroke, incapacitated patients can be treated without their consent. Absent an emergency, health care providers may be able to rely on an incapacitated patient's advance directive indicating treatment preferences or a POLST addressing current circumstances. They may have previously appointed a health care agent or surrogate decision-maker through a durable power of attorney for health care. Many states outline a hierarchy of surrogate decision-makers—usually beginning with the spouse—for those without such documentation. But, none of these are available to help the unrepresented patient; none of these can tell the medical team what Juan, Deepak, or Sara would want them to do.

Like all patients, unrepresented patients have a right to medically and ethically sound decisions made on their behalf and in their best interest, that is, decisions with which reasonable people of good will would agree in similar circumstances considering the patient's beliefs, values, and cultural, ethnic, and religious perspectives, if known. Unfortunately, that right can be lost in the hodgepodge of procedures governing their care.

Current decision-making practices for the unrepresented vary widely across the country, and this variation leads to inconsistency and invisibility in how these patients are identified and treated. When present, laws differ from state to state and county to county. Absent clear guidelines from the law, few systems or processes are in place to guide decision-making for unrepresented patients, resulting in substantial differences among providers, hospitals, and locales in how medical decisions are obtained and documented. Even when present, decision-making procedures often lack adequate safeguards, necessary transparency, and consistent application.

The *Ethical and Religious Directives* are of little direct help as they too assume that patients can decide for themselves, for example, appreciating the distinction between proportionate and disproportionate means of preserving life and choosing appropriately (directives 56, 57). Further, directive 32 reads: "While every person is obliged to use ordinary means to preserve his or her health, no person should be obliged to submit to a health care procedure that the person has *judged, with a free and informed conscience,* not to provide a reasonable hope of benefit without imposing excessive risks and burdens on the patient or excessive expense to family or community" (emphasis mine). But there is no ability to judge, no discernible access to the voice of conscience of the incapacitated patient. Ideally, a surrogate decision-maker can render a decision faithful to the patient's intentions and values or in the patient's best interest thereby providing free and informed consent or, in some cases, informed refusal as would the patient if capable (directives 25, 26, 27). But, there is no surrogate to decide. How do we answer the persistent and urgent question of what to do for these most vulnerable patients? What would we want done if we found ourselves incapacitated and alone in the ICU?

In general, institutions use one of the three following approaches—either formally or informally—to address decision-making for unrepresented patients in nonemergency situations when informed consent is needed: (1) the primary physician alone or in consultation with one or more other physicians decides; (2) the ethics committee (or subcommittee) or an interdisciplinary committee convened specifically for this purpose decides; or (3) decisions are made by a court-appointed guardian,[18] which, in most states, is the sole legally sanctioned remedy to this problem.[19]

The Courts as Decision-makers

Notably, petitioning the court to appoint a guardian is a glacially slow, cumbersome process, often taking months, if not a year or more, and routinely failing to meet the real-time need of the patient for treatment decisions and the treating team for guidance.[20] In almost all cases, guardianship should be the last resort. Although a court order authorizing, withdrawing, or withholding medical intervention may be pursued, it is often discouraged. The California Probate Code goes so far as to state that absent controversy, "a court is normally not the proper forum in which to make health care decisions, including decisions regarding life-sustaining treatment."[21] Where to turn?

Physicians as Decision-makers

Since the law and the *Directives* are largely silent, and large numbers of hospitals do not have formal written procedures for making decisions, physicians often assume sole authority, without consultation or oversight, over decision-making for incapacitated patients lacking surrogates. Douglas White and colleagues have published two studies—one focused on seven months of medical ICU admissions in a West Coast teaching hospital and

---

[18] Rebecca L. Volpe and Deborah Steinman, "Peeking Inside the Black Box: One Institution's Experience Developing Policy for Unrepresented Patients," *Hamline Law Review* 36, no. 2 (2014): 265–74.

[19] Thaddeus Mason Pope and Tanya Sellers, "The Unbefriended: Making Healthcare Decisions for Patients without Surrogates," *Journal of Clinical Ethics* 23, no. 2 (2012): 178.

[20] Thaddeus Mason Pope, "Making Medical Decisions for Patients without Surrogates," *New England Journal of Medicine* 369, no. 21 (2013): 1976–78.

[21] California Probate Code §4650(c).

the other on six months of medical ICU admissions in seven medical centers across the country. These studies indicate that most medical decisions—including end-of-life decisions—for unrepresented patients, who account for 5 percent of ICU deaths, were made by physicians without judicial or institutional review.[22] Such ad hoc, nontransparent, inconsistent decision-making is ethically troubling. Although treating clinicians have a vital role to play in making decisions for unrepresented patients based on their medical expertise and duty to act for their patients' good, "serious ethical problems arise when they are asked to exceed their socially sanctioned role of advisor to be the sole decision-maker."[23]

Although physicians are able to make time-sensitive and medically informed decisions for the patient, such unilateral decision-making introduces potential conflicts of interest that may compromise a clinician's ability to act as decision-maker. For example, financial conflicts of interest may result in overtreatment in a fee-for-service model and undertreatment in a capitated model.[24] Since conflicts of interest can affect decision-making in unrecognized and unintended ways, it may be impossible for physicians to reliably identify and manage these conflicts. Inconsistency, lack of procedural fairness, and an erosion of public trust are further concerns.[25] In addition, sizable differences exist in how physicians and the general public evaluate and reason under critical care conditions.[26] The *Ethical and Religious Directives* explicitly recognize the health care professional-patient relationship warning against "manipulation, intimidation, or condescension" and either acting independently of the other (introduction to part 3). Concern for the physician assuming sole decision-making authority has led many states to ban the practice.[27]

Despite this caveat, many decisions about care for unrepresented patients in both hospitals and nursing homes are made by physicians alone. Over a dozen states authorize attending physicians to make medical decisions for

---

[22] Douglas B. White, J. Randall Curtis, Bernard Lo, and John M. Luce, "Decisions to Limit Life-Sustaining Treatment for Critically Ill Patients who Lack Both Decision-making Capacity and Surrogate Decision-makers," *Critical Care Medicine* 34, no. 8 (2006): 2053–59; Douglas B. White, J. Randall Curtis, Leslie E. Wolf, Thomas J. Prendergast, Darren B. Taichman, Gary Kuniyoshi, Frank Acerra, Bernard Lo, and John M. Luce, "Life Support for Patients without a Surrogate Decision Maker: Who Decides?" *Annals of Internal Medicine* 147, no. 1 (2007): 34–40.

[23] Douglas B. White, Albert Jonsen, and Bernard Lo, "Ethical Challenge: When Clinicians Act as Surrogates for Unrepresented Patients," *American Journal of Critical Care* 21, no. 3 (2012): 206.

[24] Ibid., 204.

[25] Ibid., 202–7.

[26] Anders Rydvall and Niels Lynöe, "Withholding and Withdrawing Life-Sustaining Treatment: A Comparative Study of the Ethical Reasoning of Physicians and the General Public," *Critical Care* 12 (2008), http://ccforum.biomedcentral.com.

[27] See, e.g., California Probate Code §4701.

unrepresented patients, either solo or in consultation with a second physician and perhaps the ethics committee. This is understandable in that physicians are present, proficient, and relatively prompt in their decision-making. But their potential conflicts of interest and recognized and unrecognized biases regarding, for example, disability, race, and culture may cloud their ability to render solid, defensible patient-centered decisions on their own.

Conflicts of interest and clinician bias, while always potential concerns, are less problematic when the patient is capable of representing his or her own interests or has a surrogate to represent those interests. During the process of shared decision-making, ideally there is a sharing not only of information but also of values and commitments. Physicians ask about life goals and treatment preferences in an effort to tailor possible medical intervention to meet patient aims. Ordinarily, the patient or surrogate has the final say over the treatment plan. But incapacitated patients have no say, no ability to discern influential conflicts of interest or appreciate potential bias, no ability to disagree with the plan. It is simply impossible for these patients to know if the physician is trustworthy and fair-minded or if their treatment goals will be met.

Ethics Committees as Decision-makers

"The best answer to the question of 'who will decide if not the clinician' remains unsettled."[28] Appointing the ethics committee or a similar body to make decisions on the patient's behalf reduces concerns about physician conflict of interest, introduces multiple points of view, and allows decision-making to keep pace with a rapidly developing clinical course. Although not ideal, it is a defensible process while awaiting a more satisfying solution.

This was the approach taken in 2001 when, noticing an increase in hospital admissions of unrepresented patients and questions about decision-making for them, the Santa Clara County Medical Association (SCCMA) proposed a Model Policy for Health Care Decisions for Incapacitated Patients without Surrogates,[29] a version of which has now been adopted by eight hospitals in Santa Clara County and two hospitals in San Mateo County, neighboring counties in California. At the time of adoption, three of these hospitals were members of the Daughters of Charity Healthcare System. The policy goals are "to make and effect health care decisions in accordance with a patient's best interest, taking into consideration the patient's personal values

---

[28] White, Jonsen, and Lo, "Ethical Challenge," 206.

[29] See Santa Clara Medical Association, "Recommendation for Establishing Policy on Health Care Decisions for Incapacitated Patients without Surrogates," February 2001; "A Preface to the Santa Clara County Medical Association Ethics Committee Model Policy on Health Care Decisions for Incapacitated Patients without Surrogates," July 2001, http://www.sccma-mcms.org.

and wishes to the extent that these are known" and "to establish uniform procedures" to manage medical decision-making for unrepresented patients.

In the absence of a valid advance directive, a valid POLST (or equivalent), and a willing, capable surrogate, the Model Policy empowers the ethics committee, composed of medical professionals and members of the community, to act as the decision-maker for incapacitated patients. Acting as the surrogate in this particular instance importantly changes the role of the ethics committee from advisory only to that of decision-maker. The ethics committee provides timely decision-making that is independent of but, deliberately, informed by the attending physician and members of the medical team. Ethics committees are by design multidisciplinary, accustomed to considering thorny cases, and able to weigh both medical and nonmedical considerations in determining the best interest of a particular patient. Relying on committee members from various disciplines—including nonmedical community members and a member of the spiritual care team—militates against both groupthink and bias on the part of physicians, the medical team, or any single discipline. Involving someone with a similar cultural background or religious tradition in the decision-making process, when possible, is encouraged. A committee approach ensures that the decision rests on many shoulders, not just those of the clinician, and extends the practice of shared decision-making to unrepresented patients.

Initially, an "ethics consultant"—usually one or more members of the ethics committee—provides advice about the decision-making process and ensures that medical decisions are made in accordance with the procedures outlined in the policy. The consultant must make all reasonable efforts to learn about the patient's medical treatment preferences. When possible, patients themselves are consulted, as those who lack the capacity to fully understand their medical circumstances and options, if conscious, may be able to provide important insight into their values and wishes and actively participate in decision-making.

One of the notable aspects of the model policy is that it empowers the social worker to look diligently for a surrogate decision-maker—talking to homeless people in the park Juan frequented; calling the main library in Calgary and eventually Deepak's parents in India; perusing the chart from the nursing home and talking to staff to find Sara's long-lost nephew. The policy's support of the time and effort expended by social workers often results in more information and, at times, a willing and grateful surrogate decision-maker.

If the decision under consideration involves withholding or withdrawing life-sustaining intervention(s), a multidisciplinary subcommittee of the ethics committee becomes the surrogate decision-maker and advocates on behalf of the patient by inquiring about the patient's capacity, the diagnosis and prognosis, the attempts to locate a surrogate and determine patient preferences, other options, and the likelihood of restoring the patient to an "acceptable quality of life." The subcommittee can ask for additional medical opinions, further investigations into the surrogate availability, and treatment preferences. When ready, the subcommittee makes an independent finding regarding the proposed withholding or withdrawing of medical intervention.

In a case in which there is no general agreement among subcommittee members or complete disagreement, the chief of staff or designee must be included in the decision-making process to assist in resolution. In cases in which the decision authorizes the withholding or withdrawing of life-sustaining intervention, the chief of staff must approve of the decision. Irresolvable conflicts can be referred to court for legal resolution but only "in extreme circumstances." Any implementation of a decision to withhold or withdraw life-sustaining intervention is the responsibility of the primary treating physician.

Process and accurate record-keeping are important, as is retrospective review of each case. The process must not only be timely, efficient, and cost-effective but also render decisions in the best interest of the patient and consistent with patient values as best as can be known, not solely in the interest of the institution, providers, and payers.

Upstream Solutions

The Model Policy provides the interdisciplinary collaboration and perseverance needed to address the wicked problem of unrepresented patients. But a better solution would be simultaneously to attack the issue upstream from the problem by encouraging and enabling advance care planning, including the appointment of a surrogate decision-maker, in an attempt to prevent patients from falling into the ranks of the unrepresented in the first place. Modern medical technology has given us unmatched opportunities for health—ameliorating degenerative processes, preventing and curing disease, alleviating pain and other symptoms. But sometimes this same technology becomes fearsome—prolonging a terminal disease, forestalling death, burdening patients and families with unprecedented decisions. These decisions become excruciatingly difficult when there is no guidance from the patient as to what is to be done. An advance directive can provide needed guidance to family and friends and, in the case of unrepresented patients, to strangers—physicians, nurses, members of the ethics committee, the court— for whom such guidance is arguably more vital. Deciding for a loved one who is knocking on heaven's door is hard; deciding for the stranger who knocks is excruciatingly difficult. An advance directive provides a window into patient wishes, interests, and values that can direct deliberation and decisions made on behalf of these most vulnerable persons.

All of us, as future patients, should advocate for a fair, transparent, efficient, and cost-effective model for medical decision-making for those who
cannot decide for themselves and do not have someone to decide on their
behalf. We can keep ourselves and others from slipping into this group by
insisting that advance directives be considered, a surrogate decision-maker
appointed, and, when the time comes, a POLST form executed. Those of us
in health care can identify and seek out those family members, neighbors, and
patients who have not nurtured close relationships with family and friends and
are apt to become isolated and alone and encourage them to document their
health care wishes and appoint a surrogate decision-maker. To quote Dubler
once again, "We owe these patients the highest level of ethical and medical
scrutiny; we owe it to them to protect them from over-treatment and from
under-treatment; . . . we owe it to them to help them live better or to die in
comfort and not alone."[30] This is what we must do for the least of these; we
must care deeply not only if they live or die but how they live out their lives
and die.

Unrepresented Patients in the
Catholic Health Care Context

Catholic health care is rooted in God's love and the healing ministry of
Jesus, which gives rise to a set of commitments including respect for intrinsic
human dignity and a particular concern for those whom Jesus called "the
least of these." Catholic health care includes more than one thousand health
care facilities in all fifty states. One in six patients is cared for in a Catholic
hospital, resulting in over 5 million admissions per year and over 101 million
outpatient visits.[31] With commitments to the intrinsic dignity of the human
person, deep care for the poor and the marginalized, and robust promotion of
the common good, Catholic health care is well situated to address the "wicked
problem" posed by patients who cannot make their own medical decisions
and lack an identifiable, capable, and willing decision-maker. The commitment to the communal nature of conscience, rooted not only in one's ability to
discern and do the good but in a life that is lived in and shaped by community,
sparks the moral imagination to consider what it means to bear responsibility
for the other, exercising mercy and justice on behalf of those marginalized by
illness and the inability to make decisions in a culture steeped in autonomy.

So long as legally supported decision-making processes remain elusive,
the commitment to care for the least of these compels the development of

---

[30] Karp and Wood, *Incapacitated and Alone*, 1.

[31] Catholic Health Association, "Catholic Health Care in the United States," January
2016, www.chausa.org.

policies that structure decision-making in a way that is consistent, transparent, workable, timely, deliberative, and in the best interest of the patient. Attending to the mandate to care for the least of these demands procedures and policies that demonstrate respect for the patient as a person and support decision-making that is:

- Patient centered
- Consistent with patient values and preferences as best as these are known
- In the patient's best interest, striking a balance between the dangers of undertreatment and overtreatment
- Timely and efficient
- Cost-effective

Catholic health care is committed to respect for human dignity, care for the poor, and fostering the common good. Directive 3 states that "Catholic health care should distinguish itself by service to and advocacy for those people whose social condition puts them at the margins of our society and makes them particularly vulnerable to discrimination. . . . In particular, the person with mental or physical disabilities, regardless of the cause or severity, must be treated as a unique person of incomparable worth, with the same right to life and to adequate health care as all other persons." Surely, this must compel us to advocate on behalf of incapacitated persons who have no Joe or Katy—who have no other voice but ours—and to develop policies that reflect caring deeply how they live and die.

Conscience, Race, and Health Care Disparities

Catholicism and the Formation of Conscience in Light of a Black Liberation Bioethics

Shawnee M. Daniels-Sykes

> Always be ready to give an explanation to anyone for a reason for your hope, but do it with gentleness and reverence, keeping your conscience clear, so that, when you are maligned, those who defame your good conduct in Christ may themselves be put to shame. For it is better to suffer for doing good, if that be the will of God, than for doing evil.
>
> —1 Peter 3:15–17

To grasp the central problem raised by the consideration of conscience, Catholic health care, and race, it is important to understand two things about the theology of conscience. First, conscience is the scene of the encounter between the person and God. As *Gaudium et Spes* says, "Conscience is the most secret core and sanctuary of a man. There he is alone with God, Whose voice echoes in his depths."[1] Second, however singular the nature of this encounter between the person and the divine, it is also the case that conscience is profoundly shaped for good or ill by the culture that persons inhabit.[2] I note these two things because it will be the argument of this chapter that the principal task of Catholic health care in addressing the conscience of African Americans is to recognize the powerful and damaging cultural

---

[1] *Gaudium et Spes, The Pastoral Constitution on the Church in the Modern World,* 16.

[2] Bryan N. Massingale, "The Challenge of Unconscious Racial Bias," in *Conscience and Catholicism: Rights, Responsibilities, and Institutional Responses*, ed. David E. DeCosse and Kristin E. Heyer (Maryknoll, NY: Orbis Books, 2015), 56–61.

forces—cultural forces intimately linked to structural inequalities—that have shaped African Americans' approach and access to health care.

The January 17, 2016, *New York Times* article titled "In Rural Alabama, a Longtime Mistrust of Medicine Fuels a Tuberculosis Outbreak" provides a tragic but helpful way to understand the contextual problem of race, conscience, and Catholic health care.[3] The author recounts that Marion County, Alabama, is in the midst of a horrendous tuberculosis outbreak, so grim that it has posted an incidence rate about 100 times greater than the state's and worse than in many developing countries. Residents, local officials, and medical experts agree that underlying the struggle to combat this epidemic are generations of African Americans' experiences of limited health care access, endemic poverty, and deep-seated mistrust of the health care system.

Many African Americans' mistrustful dispositions are mainly grounded in the extensive history of institutionalized racism[4] in the US health care system—a history from which Catholic health care institutions have not been exempt. That is, when the health care system has historically set up pervasive racial barriers to access and for centuries has provided racially disparate treatment and care for African Americans, these conditions deeply harmed all health care institutions that purported to participate in this important healing ministry. Bioethicist and lawyer Patricia A. King unpacks the devastating dimensions of this history of racism as it relates to health care:

> African Americans [blacks] suffered injustices in at least three ways. First black health needs were dismissed, except to the extent that they were relevant to the health status of whites. Second, since blacks were not only regarded as inferior, but were powerless, it was permissible to exploit their helplessness in education and experimental endeavors to further the health needs of whites. Finally, the assumption, stereotypes, and myths that evolved and sustained faith in white superiority became obstacles to the creation, implementation, and interpretation of efforts to improve black health status.[5]

---

[3] Alan Blinder, "In Rural Alabama, a Longtime Mistrust of Medicine Fuels a Tuberculosis Outbreak," *New York Times*, January 17, 2016, 1–4, www.nytimes.com.

[4] Institutionalized racism is defined as any system that asserts that there is a biologically and scientifically unalterable basis to differences and, for example, allows the dominant white group to believe and think that African Americans are not fully human, unequal to them, inferior, disposable, and/or can be used and abused for any monetary or intellectual gains. It also comprises those policies, practices, and activities, which injure or damage an individual or group based on race.

[5] Patricia A. King, "Race, Justice, and Research," in *Beyond Consent: Seeking Justice in Research*, ed. Jeffrey P. Kahn, Anna C. Mastroianni, and Jeremy Sugarman (Oxford: Oxford University Press, 1998), 91.

These realities of racist health care, I believe, have traumatized and crippled the consciences and well-being of many in the African American population. One way of capturing this damage, especially as it relates to conscience, is in terms of the concept of "black internalized oppression." Internalized oppression for Paulo Freire, writing in *Pedagogy of the Oppressed*,[6] means that "the oppressed, having internalized the image of the oppressor and adopted those guidelines, are fearful of freedom."[7] The oppressed accept their life of dread, fear, and mistrust, their vulnerability, and their exploitation, done unto them at the hands of their oppressors. African American psychiatrist Dr. Alvin Poussaint also speaks of such a corrosive, internalizing process among African Americans in response to years of health care mistreatment. He says, "The legacy of hundreds of years of official representation and misinterpretation of black behavior is a morass of harmful myths and stereotypes about African-Americans' behaviors and mental health, including faulty beliefs, that have been internalized by blacks themselves—with devastating results."[8] Deep inside themselves, many African Americans harbor the pain and the memories, the fears, the confusions, and negative attitudes that are the results of long-term overt or covert medical and clinical abuse, neglect, and maltreatment.

In this chapter, first I discuss Catholic health care as an expression of Jesus' healing ministry and in light of seeing race through the lens of being color-blind or the lens of difference. Second, I offer concrete examples of racial oppression in clinical research and health care. Finally, I invite Catholic health care leaders, providers, and staff to consider more deeply what it means to respect the consciences of African American patients and clients. For this, I draw on the works of Catholic theologian Bryan Massingale[9] and sociologist Joe R. Feagin.[10] Massingale discusses the notion of unconscious racial bias, and Feagin offers practical suggestions for how to foster respect for the consciences of African Americans living in a culture of racism.[11] In tandem with their work, I call on tools drawn from an African American liberation bioethics.

---

[6] Paulo Freire, *Pedagogy of the Oppressed: New Revised 20th Anniversary Edition* (New York: Continuum, 1994), 40.

[7] Paulo Freire, *Pedagogy of the Oppressed* (New York: Herder and Herder, 1970), 31.

[8] Alvin F. Poussaint and Amy Alexander, *Lay My Burden Down: Unraveling Suicide and Mental Health Crisis among African Americans* (Boston: Beacon Press, 2000), 63.

[9] Massingale, "Challenge of Unconscious Racial Bias," 64–68.

[10] Joe R. Feagin, *Racist America: Roots, Current Realities, & Future Reparations* (New York: Routledge, 2000), 254–55.

[11] Massingale, "Challenge of Unconscious Racial Bias," 64–68.

Catholic Health Care and the Persistence
of Institutionalized Racism

The values of Catholic health care emerge from a long-standing, deeply rooted biblical tradition that illuminates the ministry and mission of Jesus Christ. In Jesus' healing ministry, he cleanses a man with leprosy (Mt 8:1–4; Mk 1:40–42); he cures a woman who was hemorrhaging (Mt 9:20–22; Mk 5:25–34); and he brings a young girl back to life (Mt 9:18, 23–25; Mk 5:35–42). Flowing from Jesus' healing commitments are principles and practices that constitute Catholic health care, such as respecting human dignity, treating patients in a holistic way, prioritizing the needs of the poor, contributing to the common good, and stewardship of economic resources.[12] Successive iterations of the *Ethical and Religious Directives for Catholic Health Care Services*[13] have made concrete these general value commitments—commitments that arise from the fundamental theological commitments at the heart of Catholic health care.[14]

This brief illustration of what makes Catholic health care institutions Catholic reminds us of the theological and spiritual underpinnings of mission and ministry. Sister Carol Keehan, chief executive officer of the Catholic Health Association, writes about the moral problem concerning enduring health disparities. She states that "the primary goal of Catholic health care is to protect the human dignity and honor of the needs of the people we serve."[15] She goes on to note, however, that "when people receive substandard care or experience poor health outcomes simply because they are minorities, our health system is failing. It is failing to provide quality care that is *blind* to racial, ethnic, or socio-economic status. It is failing to meet the needs of millions of people."[16]

In essence, when there is a perceived breach or a threat to the health status of anyone who enters into Catholic health care, employees of Catholic health care facilities are mandated, indeed required, to respond in appropriate manners that parallel Jesus' healing ministry. But the metaphor of blindness is a tricky concept. I understand Sister Keehan to be saying that just as social justice should be blind, so too should the delivery of health care: No attributes like race, class, gender, or religion should cause a person or group to receive less health care than they deserve. This is certainly true, and Sister Keehan's

---

[12] United States Conference of Catholic Bishops, *Ethical and Religious Directives for Catholic Health Care Services*, 5th ed. (November 2009), 10–11.

[13] Ibid., 2.

[14] See Kevin O'Rourke and Thomas Kopfensteiner, "A Brief History: A Summary of the Development of the Ethical and Religious Directives for Catholic Health Care Services," *Health Progress* (November–December 2001): 18.

[15] Carol Keehan, "Ending Healthcare Disparities: An Urgent Priority and a Growing Possibility," *Frontiers of Health Services Management* 30, no. 3 (Spring 2014): 32.

[16] Ibid., 32. I italicized the word "blind."

concern sounds a prophetic call for Catholic health care. But the metaphor of blindness also, I believe, can work against doing social justice. Thus I believe that leaders, providers, and staff members of Catholic health care institutions must also *not* be blind to racial, ethnic, or socioeconomic differences. I offer as an explanation what Michael Omi and Howard Winant maintain: That "whites tend to locate racism in color consciousness and find its absence in color-blindness."[17] One's ethnic, social, and racial status in the society in which we live is what is revealed for all to see. We all *see* racial differences and encounter people of various statuses. We should never be blind to one's particular physical and spiritual characteristics, language, gender, sexual orientation, and creed, among others.

Please understand that I am not denying that the absolute spiritual and theological sensibilities of being blind to differences allows us to see that all human beings are created in the image and likeness of God and, thus, that we are all brothers and sisters together in Christ Jesus. This understanding also coheres with the passage in Paul's Letter to the Galatians (3:28), that "there is no Jew nor Greek, there is neither slave nor free person, there is not male and female; for you are all one in Christ Jesus." Nevertheless, in any perspective that calls us to be blind to racial, ethnic, and social statuses, I believe what is implicit and missing from the conversation are the three points that Bryan Massingale makes about racism:

1. *We do not know what we are talking about*—that we lack clarity and agreement as to what constitutes "racism" in a so-called post-racist society;
2. *We do not know how to talk about it*—especially in mixed-race settings. The various racial and ethnic groups talk about "race" among themselves and in "safe" company. But we don't know how to talk about race productively in an interracial situation, where we often are inhibited by concerns of not wanting to appear insensitive, ignorant, or intolerant;
3. *We really don't want to talk about it*—even unwillingly—to address the core reasons for racial tensions and inequality in the United States, namely that a specific racial group benefits from our nation's racial hierarchy.[18]

Hence I believe that, in terms of health care, perspectives that call us to be blind to racial, ethnic, and social statuses coincide with people not knowing

---

[17] Michael Omi and Howard Winant, *Racial Formation in the United States: From the 1960s to the 1990s* (New York: Routledge, 1994), 70.

[18] Bryan Massingale, *Racial Justice and the Catholic Church* (Maryknoll, NY: Orbis Books, 2010), xi–xii.

or not understanding the long-standing history of maltreatment in health care endured by African Americans; nor do they know why the consciences of many African Americans are wary, mistrustful, suspicious, and fearful of accessing the health care system. It will be helpful next to look to history to understand the roots of this mistrust. Blindness to race must not be a barrier to understanding the history of the oppressive imposition of difference on generations of African Americans.

The History of African American Maltreatment in Medicine and Clinical Research

During the period of African chattel slavery in the early seventeenth century, African Americans were the subjects of research and medical abuses. According to bioethicist Harriet Washington,

> Enslavement could not have existed and certainly could not have persisted without medical science. Physicians were very much dependent upon slaves, both for economic security and for the enslaved "clinical material" that fed the American medical research and medical training that bolstered physicians' professional development.[19]

"The Dissecting Hall" illustrates further this notion about "clinical material":

> Yuh see dat house? Dat great brick house? Way younder down the street?
> Dey used to take dead folk een dar wrapped een a long white sheet.
> An' sometimes we'an a nigger'd stopped, a-wondering who was dead.
> Dem stujent men would take a club an' bat im on de head.
> An' drag dat poor dead nigger chile right een dat 'section hall to 'vestigate
> 'is liver—lights—
> His gizzard an' is gall.
> Tek off dat nigger's han's an' feet—
> His eyes, his head, an 'all, an' w'en dem stujent finish Dar was nothin' left at all.[20]

---

[19] Harriet A. Washington, *Medical Apartheid: The Dark History of Medical Experimentation on Black Americans from the Colonial Times to the Present* (New York: Doubleday, 2006), 26.

[20] I found this conversation in an article by Todd L. Savitt called "The Use of Blacks

In essence, African Americans during this early period of history had little control over medical decisions made to use their body parts or even to use their corpses for medical research.[21] Medical personnel believed that African Americans were different from whites and thus could be dominated and oppressed because they were considered inferior. Further, from research on human bodies, scientists documented that whites allegedly had the largest skulls and the largest brains and were thus superior and more intelligent with the best character of all human beings.[22] To the contrary, African Americans allegedly had the smallest skulls, the smallest brains, and were, therefore, considered unintelligent with no character.[23] These same myths and stereotypes persist today in discussions around deficiencies in African Americans' intellectual understandings of health and disease.

In the eighteenth and nineteenth centuries, white medical researchers and physicians practiced on African Americans to develop their clinical techniques and skills. The father of gynecology, Dr. Marion Sims, for example, in the nineteenth century used African female slaves to perfect his vaginal-vesicular surgical procedure.[24] Sims performed painful surgeries on twenty-six women who had vaginal fistulas. His experimentation led to the development of a forerunner of the modern speculum. Moreover, also in the nineteenth century, Dr. Robert Jennings was credited with the development of a successful vaccination against typhoid infections that resulted from his successful experimentation on thirty slaves and free blacks.[25] Important reasons for poor health for African Americans are deeply intertwined with and stem from such examples of racist medicine.

Such medical experimentation is not a relic of a distant past. Two examples of twentieth-century medical experimental abuse and neglect toward African Americans reveal the dramatic persistence of this exploitative fascination. The first example concerns a thirty-one-year-old woman named Henrietta Lacks. She was a poor Southern black tobacco worker, who worked the same

---

for Medical Experimentation and Demonstration in the Old South," *Journal of Southern History* 48 (August 1982): 341–42. In a footnote he gives credit to Anne Donato for the reference, which is preceded by *Scribe* 1 (December 1951): 17. Unfortunately, I was not able to find the primary source to verify this conversation.

[21] Savitt, "Use of Blacks for Medical Experimentation and Demonstration in the Old South," 331–48.

[22] Washington, *Medical Apartheid*, 35.

[23] Ibid.

[24] L. L. Walls, "The Medical Ethics of Dr. Marion Sims: A Fresh Look at the Historical Record," *Journal of Medical Ethics* 32 (2006): 342–50; Leon R. Kapsalis, "Mastering the Female Pelvis: Race and the Tools of Reproduction," in *Skin Deep, Spirit Strong: The Black Female Body in American Culture* (Ann Arbor: University of Michigan Press, 2002), 263–300.

[25] Barbara L. Bernier, "Class, Race, and Poverty: Medical Technologies and Socio-Political Choices," *Harvard Blackletter Law Journal* 115 (1994): 119.

land as her slave ancestors. In February 1951, Lacks walked through the doors of Johns Hopkins Hospital in Baltimore, Maryland, bleeding profusely from untreated cervical cancer. It turns out that her cancer cells had a remarkable generative capacity, a fact made evident in the course of her treatment. Indeed, during that treatment, she had her cancer cells taken from her without her knowledge or informed consent. She did not live to see that she would make Dr. George Gey famous only ten months after she died; he used Lacks's peculiar and highly generative cells to develop a medical specialty called cell-line, or HeLa cells that were thought then and have proved to be capable of becoming cells for healing.[26] Her cells, for instance, became noteworthy and vital to the development of the polio vaccine; to uncover secrets of cancer research; and to lead to important advances like human cloning and gene mapping. Because of this demonstrated therapeutic capacity, the cells have been bought and sold for years by medical scientists and researchers.[27] Years later, Henrietta Lacks's family members were made aware that the HeLa cells had become one of the most prized biological specimens in medicine. They remain hopeful that one day they will also share in the financial profits or royalties for the worldwide usage of their relative's cells in advancing medicine and scientific research.[28] Lacks and her family members were exploited because they never gave permission for use of the cells and accrued no financial benefit from, literally, their own flesh and blood.

A second noteworthy medical experimentation pertains to the United States Public Health Services Study, more popularly known as the Tuskegee Syphilis Study, which lasted from 1932 to 1972. Driving this longitudinal study is "a striking parallel developed between the tone of race relations and the extent to which physicians attributed the incidence of syphilis among blacks to physical inferiority and sexual promiscuity as intrinsic to their racial characteristics."[29] Recall my previous discussion about the alleged intellectual inferiority of African slaves who have smaller brains than those of white people. Sexual promiscuity is another stereotype attributed to African Americans; the principal investigators believed such promiscuity contributed to the spread of a sexually transmitted disease like syphilis.

The Tuskegee Syphilis Study involved 399 poor, uneducated African American men from Macon County, Alabama. It is important to note that another 201 men constituted the control group, and that these men had contracted syph-

---

[26] W. Michael Byrd and Linda A. Clayton, *An American Health Dilemma: Race, Medicine, and Health Care in the United States: 1901–2000* (New York: Routledge, 2002), 285–86; see also Rebecca Skloot, *The Immortal Life of Henrietta Lacks* (New York: Crown, 2010).

[27] Skloot, *Immortal Life of Henrietta Lacks*.

[28] Ibid., 152–98, 312.

[29] James H. Jones, *Bad Blood: The Tuskegee Syphilis Experiment*, new and exp. ed. (New York: Free Press, 1993), 23–24.

ilis and were not injected with the disease by the principal investigators of this experiment. Nevertheless, "in the early 1930s treatment for syphilis consisted of mercury and two arsenic compounds called arphenamine and neoarsphenam-ine."[30] The experimental group continued to receive this chemical treatment, while the control group received a placebo. Although in the early 1940s peni-cillin was approved by the Federal Drug Administration of the United States to treat and cure syphilis, the investigators of this US-government-sponsored experiment ignored this approval of penicillin for syphilis. Rather, their main goal was to watch the progression of untreated syphilis in these men. Syphilis is a three-staged progressive debilitating disease, where in the third stage the disease affects the brain, neuromuscular system, and all internal organs. Ulti-mately, the person dies ten to twenty years later.[31] In 1972, a federal government panel of experts determined that the Tuskegee Syphilis Study was unethical because penicillin was intentionally ignored and withheld from these men; the study had to be shut down.

For too many African Americans, the knowledge of these aforementioned medical experiments and the history of structural injustices in health care have left an indelible mark on their consciences. Moreover, efforts to rectify this history have been mixed. For instance, Title VI of the 1964 Civil Rights Act sought to rectify the legacy of racist medicine by outlawing discrimination. However, the effects of the law were decidedly mixed. David Barton Smith said that the Civil Rights Act left intact "unaddressed racial disparities and practice patterns of physicians."[32] We can see these disparities and patterns still evident in the results of the 2003 Committee on Understanding and Elim-inating Racial and Ethnic Disparities in Health Care convened by the Institute of Medicine in Washington, DC.[33] For instance, committee members reported continual unethical behaviors in health care connected with racial and ethnic bias and stereotyping. That is, even when patients are medically insured, if they are African Americans some health care providers do not order the necessary diagnostic and screening tests to rule out a chief complaint. Some providers, the report says, "give an untreatable diagnosis to a patient, or order limited treatments, or deny radiation or chemotherapy for cancer, dialysis for kidney failure, and bypass or balloon surgery and a pacemaker for heart disease cases."[34] As a result of such insufficient health care, many African Americans have become sicker and sicker from preventable and treatable

---

[30] Ibid., 7.

[31] Centers for Disease Control and Prevention, "Syphilis," http://ww.cdc.gov.

[32] David Barton Smith, "Health Care's Hidden Civil Rights Legacy," *Saint Louis University Law Journal* 48, no. 1 (Fall 2003): 37.

[33] See Institute of Medicine, *Unequal Treatment: Confronting Racial and Ethnic Disparities in Health Care* (Washington, DC: National Academies Press, 2003), 102.

[34] Emilie M. Townes, *Breaking the Fine Rain of Death: African American Health Issues and a Womanist Ethic of Care* (New York: Continuum, 1998), 117–18.

ailments. Similarly, the January 2005 issue of *Morbidity and Mortality Weekly* reported that African Americans continue to have highly disproportionate rates of medical and public health problems such as various types of cancers, HIV/AIDS, and other sexually transmitted infections, obesity, cardiovascular diseases, strokes, diabetes, hypertension, infant mortality, childhood asthma, unintentional accidents, and homicides.

Most recently, recall the January 17, 2016, news story that I shared at the beginning of this essay about rural Alabama and the long-time mistrust of medicine that fueled a tuberculosis outbreak. African Americans have not forgotten about the Tuskegee Syphilis Study. Here one can argue that African Americans are beset by a great deal of wariness and suspicion. As one physician involved in the current outbreak said: "There is a mistrust of government medicine, in the African-American community especially, because of Tuskegee. It dates back to that. We haven't dealt with the damage of Tuskegee in this state at any meaningful level."[35] The lack of attentiveness to rectify the damage from Tuskegee has not only had a local impact in the state of Alabama; the lack of addressing this medical abuse of human subjects has had national and international effects.

African Americans, Conscience, and Conscience Formation in Catholic Health Care

How might Catholic health care best approach the challenges of respecting the consciences of African American patients and of forming the consciences of all personnel concerned with the treatment of African Americans in medical institutions? I note that there has been no sustained attention to the need to respect the consciences of African Americans and to the conscience formation of providers of health care around the elimination of institutionalized racism. In general, Catholic health care institutions and in particular those in African American communities have important roles to play in rectifying racial injustice concerns through the formulation of well-formed consciences. The *Catechism of the Catholic Church* says: "The dignity of the human person implies and requires *uprightness of moral conscience*. . . . Conscience enables one to assume *responsibility* for acts performed. . . . It calls to mind the forgiveness that must be asked, the good that must be practiced, and the virtue that must be constantly cultivated with the grace of God."[36] This implies the formation of a well-formed conscience, which is a lifelong task for all human beings. But what does this mean to move toward a well-formed conscience in

---

[35] See Alan Blinder, "In Rural Alabama, a Longtime Mistrust of Medicine Fuels a Tuberculosis Outbreak," *New York Times*, January 17, 2016.

[36] *Catechism of the Catholic Church*, 2nd ed., nos. 1780–81.

light of the history of social and cultural sin of institutionalized racism in health care?

I think we have to be honest about the power of that history in light of the challenge of conscience formation. The work of Bryan Massingale can help us think through this challenge. He notes the traditional Catholic methods of conscience formation—one more rational and aimed at knowing church teaching, the other more character-based and aimed at shaping virtues—and finds them wanting in the face of the history of racism in the United States.[37] Hence, it is not enough to focus on moral principles or even on virtues—if we do so apart from an awareness of the cultural forces around racism that affect our basic moral instincts about what the patient in front of me deserves; about the nature of such patients' fears and anxieties; about our judgments regarding their degree of responsibility for their plight; and more.

Thus Massingale speaks of the persistence of "unconscious racial bias or motivation"[38] and of how conscience formation has to foster movement from the unconscious world of motivation to the world of consciousness and, hence, to the world of conscience and true moral responsibility. For him, "this reality [of unconscious racial bias or motivation] not only severely challenges our dominant understanding of racism but it also reveals the inadequacies of our current understanding of it in light of sin, culpability, and conscience."[39] The Catholic Church has pastoral documents based in Sacred Scripture, moral norms, and its social teachings, but not enough attention has been given to the powerful and damaging cultural forces—cultural forces intimately linked to structural inequalities—that have shaped African Americans' approach and access to health care.

Hence, it is important for us to stop and think about how this unconscious, racist world of motivations and assumptions affects the way, for instance, that an elderly African American woman views her options when she comes into the hospital and the way that a treatment team might see such a patient. In terms of care, what does she think she is entitled to? What might be her assumptions about her own sense of agency in light of care potentially involving advanced technology? How might she view various treatment recommendations and their worth—given how the options are presented to her? Conversely, how might the treatment team more consciously engage the possible mistrust and suspicion of such a patient? How might the team check itself, so to speak, so that the care they consider providing to her is the same as the care they would provide to anyone else in a similar situation? In response to such questions, I would like to suggest a practical solution for

---

[37] Massingale, "Challenge of Unconscious Racial Bias," 61–62.

[38] Ibid., 64–65.

[39] Ibid., 64.

conscience formation—a solution that combines Massingale's thinking (and the related thought of Joe Feagin) with what I call a black liberation bioethics. The solution requires us to think of conscience formation not so much as providing intellectual content but as fostering interpersonal connections.

Massingale argues that to penetrate this cultural cloud of racism we must move toward "a process of cultivating authentic interracial solidarity and transformative love (compassion)."[40] He builds on this notion of relationship by drawing from Joe Feagin's[41] work the following essential requirements for cultivating authentic interracial solidarity and transformative love (compassion): "an ability to hear and be present to black anger; the interior space to welcome perspectives that significantly differ from one's own; and the cultivation of genuinely affective relationships with persons of color."[42] Here whites must be able to hear past pain and trust that they are allied with another human being on this pilgrim journey of racial healing and reconciliation and that they will be kept safe from harm in this process. Joe Feagin argues that white people involved in such interracial solidarity move through three different stages:

> *Sympathy* with its limitations, it typically involves a willingness to set aside some racist stereotyping and hostility and the development of a friendly if variable interest in what is happening to the racialized other. *Empathy* is a much more advanced stage of development in that it requires a developed ability to routinely reject distancing stereotypes and a heightened and sustained capacity to see some of the pain of those in the out-group. . . . *Autopathy* is the third stage of white development, which has not been yet been fully analyzed. . . . At this stage, a white person has to intentionally put herself or himself, if only partially, into the racist world of the oppressed.[43]

I would like to join these ideas of Massingale and Feagin to practices associated with what I call an African American liberation bioethics. By speaking of bioethics in such a way, I mean to join the long, pervasive history of the mistreatment of African Americans in the health care system to the Christian promise of liberation told in the stories of the Exodus and the Paschal Mystery. To address the mistrust that afflicts the consciences of many African Americans as they travel through the health care system is to engage in acts of liberation consistent with the salvific promise of the Gospel. Thus,

---

[40] Ibid., 65.
[41] Feagin, *Racist America*, 254–55.
[42] Massingale, "Challenge of Unconscious Racial Bias," 65.
[43] Feagin, *Racist America*, 254–55.

the focus on liberation in bioethics refers to the need to be intentionally open, reflective, and thoughtful about the ramifications or implications of bioethical decision-making as it pertains to race. The end result of such decision-making must be liberation that translates into human flourishing, human dignity, and racial justice for African Americans and Catholic health care institutions. One important dimension of liberation bioethics is what I call a Lay Ministry Ally whose role is to partner with an African American patient as he or she moves through the health care delivery system. In this, I agree with Massingale that "conscience formation, especially for Christians in the United States, must include the cultivation of the qualities essential for authentic interracial solidarity."[44] Interracial solidarity thrives when we see and understand each other as truly brothers and sisters just as Jesus Christ taught us to be.

Both the African American patient and the Lay Ministry Ally (I think of it as a lay role because of the increasing number of laity taking on ministerial roles in the Catholic Church and in Catholic health care institutions) have moral responsibilities for stopping this debilitating dance that keeps recycling racism and health disparities, fear, mistrust, frustration, and despair. The Ally must have gone through thorough and extensive antiracism, cultural competency, and conscious racial awareness trainings, while also understanding that Catholic health care is animated by the healing ministry of Jesus and guided by the *Ethical and Religious Directives*.

While the partners navigate the health care delivery system together, here's hoping, too, that the Ally has grasped the essence of Feagin's stages of solidarity: In the medical context, he or she must be able to ask the appropriate questions; be comfortable with challenging medical judgments when there is a perception of unconscious racial bias or motivations; and be able to act in an authentic collaborative spirit as a mentor and monitor of threats to human dignity linked to racial injustices. I believe that in the midst of this communal relationship human lives can be made healthy and whole. Reconciliation and liberation happens, too, and is reflected in the experience of confidence and care: The confidence of a patient with a peaceful conscience navigating the health care system and the care of a medical team sure they are aware of the specific needs of the African American patient before them. The Ally plays a mediating role, assisting in the conscience formation of the patient and in the formation of leaders, providers, staff members, and stakeholders in Catholic health care.

In conclusion, my deepest hope for this work is indeed to realize some day the elimination of institutionalized racism and enduring health disparities in health care generally and in Catholic health specifically, not only because racial injustices continue to affront human dignity and the whole human

---

[44] Ibid., 67.

family but also because in the law inscribed by God we are called to love and to do what is good and to avoid evil. Through the Lay Ministry Ally process, my hope is that we might break through the accumulated layers of racial bias and foster a deeper respect for the consciences of African Americans and for all of those involved in Catholic health care. Ultimately, Jesus came so that we might all have life and flourish as creatures fearfully and wonderfully made in the image and likeness of God.

Conscience Formation of Students in Health Profession Programs in Catholic Universities

Carol Taylor, PhD, RN

Labor to keep alive in your breast that little spark of celestial fire called conscience.

—George Washington

The only tyrant I accept in this world is the "still small voice" within me. And even though I have to face the prospect of being a minority of one, I humbly believe I have the courage to be in such a hopeless minority.

—Mahatma Gandhi

I have taught health care ethics at a Jesuit university medical center for twenty-five years and rarely used the language of conscience formation to describe my work. Our students in the health professions, the patients and families they serve, and our faculty are culturally and ethically diverse. When asked if I am teaching Catholic ethics, my usual response is that I am hoping to challenge our students and practitioners to reflect on what they believe about ethically challenging situations, why they believe this, and on how these beliefs are likely to influence clinical conversations and actions. When lecturing on the clinician's role in assisted suicide, for example, I present the teaching of the Catholic Church, refer to the *Ethical and Religious Directives for Catholic Health Care Services*, and contrast these with secular arguments, including those made by health care professionals.

The invitation to write this chapter and to participate in a scholarly dialogue about conscience and Catholic health care provided a welcome opportunity to reflect on the obligation of faculty in a Catholic university to promote conscience formation of students in the health professions. This is particularly challenging in an environment where neither students nor faculty are clamoring for help in exploring how best to "form" their consciences. Although a few students are very clear about understanding conscience as a matter of following clear rules about what is ethical and what is not, the majority of the students have never devoted time to reflecting on how they calibrate their moral compass and the role conscience plays in informing and evaluating their decisions.

This chapter aims to describe pedagogical approaches to promote conscience formation as well as to suggest why conscience formation should matter in today's universities. It specifically explores the role of lay faculty teaching health care ethics to health care professionals, not theologians teaching courses in Catholic medical ethics. Although much of this content is applicable to teaching any student to reflect on the moral sense, intuition, or inner voice that animates moral action, I highlight challenges for Catholic faculty and students.

George Dennis O'Brien, writing about the future of Catholic higher education, comments on Jesuit John O'Malley's analysis of four ancient cultures that defined the purpose of higher education: the prophetic, the academic, the humanistic, and the artistic. Noting that twentieth-century universities have replaced the humanistic culture with the academic culture, he writes that the aim of education today is not character but knowledge, a theme central to David Brooks's 2015 book, *The Road to Character*.[1] O'Brien asks, "Do Catholic institutions actually convey an education in humanistic culture—or in prophetic culture, for that matter? Do they do this in the class-room? Or do they leave these things to the campus chaplain and various extracurricular activities?"[2] So what exactly is my role in promoting the conscience formation of my students in the health professions?

Bioethicist Daniel Callahan identified the three questions foundational to bioethics: (1) What kind of person ought I to be in order to live a moral life and make good ethical decisions? (2) What are my duties and obligations to the other individuals whose life and well-being may be affected by my actions? And (3) what do I owe the common good or the public interest, in my life as a member of society?[3] To the degree that I challenge every student

---

[1] David Brooks, *The Road to Character* (New York: Random House, 2015).

[2] G. D. O'Brien, "Incarnation U.: The Future of Catholic Higher Education," *Commonweal*, June 12, 1951, 15–18.

[3] Daniel Callahan, "Bioethics," in *Encyclopedia of Bioethics,* rev. ed., ed. W. T. Reich (New York: Macmillan Library Reference, 1995), 247–56.

with these questions and believe that some answers better serve the authenticity of the student and the well-being of society, conscience formation has to matter. Callahan's questions resonate with Linda Hogan's explication of conscience:

> The primary purpose in discussing [the fundamental option] is to suggest a framework between the character of the person and the choices she/he makes. What is suggested by this is an understanding of conscience as the person's orientation to and desire for goodness. . . . This is an understanding of conscience that sees an intimate connection between the kind of person one is and the actions one performs. It recognized that the formation of conscience takes place, not by some superficial adherence to rules and laws, but rather in working toward goodness rather than evil or indifference in every context, no matter how trivial. . . . It is through the person's conscience, therefore, that one can see the unity and coherence of the moral character.[4]

Ethics 101

My first degrees were in nursing, and my doctorate is in philosophy with a concentration in bioethics. I am a committed Catholic, but I am not a theologian. Although I have seldom used the language of conscience formation, I write and talk all the time about integrity. In even the briefest of presentations on ethics, I define three terms: ethics, moral agency, and integrity. In this chapter I hope to explore the role conscience plays in each of these concepts.

Ethics is the study of who we ought to be (how we should make decisions and behave or act) in light of our identity. General ethics is about who we should be and how we should conduct ourselves as humans. To the extent that religion, profession, and other commitments are part of our identity, we need to study how these commitments shape our ethical responsibilities and obligations—thus, Catholic health care ethics, medical or nursing ethics, military ethics.

Moral agency is the capacity to habitually act in an ethical manner. It entails a certain set of competencies in matters ethical as well as moral character and motivation. Central to these competencies are moral reasoning and discernment and thus conscience. Some elements of this list can be enumerated in the following way:

---

[4] Linda Hogan, *Confronting the Truth: Conscience in the Catholic Tradition* (Mahwah, NJ: Paulist Press, 2000), 133.

1. Moral sensibility: Ability to recognize the "moral moment" when a moral challenge presents itself.
2. Moral responsiveness: Ability and willingness to respond to the moral challenge.
3. Moral reasoning: Knowledge of and ability to use sound theoretical and practical approaches to "thinking through" moral challenges; these approaches are used to inform as well as to justify moral behavior.
4. Moral discernment: Ability to apprehend, insightfully, what is at stake in a moral challenge and after an analysis of competing alternatives to decide what is the best response in this particular situation.
5. Moral accountability: Ability and willingness to accept responsibility for one's moral behavior and to learn from the experience of exercising moral agency.
6. Moral character: Cultivated dispositions that allow one to act as one believes one ought to act.
7. Moral valuing: Valuing in a conscious and critical way that which squares with good moral character and moral integrity.
8. Moral motivation: A love for the good; commitment to do the morally right thing because it is the right thing to do.
9. Transformative moral leadership: Commitment and proven ability to create a culture which facilitates the exercise of moral agency, a culture in which people do the right thing because it is the right thing to do.

Moral integrity is that condition or state in which moral activity (valuing, choosing, acting) is intimately linked to a particular conception of the good and the good life. Moral integrity does not simply happen as a result of our wanting to be moral individuals. It begins with an intentional commitment to develop and own a conception of the good life. Then one practices valuing, choosing, and acting according to what fidelity to the good life demands. The goal is to develop a habitual disposition to value, choose, and act in accordance with one's moral code. Reflective practice allows us to reflect on moral activity in order to learn from it and make improvements for the future. Moral integrity is what allows the public we serve to trust us to be who we purport to be, an ethical human being, an ethical practitioner.

Approaches to Conscience

The above discussion of ethics, moral agency, and integrity does not use religious language or mention conscience specifically. Conscience is "understood as a judgment about the morality of an act to be done or omitted or already done or omitted by the person."[5] Conscience is thus essential to the identity and integrity of the Catholic and central to the exercise of moral agency. The United States Conference of Catholic Bishops in describing a well-formed conscience highlights the serious and lifelong obligation Catholics have to form their consciences in accord with human reason and the teaching of the church.

> Conscience is not something that allows us to justify doing whatever we want, nor is it a mere "feeling" about what we should or should not do. Rather conscience is the voice of God resounding in the human heart, revealing the truth to us and calling us to do what is good while shunning what is evil. Conscience always requires serious attempts to make sound moral judgments based on the truths of our faith.[6]

James Keenan writes that many Catholics today truncate the notion of conscience to that which gives us the right to dissent from teaching: "Any right to dissent derives first from the responsibilities we have to conscience—that is, to examine our own conduct, to form and inform our consciences daily and to determine the right direction of our lives."[7] Vatican II's *Declaration on Religious Freedom* cites the inviolability of conscience: "In all his activity a man is bound to follow his conscience faithfully, in order that he may come to God, for whom he was created."[8] Michael Lawler and Todd Salzman contrast two approaches to conscience. For the theologian Germain Grisez conscience is ultimately about obedience to church teaching. For the revisionist theologian Bernhard Häring, conscience is "man's innermost yearning toward 'wholeness,' which manifests itself in openness to neighbor and community in common searching for goodness and truth," and must be free and inviolable.[9] The approach to conscience that guides a faculty member will direct efforts to form conscience. One in the Grisez school merely needs to ensure that students learn church teachings and value obedience. Those in the Häring school will commit to open dialogue with neighbor and community and will be intentional about structuring these opportunities as well as cultivating

---

[5] Charles E. Curran, *The Catholic Moral Tradition Today: A Synthesis* (Washington, DC: Georgetown University Press, 1999), 172.

[6] United States Conference of Catholic Bishops, *Forming Consciences for Faithful Citizenship: A Call to Political Responsibility from the Catholic Bishops of the United States with Introductory Note* (Washington, DC: USCCB Publications, 2015), 10.

[7] James F. Keenan, "Examining Conscience," *America*, April 4–11, 17.

[8] Second Vatican Council, *Dignitatis Humanae*, 4.

[9] Michael G. Lawler and Todd A. Salzman, "Following Faithfully: The Catholic Way to Choose the Good," *America*, February 2, 2015, 17.

attention to the whispers of the Spirit within. I always tell students that when we are in a conflicted situation we should be wary of sitting at a table with people who believe what we believe because the most dangerous part of our thinking is that we do not know what we don't know. It's better to be in conversation with those who will challenge us and perhaps reveal areas of blindness.

Similarly, theologian Karl Rahner describes spirituality itself as the ultimate depth of what spiritual creatures do when they realize themselves—"when they laugh or cry, accept responsibility, love, live and die, stand up for truth, break out of preoccupation with themselves to help the neighbor, hope against hope, cheerfully refuse to be embittered by the stupidity of daily life, keep silent, not so that evil festers in their hearts, but so that it dies there—when, in a word, they live as they would like to live in opposition to selfishness and to the despair that always assails us."[10]

Pope Francis gave new meaning to these convictions in his apostolic exhortation *Evangelii Gaudium*, the *Joy of the Gospel*. Pope Francis said that the great danger in today's world, "pervaded as it is by consumerism, is the desolation and anguish born of a complacent yet covetous heart, the feverish pursuit of frivolous pleasures, and a blunted conscience." He cautions, "Whenever our interior life becomes caught up in its own interests and concerns, there is no longer room for others, no place for the poor. God's voice is no longer heard, the quiet joy of his love is no longer felt, and the desire to do good fades."[11] A particular challenge for faculty in Catholic universities is how we extend Pope Francis's invitation to Christians everywhere to a renewed personal encounter with Jesus Christ, or at least "an openness" to letting Jesus encounter them. Faculty in Catholic medical centers may actually facilitate the "blunting of conscience" deplored by Pope Francis as we teach students to respect and promote the autonomy of patients by serving as their uncritical advocates. I loved the clinician who told my students, "I often tell patients, this isn't Burger King—you don't always get it your way!"

If we are bound to follow conscience faithfully, we need to ensure that our conscience is true. Curran proposes that peace and joy are the hallmarks of a good conscience. "The human person has a God-given inclination to the true and good, which grounds the questions we are constantly raising about moral actions. When all the pertinent questions have been raised and settled, one is at peace precisely because no questions remain. The drive for truth has found its proper object. Grace, reason, affectivity and intuitions all cooperate

---

[10] Karl Rahner, "How to Receive a Sacrament and Mean It," *Theology Digest* 19 (1971): 229.

[11] Pope Francis, *Evangelii Gaudium* (2013), 3.

in this thrust for the true and good."[12] Many students share the importance of being able to put their heads on their pillows and sleep peacefully after struggling with an ethical challenge. Many students discomforted by their own ethical weaknesses return from a directed retreat or sacramental encounter profoundly at peace after richly experiencing our all merciful God.

While I would be hesitant to assign Grisez or Häring to the average health care professional student, the article by Lawler and Salzman should spark a lively discussion at a meeting of Catholic medical students or nurses. The popularity of "theology on tap" evenings sponsored by Catholic universities would also provide a rich forum to explore the role conscience plays in our moral lives.

Moral Integrity and the
Catholic Vision of the Good Life

Many of our Catholic students have paid scant attention to what the Catholic Church teaches about the Good Life. While some are "John Paul II Catholics," well versed in traditional church teachings about health care ethics, many are more familiar with privacy and liberty arguments that support contraception, abortion, same-sex marriage, and assisted suicide. Those who are aware of the church teachings on contraception, abortion, and assisted suicide will hear strong counterarguments from respected health care professionals and may feel conflicted about their responsibilities. Some who want to support patient preferences that conflict with church teachings are concerned about their ability to counsel patients while a student in a Catholic facility. Too few students have sufficient familiarity with the social teachings of the Catholic Church to feel conflicted when experiencing disrespectful treatment of vulnerable persons or health disparities linked to inadequate social resources and supports. Last, until Pope Francis, many Catholic faculty who grew up with Vatican II and who held positions that ran counter to, for example, the received tradition on contraception, were reluctant to participate in public forums with students to address the questions they had. The fear that someone would "run to the bishop" and raise concerns for the faculty and university was credible.

Clarifying the Faculty's Role in Conscience Formation

It is the rare student who asks about how best to form his or her conscience. While researching this topic, I found a set of lecture notes describing the following practices for the formation of conscience. Although I

---

[12] Curran, *Catholic Moral Tradition Today*, 186.

have not used these resources, they make sense to me. I remember my impotence after 9/11 when a member of Georgetown University's staff approached me and said, "I have not been raised in a particular religious tradition but I now have critical questions about the meaning and purpose of life." These seem to be great starting points.

1. *Community.* Immerse yourself in the common practices and life of a conscientious community (e.g., a religious congregation or church; sacraments); place your conscience in conversation with this communal conscience and allow it to challenge you while you challenge it to become better.
2. *Stories.* Listen to good stories that creatively engage and develop your moral imagination (from stories in scriptures to novels and films).
3. *Study.* Study scriptures, church teaching, lives of saints, and local and global news.
4. *Prayer and self-examination.* Find ways of praying that will help develop a rich interior life, capacity for self-examination, and a capacity for wonder and thanksgiving. Examples: meditation/reflection with God, prayer and worship with others through liturgy and Eucharist, Spiritual Exercises of Saint Ignatius. Engage in regular reflection on our moral successes and failures (e.g., journaling).
5. *Mentor.* Share your journey with someone who has already traveled far on the path that you seek. Learn from a mentor—a spiritual director, confessor, teacher, counselor, or a wise and good friend.
6. *Service.* Practice service to others that will encourage empathy, compassion, and love of neighbor.[13]

Faculty can also "blunt conscience formation" by keeping students so focused on academic performance that spiritual formation becomes an afterthought.

Part of the responsibilities of Catholic faculty members teaching ethics to Catholic health profession students is identifying the resources students can access to learn what the church teaches about health care ethics. Where points of tension exist between the received doctrine and contemporary approaches and challenges, these should be discussed frankly. Respectful communal discernment has the potential to enrich all. The emphasis should be on fostering the students' desires to form their consciences so they can make true judgments that align with God's will and bring them peace and joy and serve the public well. I believe the challenge will always be addressing the motivation to do this, which is intimately linked to the universal call to holi-

---

[13] Thomas B. Leininger, "Conscience Lecture Notes," undated materials.

ness. Jesus who came to bring us life and "life more abundantly" (Jn 10:10) is also the "way, the truth, and the life" (Jn 14:6). Fostering encounters with the living Christ that translate into desires to live freely and authentically is the goal. I am always grateful when students share comments about how their required ethics course affects their lives. Random comments from students this spring:

> This class has lit a fire in my curiosity and passion to explore ethical challenges. The more stories I hear from others the more I can understand where I stand with my moral character and what truly guides my decisions (moral compass).

> I am most certainly a better practitioner (and a better person) from the lessons learned in this course.

Since conscience can be erroneous, faculty members also play an important role in challenging suspect student judgments. I believe the witness of faculty who struggle with the complexities of modern health care while also striving to be in communion with the church and aligned with God's holy will is a powerful inducement. In George Dennis O'Brien's article on the future of Catholic higher education, he notes that the prophetic culture of a sort is clearly present in the contemporary university, citing black studies, gay studies, and women's studies. He calls these programs "witness studies" because they depend on the notion that incarnation is essential to understanding.

> If the model of most academic culture is intellect speaking to intellect, in witness studies incarnate minds speak to incarnate minds. Here the scientific model of dispassionate objectivity is replaced by a model of personal engagement. The voice that counts is the voice of someone who knows what it means to live as a female, gay, or black [committed Catholic health care professional or ethicist] in this time and place. Such disciplines can best be described as a gathering of witnesses.[14]

A witness of human excellence—for example Pope Francis or a respected mentor—is the most powerful inducement to motivation to prioritize forming a good conscience.

---

[14] O'Brien, "Incarnation U.," 18.

Pedagogical Approaches

When teaching students to reflect on ethically challenging situations, I suggest they pay attention to how they reason about how they *should* and *would* respond.

- What informs your judgment? Rephrased, how do you calibrate your moral compass? What is the basis of the "inner voice" or "intuitions" that instruct you? To what degree do religious beliefs or your relationship with a Supreme Being inform your judgments?
- Are there moral "rules" that apply?
- What counts as a *good* response? What criteria/principles do you use to inform and justify your response?
    - Promotes human dignity and the common good
    - Maximizes good and minimizes harm
    - Emphasizes just distribution of goods and harms
    - Respects rights
    - Is responsive to vulnerabilities
    - Promotes virtue
    - Other elements? (Golden rule, theological ethics, care ethics)
- What criteria/principles do you use to critique/evaluate your response?
    - My moral integrity is intact
    - I stayed out of trouble—not greatly inconvenienced
    - I made money or at least didn't lose money
    - My reputation is intact
    - "I could tell my children what I/we did and feel proud." *Washington Post* test
    - I am able to put my head on my pillow and fall asleep peacefully
    - Transparency
    - Consistency
    - Other
- Do you have a responsibility to respond? Are you personally able and willing to respond? Are there institutional or other external variables making it difficult or impossible to respond? Are you confident in your ability to respond ethically and to preserve your integrity?
- Are there any universal (nonnegotiable) moral obligations that obligate all health care professionals?
- To whom would you turn if you were uncertain about how to proceed?
    - What agency resources exist to help you think through and secure a good response? How confident are you that these resources would facilitate a good resolution of your concern?

When what we think we would do differs from what we think we should do (i.e., the ethically right decision/course of action), either our moral agency is deficient, moral distress is present (we know the right thing to do but institutional or other variables are making it virtually impossible to do so), or some combination of these. Recent literature on the consequences of unresolved moral distress of health care professionals is making it imperative for educators to better equip health professionals with resources that promote resilience and strategies to address institutional factors that compromise integrity.

Students often struggle with ethical analysis. It is not unusual for students to tell me, "I didn't know I had a moral compass, let alone know how to use it!" These same students will use the terms "refreshing" or "novel" to describe the experience of using an ethics lens to analyze a clinical challenge. These comments speak powerfully to me of the inadequacy of our academic efforts to prioritize moral agency as a prized outcome in our graduates. Health professions students come into the ethics classes with great variability in their exposure to ethical frameworks. After familiarizing students with basic approaches to doing ethics, I now incorporate the exercise below to help them to assimilate this content:

1. Briefly outline a personal or professional challenge to your moral agency/integrity. Share how you responded and what informed your ethical response. Finally, give a critique of your response.
2. Describe how you calibrate your moral compass. What do you typically "reach into" to form your moral judgments and response? What criteria do you use to evaluate the adequacy of your judgment/ response? What or which ethical frameworks have you found to be most helpful. Why? What are their strengths and limitations?
3. Prepare a description of your anticipated moral agency as you begin your professional practice. What will you bring as ethical strengths and limitations to your practice? What areas for improvement do you want to be intentional about cultivating?

There is usually consensus that while this exercise is difficult, students learn much about themselves and one another. The narratives they share witness to the importance of this reflection and its importance to the work they do and the well-being of others entrusted to their care.

My experience teaching Catholic medical and nursing students in a Catholic medical center has convinced me that the work we do to sensitize students to the important role conscience plays in forming their identity and integrity is central to our responsibilities as educators. Although neither students nor faculty may use the language of conscience, they readily grasp the need for a "moral compass" understood as the rudder that will guide them through the rough waters of challenging clinical situations. Finding a way to facilitate dialogue about how they calibrate their moral compass has paid rich dividends, especially when such dialogue is communal and students believe they are in a safe space to freely raise questions and concerns.

Contributors

Gerald Coleman, PSS, Daughters of Charity Health System
Father Coleman is a member of the United States Province of St. Sulpice (the Sulpicians). He is presently an adjunct professor of ethics in the Graduate Program of Pastoral Studies at Santa Clara University. Since 2006 he has served as corporate ethicist for the Daughters of Charity Health System, a six-hospital system located in California. His recent publications include "Direct and Indirect Abortion in the Roman Catholic Tradition: A Review of the Phoenix Case" (*HEC Forum*) and "Subjectivism, Vitalism? Catholic Teaching Avoids Extremes" (*Health Progress*).

Shawnee M. Daniels-Sykes, Mount Mary University
Shawnee M. Daniels-Sykes, PhD, is an associate professor of theology and ethics at Mount Mary University in Milwaukee, Wisconsin. She is also an adjunct associate professor at Xavier University of Louisiana. Her research and writing focuses on health disparities, the Affordable Care Act, and violent gun homicides, among other topics. She is the author of "Still We Remain: Living Religious Liberty Consciously and Unconsciously," which appeared in the *Journal of the Black Catholic Theological Symposium*, and of "Code Black: A Black Catholic Liberation Bioethics," *Journal of Black Catholic Theology.*

David E. DeCosse, Markkula Center for Applied Ethics, Santa Clara University
David E. DeCosse is the director of campus ethics programs at the Markkula Center for Applied Ethics at Santa Clara University, where he is also an adjunct associate professor of religious studies. He has written for academic journals such as *Theological Studies* and journalistic outlets such as the *National Catholic Reporter*. With Kristin Heyer, he co-edited the book *Conscience and Catholicism: Rights, Responsibilities, and Institutional Responses* (Orbis Books, 2015). He also co-edited the book *Pope Francis and the Future of Catholicism in the United States: The Challenge of Becoming a Church for the Poor* (University of San Francisco, 2015).

Roberto Dell'Oro, Loyola Marymount University

Roberto Dell'Oro is the director of the Bioethics Institute and a professor in the Department of Theological Studies at Loyola Marymount University in Los Angeles. He is the author or co-author of three books, *Health and Human Flourishing: Religion, Moral Anthropology, and Medicine*; *Esperienza morale e persona*; and *History of Bioethics: International Perspectives*. He has also published in national and international journals, such as *Theological Studies*, the *Gregorianum,* and *Health Progress*. He is working on a book tentatively titled *Method and Meaning: Hermeneutical Reflections in Bioethics*.

Kevin T. FitzGerald, SJ, Georgetown University

Kevin T. FitzGerald is a Jesuit priest, a research associate professor in the Department of Oncology, and the David Lauler Chair for Catholic Health Care Ethics at the Georgetown University Medical Center in Washington, DC. In 2014 Pope Francis named him to the Pontifical Council for Culture. His research efforts focus on the investigation of abnormal gene expression in cancer, and on ethical issues in biomedical research and medical genomics. He has published both scientific and ethical articles in peer-reviewed journals, books, and in the popular press.

Lisa Fullam, Jesuit School of Theology of Santa Clara University

Lisa Fullam, DVM, ThD, is a professor of moral theology at the Jesuit School of Theology of Santa Clara University in Berkeley, California. She is the author of the book *The Virtue of Humility: A Thomistic Apologetic*, and she co-edited the books *Ethics and Spirituality: Readings in Moral Theology No. 17* (2014) and *Virtue: Readings in Moral Theology No. 16* (2011). Her essay "Joan of Arc, Holy Resistance, and Conscience Formation in the Face of Social Sin" appeared in *Conscience and Catholicism: Rights, Responsibilities, and Institutional Responses* (Orbis Books, 2015).

Ron Hamel, Catholic Health Association, ret.

Ron Hamel, PhD, recently retired as the senior director of ethics for the Catholic Health Association of the United States. Previously, he was director of the Department of Clinical Ethics at Lutheran General Hospital-Advocate, Park Ridge, Illinois. He is a regular contributor to *Health Progress* (the publication of the Catholic Health Association); the executive editor of *Health Care Ethics USA*, CHA's electronic ethics publication; and the editor of *Making Health Care Decisions: A Catholic Guide*. His 2014 Regan Lecture at Santa Clara University was titled "Conscience and the Complex World of Catholic Health Care."

Kristin E. Heyer, Boston College

Kristin E. Heyer is a professor of theology at Boston College. Her research interests include social ethics, migration ethics, and Catholic social thought. Heyer is the author of several books, including *Kinship across Borders: A Christian Ethic of Immigration* and *Catholics and Politics: The Dynamic Tension between Faith and Power.* She has also published articles in *Theological Studies* and *Health Care Ethics USA.* She is the co-editor of the book *Conscience and Catholicism: Rights, Responsibilities, and Institutional Responses* (Orbis Books, 2015).

Cathleen Kaveny, Boston College

Cathleen Kaveny is the Libby Professor at Boston College, where she holds appointments on the faculty of both the Theology Department and the Law School. She is a recent president of the Society of Christian Ethics. Among her books are *Prophecy without Contempt: Religious Rhetoric in the Public Square, A Culture of Engagement: Law, Religion, and Morality*, and the forthcoming *Ethics at the Edges of Law: Christian Ethics and the American Legal Tradition.* She is a columnist at *Commonweal* and has appeared on the *Daily Show* to speak about the Catholic response to the Obama administration's contraceptive mandate.

Margaret R. McLean, Markkula Center for Applied Ethics, Santa Clara University

Margaret R. McLean, PhD, is the associate director and director of bioethics at the Markkula Center for Applied Ethics as well as a senior lecturer in religious studies and an affiliate faculty in bioengineering at Santa Clara University. She is a former editor for *Religious Studies Review*, reviews manuscripts for a variety of professional journals, and has for years been an ethics consultant for San Francisco Bay Area hospitals. Her article on disaster preparedness published in 2013 in *Health Progress* received a 2014 Gold Award from the American Society of Healthcare Publication Editors.

M. Patrick Moore Jr., Boston College

M. Patrick Moore Jr., JD, is a graduate of Boston College and Boston College Law School. After law school he clerked at the Massachusetts Supreme Judicial Court, the Federal Third Circuit Court of Appeals, and the Federal District Court of Massachusetts, and was an assistant attorney general for the Commonwealth of Massachusetts. He also served as associate counsel in the executive office of the governor under Governor Deval Patrick and Governor Charles Baker and as assistant deputy counsel in the executive office of the President in the White House for President Obama. He is now teaching at the Boston College Law School.

Thomas A. Nairn, OFM, Catholic Health Association
Thomas A. Nairn is a Franciscan priest and the senior director of theology and ethics at the Catholic Health Association of the United States in St. Louis, Missouri. Prior to joining CHA, he was the Erica and Harry John Family Professor of Catholic Ethics at the Catholic Theological Union in Chicago. He has published articles on medical ethics and other ethical issues in such journals as *Health Progress*, *New Theology Review*, and the *Annual of the Society of Christian Ethics*. He has also edited *The Seamless Garment: Writings on the Consistent Ethic of Life*, by Joseph Bernardin (2008). In 2014, the Vatican's Pontifical Council for the Laity appointed him as the spiritual assistant to the International Catholic Committee for Nurses and Health Care Workers.

Lawrence J. Nelson, Santa Clara University
Lawrence J. Nelson is an associate professor in the Department of Philosophy at Santa Clara University, where he is also a faculty scholar at the Markkula Center for Applied Ethics. He has served as a bioethics consultant to projects of the National Institutes of Health, the Hastings Center, and the American Thoracic Society. He also argued the end-of-life Wendland case before the California State Supreme Court. Nelson has published articles on ethics, law, and health care in publications such as the *Journal of the American Medical Association, Critical Care Medicine, the Journal of Law, Medicine & Ethics*, and the *Hastings Law Journal*.

John J. Paris, SJ, Boston College
Father Paris is the Walsh Professor of Bioethics at Boston College. He has served as consultant to the President's Commission for the Study of Ethics in Medicine, the United States Senate Committee on Aging, and the Congressional Office of Technology Assessment. He has published over one hundred articles in the area of law, medicine, and ethics; and he has served as a consultant and expert witness in many landmark biomedical cases, including the Quinlan, Brophy, Jobes, Baby K, and Gilgunn cases. His recent publications have been appeared in the *Journal of Perinatology, Nature,* and the *American Journal of Bioethics*.

Anne E. Patrick, SNJM, Carleton College
Anne E. Patrick, SNJM, was the William H. Laird Professor of Religion and the Liberal Arts, emerita, at Carleton College. She was a past president of the Catholic Theological Society of America; recipient of its John Courtney Murray award; and a founding vice-president of the International Network of Societies for Catholic Theology. She is the author of *Liberating Conscience* (1996), *Women, Conscience, and the Creative Process* (2011), and *Conscience and Calling: Ethical Reflections on Catholic Women's Church Vocations* (2013).

Carol Taylor, Georgetown University

Carol Taylor, PhD, RN, is a senior clinical scholar at the Kennedy Institute of Ethics at Georgetown University and a professor of medicine and nursing. At Georgetown, she directs an innovative ethics curriculum grounded in a rich notion of moral agency for advanced practice nurses. Her research interests include clinical and professional ethics, and organizational integrity. She is the author of *Fundamentals of Nursing: The Art and Science of Person-Centered Nursing Care*, which is now in its eighth edition, and co-editor of *Health and Human Flourishing: Religion, Medicine, and Moral Anthropology.*

Index